天野真志
AMANO Masashi
松下正和
MATSUSHITA Masakazu
編

地域歴史文化の まもりかた

災害時の救済方法とその考え方

【付・英語版】

How to Preserve Local Historical Culture
Methods and Ideas for Rescuing Materials during Disasters

日髙真吾／大林賢太郎／山内利秋／阿部浩一／市沢　哲

英語監修：根本峻瑠

JN062707

文 学 通 信

目次

第3部　資料救済への備え方

Contents

Part 3 Preparation for Materials Rescue

ご挨拶

▨ 奥村　弘（神戸大学大学院）

　本書は、科学研究費助成事業（特別推進研究）「地域歴史資料学を機軸とした災害列島における地域存続のための地域歴史文化の創成」（研究代表者奥村弘　課題番号：19H05457）の重要な成果をなすものである。

　阪神・淡路大震災以降、私たちは地域歴史資料学の全国的な共同研究を展開させてきた。その中で現代日本において打ち続く大規模自然災害だけでなく、グローバル化の進展による社会構造の大変動による人口の減少や都市を中心とした流動化の拡大、高度経済成長以来の価値意識の変化等により、地域社会を支える地域歴史文化の継承が急速に困難となっているとの危機意識を一層強めた。

　人文社会科学において歴史資料・現代資料による実証的研究は、その基礎をなすものであり、地域歴史資料の保存活用はその前提となるが、資料の保存と継承が持つ社会的価値をその社会が認識しないかぎり資料は滅失してしまう。そのような社会環境の下では、歴史資料の活用を前提とする研究は弱体化し、そのことが歴史資料保存に対するさらに市民の意識を弱め、資料の滅失を一層拡大するという、悪循環を生みだす。いまだ学術的認知を受けていない歴史資料を保全するためには、研究者コミュニティ自身が地域住民と共同し、地域歴史資料の市民社会での価値を発見、価値づけることが必要であり、そのための新たな方法論と研究分野が必要であるとの関係者間の共通認識が、本研究開始の背景にあった（奥村弘編『歴史文化を大災害から守る─地域歴史資料学の構築』東京大学出版会、2014 年）。

　このような市民社会形成の基礎学として地域歴史資料学のあり方は、大学を中心とした専門知と地域社会を基盤とした社会知を関連づけ、戦後の日本社会を支える市民的価値の形成を進めていくことを目指した第二次大戦後の

日本の歴史学の課題を引き継ぐものでもあり、大規模自然災害への対応を通した実践的研究の中で、その内容が豊富化されてきたものである（奥村弘『大震災と歴史資料保存—阪神・淡路大震災から東日本大震災へ』吉川弘文館、2012年）。

　本研究では、この点を重視し、実践的研究のリーダーである天野真志・松下正和が中心となって、大規模自然災害時における歴史資料救済活動の実践的手法、地域歴史資料の防災・減災についての考え方を集約し、分析を進めてきた。本書では、その成果として、具体的な大規模災害の場で実践活動の手がかりとなるよう体系的な考え方を提示するものである。日本各地で活用していただくとともに、皆様からご意見をいただき、より良いものにしていきたいと考えている。

　なおこのような日本での動向は、世界的な規模での社会変動と呼応しており、世界各地の歴史学や歴史資料保存の新たな動向とも関係性を持つものである。これについては、本科研グループによる、ションコイ・ガーボル、奥村弘、根本峻瑠、市原晋平、加藤明恵『ヨーロッパ文化遺産研究の最前線』（神戸大学出版会、2023年）を参考にしていただければ幸いである。

はじめに

▨ 天野真志（国立歴史民俗博物館）

■ 地域住民を主体とした被災資料の救済活動を広げていくために

　自然災害が多発する現代社会において、災害対策は宿命的な課題である。自然災害は、人命や人びとの生活のみならず歴史文化に関わる多様な事物にも大きな被害を与え、被災した諸資料の救済活動が各地で実施されている。大規模災害が頻発し、今後も多くの地域が被災の危険性を抱えるなか、各地に伝わる多様な歴史文化資料の災害対策が議論されている。特に、各地の「資料ネット」に代表される地域を主体とした歴史文化の保存・継承活動は、災害時における資料の救済活動を積極的に展開している。そのなかで、破損や水濡れなど、通常とは異なる取り扱いが求められる被災資料についても、その対応をめぐりさまざまな試行錯誤が行われてきた。

　これまで、阪神・淡路大震災から東日本大震災を経て現在に至るまで、被災資料救済の対応に関わる救済技術の紹介やマニュアルが多数提示されている。災害対応経験を通したこれらの成果は、詳細な応急処置法や修復技法や具体的な機器等が多数紹介されているが、被災の状況は地理的状況や災害程度等によって大きく変容し、救済対象となる資料の状態も一様ではない。そのため、これまでの災害対応実践を踏まえた対策を行うためには、具体的な実践事例に基づいた、災害対策の考え方を提示することが求められる。被災した資料と対峙するなかで、どのような目的の下で何を考えるべきなのか。またいかなる観点に基づいて観察し、どこまでの対応策の検討が必要になるのか。被災資料との向き合い方、具体的な対応策の検討や技術選択の考え方を示すことは、地域住民を主体とした被災資料の救済活動を広げていくためにも重要なテーマである。

　以上の課題を踏まえ、本書では被災地域での活動を想定した救済活動について、被災資料を発見してから一時保管・応急処置に至るまでの対応策、および技術選択を判断するための考え方と、地域歴史資料の防災・減災についての考え方を提示する。災害対策の進展に伴い、被災対応に関する膨大な事例が蓄積され、具体的な技法が各所で公開されるなか、本書の企画に際して重視したのは、以下の2点にある。

■ 災害対策の目的・考え方を整理する

　1点目として、災害対策の目的・考え方を整理することである。前述の通り、歴史資料の救済に関する多様な事例が蓄積され、技術開発やマニュアル策定が各所で進められており、資料保存という取り組みのなかで災害対策は重要なテーマとして認知されつつあるといえる。その反面、詳細な技法が多数紹介されるなかで、それらがいかなる場面で有効な技術であるのか、何を目的にどの程度処置を施すべきなのか、といった実践に向けた情報整理は大きな課題となっている。被災した歴史資料を取り扱うのは、必ずしも保存・修復技術に精通した専門家とは限らない。特に日本の場合、自治体職員や地域住民等が初期対応を担う場面も珍しくなく、多様な担い手が技術選択や到達点の設定などを設定することも多い。そうした状況を踏まえ、膨大に蓄積された情報のなかから技術を選択し、適切な措置を施すための留意点を整理することは急務の課題でもある。すなわち、災害対策としての資料保存を実務面から整理し、具体的な作業工程や到達目標を設定するための考え方を提示すること、これが本書で目指す第1の目的である。

■ 災害対策への備え方・対話の目的を整理する

　2点目は、備え方・対話の目的を整理することである。災害対策は資料を保存・継承する上で一つの局面である。災害現場から資料を救済し、消滅の危機を脱することは、資料保存における大きな目的であるが、中長期的視野で保存・継承を考えた場合、資料に対する物理的なアプローチにとどまらず、

資料をとりまく人や社会との関わりを検討することが求められる。特に近年では、専門家・専門知の市民社会との関わりが注目され、資料保存・継承の現場においても、多様な専門家が資料救済の現場や保存・継承の過程で人びとといかなるかたちで対話を重ねていくかが模索されている。本書では、資料をとりまく人と地域との関わりに注目し、救済から継承に至る経過のなかで実践を重ねるいくつかの取り組みを通して、社会のなかで活用される専門知のあり方について考えることを課題としている。

■ 実践活動の手がかりに

　本書は3部によって構成している。**第1部「資料救済の前提」**では、災害時における諸方との連絡・連携について、地域をとりまく関連組織・団体との向き合い方を紹介する。**第2部「資料救済・保存の考え方」**は、紙資料・写真資料・民具資料・美術資料を対象として、被災資料を救済するために、緊急対応として求められる到達点と保存のための留意点などを提示する。**第3部「資料救済への備え方」**では、災害に備えたシミュレーションや地域とのコミュニケーションの目的を紹介する。地域社会の存続に向けて、さまざまな専門知識・技術の活用や多様なアクターとの連携が模索されるなか、歴史文化の継承に関しても多様な「専門知」と「社会知」を導入した地域実践が進められようとしている。災害多発期における現代社会において、地域の履歴をいかなるかたちで守り伝えることができるのか。本企画が各地域における歴史文化の保存と継承に関する実践活動の手がかりとなることを期待する。

　なお、本書には、各章で紹介した事象を幅広く伝えるために、英訳版もあわせて掲載している。これまで国内で取り組まれてきた取り組みが、国際的にいかなる事例として捉えられるのか、今後の議論を期待して企画した。資料保存・継承の国際的連携の一助となれば幸いである。

第1部

資料救済の前提

第1章

災害発生時における地域と資料

▨　天野真志（国立歴史民俗博物館）

はじめに

　我々は、地震や風水害などのさまざまな自然災害と向き合いながら生活している。多発する自然災害との対峙は、地域社会をとりまくあらゆる方面で検討と実践が行われているが、歴史や文化に関する分野でも、いかにして各地に伝来する資料を守り伝えるかが検討されている。

　地域に伝来する歴史的・文化的なものは多様である。具体的には、古文書と総称される文字記録や掛軸などの美術資料、人びとの生活文化を理解するための民具などが想起されるが、近年では写真や音声・動画といった視聴覚記録も地域の歴史文化情報として注目されている。これらの存在は、「文化財」や「文化遺産」、「歴史資料」など、さまざまな言葉で呼ばれているが、ある一定の空間において歴史的・文化的価値を共有・共感されたモノを捉える点で共通している。本書では「歴史資料」ないし「資料」と呼ぶが、資料の捉え方に関して、近年では「地域歴史資料」という考え方が広がりつつある。「地域歴史資料」とは、資料そのものだけではなく、資料に関与する主体や経緯に注目し、地域という空間で人びとが「歴史資料」なる存在を認識していく取り組みを検討・実践するものとして理解される。こうした視角を念頭に置くなら、地域に伝わるさまざまな資料を地域が主体となって保存・継承するための方法が必要となり、特に自然災害などで歴史資料が危機的な状態に陥った際に実践するための具体的な対応策が求められるだろう。

以下では、各地域における歴史資料の災害対策について、これまでの経過を概観し、地域を主体とした資料救済の考え方について検討してみたい。

1．災害対策の経過

　自然災害の発生にともない、被災地の救援に向けた諸活動が行われる。歴史文化の災害対策として行われるのが資料の救済活動であるが、これらの活動は、主に人命救助やライフラインの復旧活動など、生命や人びとの生活に直結する救援活動が落ち着きを見せ始めた頃から本格化する。被災から一定の期間が経過して救出される資料の多くは、破損や水濡れ等により劣化・消滅のリスクを多分に抱えていることが想定される。そのため、がれきの撤去や清掃活動の過程で廃棄されることも少なくないが、国宝や重要文化財といった象徴的な存在だけでなく、地域に伝わる多様な資料をこうした危機的な状況から救い出し、地域住民等と協働して守り伝える取り組みが実践されている。

　日本においてこうした取り組みの重要性が強く提起されたのは、1995 年阪神・淡路大震災を直接の端緒とする。文化庁を中心とするレスキュー事業が展開する一方で、個人宅など民間に伝わる多様な資料の救済が課題となり、ボランティア活動として地域の資料を守り伝える取り組みが目指される。この後、各地で災害が多発するようになると、同様の取り組みが各被災地で実践され、「資料ネット」と総称される活動が全国に広がっていく。

　地域を主体とした災害対策の実践について、資料ネットなどを中心に行われたいくつかの事例を確認し、地域における活動の傾向と特徴を考えてみたい。「資料ネット」活動のなかで具体的な資料の救済方法が議論されるようになるのは、2004 年頃からである。2004 年台風 23 号が通過して各所に被害が発生した兵庫県では、歴史資料ネットワークが被災地調査を実施し、その過程で確認された水濡れ資料の救済活動を行っている。この活動は、主に個人宅に伝来した古文書等紙媒体資料が対象とされ、神戸大学文学部を拠点として関西圏の大学生や自治体関係者、博物館学芸員、地域住民によるボランティア活動として対応が行われた（松下正和・河野未央編『水損史料を救

う』岩田書院、2009年)。

　2005年に台風14号が各地を襲うと、宮崎県延岡市(のべおかし)において個人宅に伝わる写真資料の救済活動が行われている。救出されたのは1940年代以降の写真類であり、固着部の展開と乾燥作業に加え、デジタル化による画像の保存が行われている(山内利秋「台風被害にあった写真資料の保存と修復について」『文化財情報学研究』4、2005年、山内利秋・増田豪「宮崎県における文化資源災害救助対策の現状と課題」『九州保健福祉大学研究紀要』8、2007年)。このときの活動を契機として宮崎歴史資料ネットワークが設立し、宮崎県域における資料保存・継承のための活動が組織されている。

　その後、いくつかの水害における資料救済の取り組みが確認されるが、これらの活動で大きな転機となったのが、2011年東日本大震災であろう。東日本太平洋沖各地における津波被害は、膨大な地域資料に深刻な被害もたらした。この災害によって博物館等の収蔵施設にも被害が発生し、被災地域に対して歴史・民俗・考古・美術など、歴史文化に関わるあらゆる分野にわたる救済活動が展開した。また、劣化・消滅の危機に瀕する資料に対して多様な専門家が検討を重ね、被災資料に対する具体的な実践が進められた。そうしたなかで各地の資料ネットでも個人宅に伝わる資料を中心に救済活動を実

図1　2018年西日本豪雨時における広島での活動(2018年7月30日撮影)

施し、資料の保存・継承に向けた模索が進められた。特に資料ネットの取り組みでは、地域住民を含む多様な人びとによって救済活動を展開し、地域を主体として資料を救い出し、守り伝えるための対話と実践が重視されている[図1]。

　東日本大震災以降、2015年の関東・東北豪雨や2016年熊本地震、2018年西日本豪雨、2019年東日本台風など、各地で大規模な豪雨・台風被害が多発している。これらの被害と対峙し、各地で多発する地震や風水害でも資料ネットの取り組みが実施され、現在に至るまで資料の継承に向けた模索が続けられている。

2. 災害対策の実務と担い手

2.1.「レスキュー」の展開

　災害時における資料救済活動は、「レスキュー」と表現されることが多い。1995年阪神・淡路大震災頃より、被災地からの資料救済活動が「文化財レスキュー」と呼ばれるようになり、2011年東日本大震災以降こうした呼称が定着しつつある。近年用いられる「レスキュー」は、単に危険な場所から資料を救出する行為にとどまらない。例えば建石徹は、「文化財レスキュー」を、「被災時の文化財救出活動のうち、主に動産文化財等を対象として、被災地から救出・輸送し、保管（一時的な保管を含む）し、必要な応急処置をするところまで」と定義している（建石徹「文化財レスキューとその活動」、高妻洋成・建石徹・小谷竜介編『入門　大災害時代の文化財防災』同成社、2023年、p.43）。この考え方は、東日本大震災時に実施された「東北地方太平洋沖地震被災文化財等救援事業（文化財レスキュー事業）」が、「緊急に保全措置を必要とする文化財等について、救出し、応急措置をし、当該県内又は周辺都県の博物館等保存機能のある施設での一時保管を行う」ことを目的に掲げて活動したことを背景としており[1]、以後の災害対策でもこの認識が継承されている。

　津波被害や台風・豪雨による浸水被害が多発する状況のなか、近年の「レスキュー」活動では、安全な場所への移動のみで救済活動は完結し得ず、資

料を水濡れ被害などの危機的な状況から脱することが目的とされている。

　では、一連の活動はどのような主体が担っているのだろうか。東日本大震災のような広域にわたる被害が発生した場合、全国規模での包括的な対応が行われるが、局地的な災害に関しては、一般的に各自治体や近隣博物館、大学等が中核となって活動が進められる。特に「資料ネット」に象徴される活動では、主に大学教員や博物館学芸員、アーキビストなど多様な領域の専門家に加え、地域住民やその地域に関わりのある人びとによって構成される。専門領域にとらわれず、地域住民との対話を通して多様な価値観に注目した地域歴史文化の調査・保存・継承を目指す取り組みが「資料ネット」の特徴といえる。反面、各地の「資料ネット」には必ずしも保存や修復に関する専門家が存在しているわけではなく、被災資料の取り扱いに関しては試行錯誤が続けられている。大規模な資料群が被災した場合、膨大な被災資料の対応に際して作業者が求められるが、多くの場合市民ボランティアなどにより作業が進められている。これらの蓄積を通して、被災直後から一時保管に至る対応過程が多数報告されており、一連の経験を踏まえた災害対策の実務に関する到達点と課題の整理、今後の対策に備えた提起が求められている。

2.2. 災害対策の広がり

　東日本大震災以降、資料救済の取り組みはいくつかの転換を迎える。その一つに、保存・修復の専門家による積極的な地域活動への関与があげられる。もちろん、それまでにも民俗資料や美術資料などを中心に、専門家を主体とした地域資料の救済は盛んに行われていたが、資料ネットや地域住民などと連携した救済活動の実践は、東日本大震災以降多様な広がりとして確認することができる。

　例えば、彫刻文化財の保存修復を専門とする岡田靖は、東日本大震災時に地震や津波により損傷・崩壊した地域に伝来する仏像類の救済活動を被災地で実施した。その際岡田は、仏像の修復を行う際、資料を工房に移動するのではなく、現地で修復作業を実施し、修復の過程を一般公開して地域住民と共有する方法を採っている。この目的について岡田は地域のシンボルとしての仏像が修復されていく過程を、被災地の復興過程とリンクさせながら感じ

てしてもらうことを挙げる（岡田靖「東日本大震災における彫刻文化財の被災後の対応と被災前の対策について」『東海国立大学機構大学文書資料室紀要』29、2021年）。被災からの復旧・復興過程で地域住民と救出資料の内容を確認しながらその地域的意義を共感するこうした取り組みは、被災民具の救済活動でも行われ（加藤幸治『復興キュレーション』社会評論社、2017年）、被災資料から地域資料へと位置づけ直す営みとしても注目される。

　また、救済活動が具体化・多角化しつつあることも、近年の特徴として指摘できるだろう。「レスキュー」の範囲が一時保管に至る救済活動の総体を指す行為と規定されると、地域を拠点とした一連の活動も、被災資料に対する具体的な対応が模索されるようになる。特に、多くの実践が行われる古文書などの紙資料に関しては、東日本大震災の経験を踏まえた取り組みが各地で行われ、水濡れ資料の乾燥やカビ・臭気対策、固着した資料の対応などさまざまな課題への模索が進められる。これらの活動は、保存・修復の専門家の指示に基づく場合もあるが、多くは自治体の文化財担当者や博物館学芸員、大学教員、地域住民が中心となることが多く、資料ネットなどを主体としたボランティア活動として実施されている。

3. 資料救済の目的と到達点

　これまで確認したように、地域を主体とする近年の資料救済の活動は、保存・修復の専門家に限定されない人びとが主体となる場合が多い。そのため、高度な技術や専門的な機器を用いない形態が各所で模索・実践されているが、対象となる資料の被災状況によって対処すべき課題は一様ではない。これまでに、被災地域の状況や対応人員の性格に応じて多様な実践例が報告されており、経験に基づいたマニュアルなども多岐にわたる。これらを概観すると、同じ言葉を用いているがその目的や手段が異なる場合も散見され、「レスキュー」に含まれる活動の経過やその到達点が必ずしも共有されているわけではない。「レスキュー」という活動を、被災地対応に関わる現場作業の総称として理解し、これまでの取り組みを今後の災害対策に向けた実践例として検証するためには、「レスキュー」で求められる作業の考え方を含めて

整理する必要がある［図2］。

　「レスキュー」の過程で重要な作業となるのが応急措置（処置）である。この目的については、日髙真吾が次のように明示している。

　　応急措置は、被災した文化財の劣化を食い止めるための作業であり、次の段階である本格修復までの間をつなぐための処理である。同時に前述してきた一時保管場所を清浄に保つためにも重要な作業である。
　　（日髙真吾「大規模災害時における文化財レスキュー事業に関する一考察」『国立民族学博物館研究報告』40-1、2015年、p.39）

　これによると、応急措置とは「本格修復」を検討・実施するまでの一時的な対応であり、資料の劣化進行を抑制することに加え、保管される空間の環境維持も射程に収めている。ここでは、修復を行うための事前対応として応急措置が位置づけられ、修復行為とは明確に区別されるものとして捉えている。そもそも、「レスキュー」という言葉に象徴されるように、災害対策の過程ではあくまで緊急的な措置が念頭にあり、資料の解体・洗浄などを伴う修復行為は必然ではない。しかし、頻発化・激甚化する近年の自然災害は「レ

救済　　　　　　　　応急処置　　　　　　　一時保管

資料が当面する消滅および急速な劣化の回避

図2　「レスキュー」のイメージ

19

スキュー」を長期化させる傾向にあり、長期間一時保管が求められるなかで応急措置の範疇を超えた作業が実施される場合も確認される。

　では、応急措置では、いかなる状態に資料を導くことが求められるのだろうか。被災地域では多様な媒体の資料が大量に被害を受けるため、すべての資料を即座に完全な状態に戻していくことは現実的ではない。そのため被災現場では、より多くの資料に対して応急的な処置を施し、資料の急速な劣化を回避・抑制する手段を講じることが要請され、その後に想定される活用・継承のための保存・修復に移行するための作業計画の立案・実践が重要となる。代表的な資料に関する具体的な方法などについては第2部の諸論考を参照されたいが、ここではその応急措置に関わるいくつかの点を整理しておきたい。

　まず、応急措置の目的についてである。対象となる資料によって程度の差はあるが、基本的には資料の劣化進行を抑制することが第一の目的とされる。すなわち、災害等によって資料にもたらされる深刻なリスクを除去することが課題となる。例えば、水損被害を受けた資料に対しては、水濡れ状態を脱することが第一の目的となり、冷凍による一時的処置や乾燥に向けた対応が求められる。また、地震による倒壊・破損被害に際しては、破損した部品の回収や破損部の確認が想定されよう。

　次に、応急措置の到達点であるが、どの程度までを応急措置として対応するかの基準は、各地の取り組み状況によって異なっている。応急措置の段階は、あくまで一時的な処置と位置づけ、資料の形状変更を伴わない乾燥作業やカビ等劣化要因の抑制に注力し、一時保管空間に安置するための簡易的なクリーニングにとどめることが理想的状況であろう。より具体的には、2〜3年程度の一時保管に耐えうる状態に導くことが、応急措置の到達点として理解されるだろう。しかし、東日本大震災に代表される大規模被害時には、広域におよぶ被害によって「レスキュー」活動が長期化し、結果として一時的な処置にとどまらない処置が応急措置の段階で実施されている。なお、この点に関連して、東日本大震災以降「安定化処理」という用語が使われることがある。「安定化処理」とは、応急措置の範疇を超えた、修復行為にも踏み込んだ処置を想定した行為であり、大規模災害により修復作業に至るまで

の長期的な一時保管が求められる状況のなかで生じた措置と捉えられる。特に、美術品などのように、救出段階からある程度の専門的技法や知識が要求される資料を想定した概念と捉えられることができよう。こうした理解を前提として、本書では、基本的に「安定化処理」ではなく応急措置の段階を想定し、実践とその考え方について紹介していく。

　以上のように、「レスキュー」として捉えられる活動は、救出とその後の対応としての応急措置、一時保管の3段階が想定される。そのうち応急措置については、将来的な修復を見通した一時的な対応とすることが原則となるが、被災状況や資料の性質によって、場合によっては修復に関わるような解体・洗浄行為を含む場合が発生する。この点に関しては、「応急措置の在り方を考える場合、被災した文化財の状態の安定化だけを求めるのではなく、その後の活用も視野に入れながら実施する、文化財の保存修復の方法論も取り入れた応急措置の在り方を模索する必要があると考える」との指摘があり[2]、技術的な議論に終始せず、資料が置かれる社会的環境に即した考え方を議論する必要性が提起されている。そのためには、活動主体のなかで資料を遺し伝える目的や認識を共有し、活動の到達点を協議・確認しておく必要があるだろう。

おわりに

　本章では、災害対策としての資料保存について、その経過と現況を確認し、災害時における資料の「レスキュー」活動について整理した。個人宅など地域に伝来する資料の多くは、蔵や物置など、必ずしも安定しない保存環境下で管理されることが多く、また金銭的にも修復・保存に関わる公的支援が受けづらい傾向が看守される。こうした資料が被災した場合、多くの場合で資料ネット等のボランティア活動が主体となって「レスキュー」が実施される。地域の自治体や博物館等による活動でも、対象となる資料を熟知した専門家が配置されているとは限らず、「レスキュー」活動においては、専門家以外の人びとが主体となって対応を余儀なくされることが多々発生する。そうした状況に備えるためには、まず資料の「レスキュー」に関する基本的な考え

方を認識しておくことが必要となる。また、処置に関わる専門的知見を有する分野や専門家の存在を理解することも重要となろう。

注

1　2011年3月30日付文化庁次長決定「東北地方太平洋沖地震被災文化財等救援事業（文化財レスキュー事業）実施要綱」https://www.bunka.go.jp/earthquake/rescue/pdf/bunkazai_rescue_jigyo_ver04.pdf（2023年12月25日最終閲覧）

2　日髙真吾「大規模災害時における文化財レスキューの課題」（『国立歴史民俗博物館研究報告』214、2019年、p.50）

参考文献

・奥村弘編『歴史文化を大災害から守る』（東京大学出版会、2014年）

・松下正和・河野未央編『水損史料を救う』（岩田書院、2009年）

・日髙真吾『災害と文化財』（千里文化財団、2015年）

・天野真志・後藤真編『地域歴史文化継承ガイドブック』（文学通信、2022年）

・高妻洋成・建石徹・小谷竜介編『入門　大災害時代の文化財防災』（同成社、2023年）

第 2 章

資料救済に関わる人びと

▧ 松下正和（神戸大学）

はじめに

第 1 章でも述べられているように、資料救済は、必ずしも文化財の取り扱いや資料修復などの専門家だけが関与するものではない。特に各地の史料ネットが主に救済対象としている民間所在資料の場合は、大学や行政の文化財関係者のみならず地域住民や被災地外のボランティアを含む多様な人びとによってレスキューが行われる。

現在の日本は人口減少や高齢化が加速し、自然災害も頻発するようになり、資料救済の担い手が少なくなりつつある中で、対応すべき資料救済の事案は増加する一方である。このように限られた人的・金銭的・物的資源の中でいかに効率的に資料救済を行うかが課題となっているのが現状である。資料レスキューの技術論や効率論とともに、資料を残してきた人びとや地域社会が今後も存続するための方策も見据えた上で、資料救済を位置づける必要があるのではないか。

よって、本章では、1995 年の阪神・淡路大震災を契機として設立されたボランティア団体である歴史資料ネットワーク[1]（事務局：神戸大学文学部内）や兵庫県内での活動を中心に、災害発生時にはどのような関連機関や団体、人びととの連携の中で、資料救済が行われてきたのか、またとりわけ文化財指定がなされておらず、被災時に公的支援を受けにくい、民間に所在する多様な資料を含む私有財産としての「未指定文化財」の保全と活用をめぐ

る現状と課題について、大学に身を置く立場から述べてみたい。

1. 広域連携体制の整備状況

1.1. 全国的な文化財・被災資料救援体制の進展

　1995年阪神・淡路大震災を契機に「歴史資料ネットワーク」が成立して以降、大規模災害が全国で発生するたびに、また災害前の備えとして、現在では30団体を超える資料ネット組織が全国各地に設立され（天野真志・後藤真編『地域歴史文化継承ガイドブック』文学通信、2022年）、2015年度以降は、「全国史料ネット研究交流集会」を開催し、各地の資料ネット相互の情報交換とネットワークの構築を進めている。また東日本大震災時に結成された文化財救援レスキュー事業でのつながりを元にして、歴史資料ネットワークも含むさまざまな文化遺産に関係する27団体（2023年6月段階）が参加する「文化遺産防災ネットワーク推進会議」が結成され、日常時から情報共有を図り、災害発生時には救援活動を迅速かつ効果的に行うネットワークを構築している。2020年には独立行政法人国立文化財機構の本部施設として文化財防災センターが設置され、文化財防災の体制作りや技術開発、発災時の救援活動の支援を行っている（高妻洋成・小谷竜介・建石徹編『入門大災害時代の文化財防災』同成社、2023年）。さらには、国立歴史民俗博物館を主導機関とする人間文化研究機構は、東北大学や神戸大学とともに、「歴史文化資料保全の大学・共同利用機関ネットワーク事業」を立ち上げ、各地の史料ネット等と連携し、災害時の相互支援体制や広域ネットワークの構築を進めている。このように全国的な支援体制がさまざまなレベルで作られており、災害で被災するさまざまな文化財や資料に対応するための体制や、全国の組織をつなぐネットワーク化は、阪神・淡路大震災発生時と比して、格段に進展している。天災・人災ともに多様化・複合化する災害に対応するためにも、今後も多様な分野からなる災害関連のネットワーク化が必要になってくると思われる。

　また広域連合の枠組みを利用した文化財などの救援体制も構築されつつある。例えば、2013年にはすでに中国・四国地方の9県並びに広島市及び岡

山市が「中国・四国地方における被災文化財等の保護に向けた相互支援計画」を策定している。また、関西では南海地震を想定し「近畿圏危機発生時の相互応援に関する基本協定に基づく文化財の被災対応ガイドライン」が 2018 年に策定されている。基本協定構成府県は、福井・三重・滋賀・京都・大阪・兵庫・奈良・和歌山・徳島及び関西広域連合（鳥取を含む）となっている（下線部は関西広域連合構成団体）。東日本大震災でも明らかになったように、大規模災害時には被災県のみでの災害対応は困難であり、複数県にまたがる支援体制の役割が大きくなる。例えば兵庫県では、当時の近畿 2 府 4 県の教育委員会による相互支援の枠組みを用いて、2004 年台風 23 号により被災した兵庫県豊岡市・日高町の水損資料の真空凍結乾燥処理が滋賀県立安土城考古博物館によって行われたこともあった（松下正和・河野未央編『水損史料を救う　風水害からの歴史資料保全』岩田書院、2009 年）。

　このように広域連合を基盤とする総合的な計画の元に、文化財に関する個別の計画の策定が進みつつあり、実際に広域支援も行われている。今後は未指定文化財の分野においても、各地の資料ネットによる発災時にカウンターパート式の支援の仕組みがさらに整備されることを期待したい。

1.2. 未指定文化財の保全に関する連携体制の課題

　先述のように全国各地に資料ネットが設置され、毎年「全国史料ネット研究交流集会」が開催されるようにはなっているが、実際に大規模災害が発生した際に、個々の資料ネットでは情報集約は行っているものの、未指定文化財の被害情報を集約し、被災地への人的・物的・金銭的支援やノウハウを効率よく提供するためのプラットフォームはいまだにない。もちろん、個々の資料ネットによる被災地支援を否定するものではなく、また中小規模の災害は各地の資料ネットが主体になり活動することが望ましい。ただ大規模災害が発生した場合に、各地の団体が別々に被災地に情報提供を求めることを行えば、被災地の行政などは度重なる問い合わせの応対だけで過度の負担を強いられる恐れがある。特定の資料ネットが情報集約のセンターになるなど、場合によっては被災地の負担が少なくなるように連絡窓口を一本化することも考える必要がある。

人命救助や避難所対応、ライフラインの復旧が一段落し、被災地の文化財担当職員が本来の文化財対応業務に戻った際に被害調査・復旧活動をしやすくなるよう、被災地外の史料ネットはそれまでに後方支援体制を整備することも必要であろう。具体的には、被災地の資料所在情報や被害状況の把握、レスキューノウハウを持つ人材や応急処置に使用する物品の用意、補助金や募金などを利用した活動資金の確保、被災資料の受け入れ（応急処置・目録作成など）などがある。またの新型コロナウイルス感染症（COVID-19）の流行を契機として、Zoom や MicrosoftTeams、GoogleMeet などのオンライン会議が普及したこともあり、必ずしも直接的に被災地入りをしなくても可能な支援内容が増えてきている。公共インフラに比べ、文化に関わる復興は長期的なものとなる。特に大規模災害時には、後方支援を含めた長期的な支援体制を構築することで、現地入りができない人びとも含めた多様な関与を引き出すことができるのではないだろうか。

2. 県内の整備体制

2.1. 都道府県・市町村の地域防災計画内の未指定文化財対応

　災害対策基本法で定める国の防災基本計画と関連し、都道府県の地域防災計画や市町村の地域防災計画がある。以前にも、地域防災計画の中に文化財保護の項目を盛り込み、災害復旧時において、被災文化財等の保全を復興業務の一環に位置づけることの重要性を指摘したことがある（松下正和「民間所在史料保全のためのネットワーク形成」奥村弘編『歴史文化を大災害から守る』東京大学出版会、2014 年）。近年は、指定文化財のみならず、未指定文化財に対しても、所在情報の把握や目録作成、保全や取り扱いの周知、被害状況の把握、情報共有、マニュアルの作成などを明示している県も増加している（秋田、新潟、石川、佐賀、和歌山、山形、大分県などが参考になる）。項目名に「指定文化財等」と「等」を明記することで、指定文化財及び登録文化財以外の文化財にも対応を可能とすることが期待できる。

　また近年は、都道府県単位で「文化財災害対応マニュアル」が策定されつつある。例えば、兵庫県は行政向けのマニュアルを 2021 年に、文化財所有

者向けのマニュアルを 2022 年に策定している[2]。行政上の手続きが必要な
ものについては、指定・登録の文化財に限定されているが、このマニュアル
で対象とする文化財は、指定・登録・未指定を問わないものとなっている。
また、風水害時の対応の際には、歴史資料ネットワークに対する歴史文化資
料保全への支援要請を行うことも文中に盛り込まれている。

　災害発生後に「動きたい人」を支援するためにも、市町村の地域防災計画
や文化財災害対応マニュアルも含め、全国の自治体において未指定文化財へ
の対応が明記されるように、呼びかけを今後とも進めていきたい。

2.2. 文化財保存活用大綱と文化財保存活用地域計画における資料ネットの位置づけ

　2018 年の文化財保護法の改正によって、都道府県による文化財保存活用
大綱の策定と、市町村による文化財保存活用地域計画の作成や文化庁長官に
よる認定が、新たに制度化された。

　文化財保存活用大綱では、防災・災害発生時の対応が基本的な記載事項と
して定められている。この策定を機に大学や史料ネットなどの民間団体との
連携を明記し、災害時の協力体制を構築することが期待される。兵庫県の場
合、歴史資料ネットワークの名はないものの、神戸大学など文化財に関連す
る大学名を明記して日常的な連携関係も位置づけられている。

　また文化財保存活用地域計画については、2023 年末段階で 139 の自治体
により作成されており[3]、地域計画の作成に際して、未指定文化財のリスト
が添付されている自治体もある。災害発生時に未指定文化財の所在情報が明
らかでない場合、救出のための初動が遅れることは、阪神・淡路大震災以来
指摘されている（奥村弘『大震災と歴史資料保存』吉川弘文館、2012 年）。
その点からも、今回の地域計画作成により未指定文化財の把握と情報公開（た
だし、盗難などの防犯対策に留意）の進展が特に期待される。

　さらには兵庫県内の場合、歴史文化遺産の被害調査や保存・活用などにつ
いての連携先として、歴史資料ネットワークを挙げる市町が増えつつある
（2023 年 12 月末現在、神河町・香美町・明石市・神戸市・福崎町）。このよ
うに、大綱や地域計画の中に各地の資料ネットを位置づけるよう提言するこ

とも今後は重要ではないだろうか。

2.3. 文化財関係団体間の連携

　業界団体ごとの連絡・協力ルートを平時からいかに確保しているのかも重要なポイントになるだろう。前者の文化財系ルートとともに、社会教育系のルートの整備が望まれる。例えば、兵庫県博物館協会は、2017 年から、被災館園の救援のために、会員館園職員に対して派遣要請をする規定を含む規約（「災害時の相互協力及び関係機関・団体との連絡と協力に関する規約」）を作り、会員館園が相互に締結している。災害救援をしたいという学芸員に対し派遣依頼を出すことで、職員がボランティアとしてではなく業務として動くことができるというシステムになっている。他には、岐阜県博物館協会では、災害発生後に被害の有無の確認とともに文化財担当者への連絡をするようにしている。実際に連絡をしてみるとつながらないこともあり、その原因に対処することで実際の防災訓練にもなっているという（正村美里「もの部会【報告】令和 2 年 7 月豪雨における被災アンケート実施と結果について」『岐阜の博物館』187、2020 年）。平時からの連絡網の構築と確認は災害時の支援・受援にとっても重要なポイントになるだろう。

　また、資料ネットと行政そして多様な文化財関係団体との間で、災害時や日常時の連携・協力関係を構築するために、規約や協定を締結している県もある。例えば、和歌山では 2015 年に「和歌山県博物館施設等災害対策連絡会議」が設立され、未指定や個人蔵も含む県内の被災文化財に対し、救援・保全を図るための協力関係を構築している。歴史資料保全ネットワーク・和歌山や、和歌山大学をはじめとする研究機関、博物館、図書館、県、市町村教育委員会などが参画している。同様の取り組みが、岡山・徳島・愛媛などにもある。

　兵庫県には現在このような規約はないものの、歴史資料ネットワークが県内の被災歴史資料を調査する際に、兵庫県教育委員会文化財課から県内市町教育委員会に対し、歴史資料ネットワークの調査への協力依頼についての公文書を発出した事例もあり、すでに両者の連携関係が構築されている。また、兵庫県教育委員会文化財課・神戸大学大学院人文学研究科地域連携センター・

歴史資料ネットワークの三者で、「兵庫県文化遺産防災研修会」を毎年開催し、県内の文化財担当職員等に対して、被災文化財の応急処置実習を行っている。また、先述のような他県の先進的取り組みに学びつつ、動産文化財・不動産文化財の枠を超えて災害時に被害調査を行うために、歴史資料ネットワークは、建築士が多く所属する「ひょうごヘリテージ機構」のヘリテージマネージャーのメンバーや、兵庫県博物館協会、兵庫県教育委員会事務局との間で協議を重ねている。以上のような文化財の関係機関・団体間の連携関係を日常的に構築することで、災害時の資料救済活動をよりスムーズなものにすることが可能になるだろう。

3. 多様なセクターとのつながり

3.1. 被災時の対応

　被災地の行政職員は防災指令が発令されると必ずしも文化財業務に従事できるとは限らない。文化財業務に戻ったとしてもまずは指定文化財の調査からはじまる。よって主に未指定文化財の保全を行う歴史資料ネットワークは、可能な限り被災地に負担をかけないために、人命救助や避難所設営が行われているような災害発生直後には、連絡を取ることを控えている。ライフラインも復活し、被災者の避難生活が終わるなど、ある程度の余裕ができた段階で、文化財担当職員や地方史研究団体のメンバー、被災地域の自治会長らとともに被災地入りをすることにしている。被災地側からの受け入れ体制や了承がない状態で、我々被災地外の人間だけで訪問することはない。民間所在の被災資料を対象とする救済活動は、まずは被災地の復興の邪魔にならないよう留意することが大前提となる。また被災資料を保全する際には、それらの一時保管場所を事前に確保しておくことが望ましい。そのためにも、行政や大学、被災地域住民との協力が欠かせない（松下正和・河野未央編『水損史料を救う　風水害からの歴史資料保全』岩田書院、2009 年）。

　ただし、被災地入りが遅れると資料の廃棄が進むことが阪神・淡路大震災以来指摘されている（奥村弘『大震災と歴史資料保存』吉川弘文館、2012 年）。民間所在の未指定文化財・資料の廃棄は、特に災害発生後に行われる「無料

のゴミ出し」や家屋の公費解体が始まることにより、一気に加速する。その
ため、所蔵者に対して、資料廃棄を防止する呼びかけや、一時保管や応急処
置などの相談窓口の周知が重要となる。近年では被災地の自治体や博物館な
どのウェブサイトでも、歴史資料の廃棄防止呼びかけや被災資料相談窓口を
周知する事例が増えている。

　インフラが途絶している大規模災害時の直後でない限り、歴史資料ネット
ワークは、役場からの広報（広報誌、被災者支援のための配布物、自治会連
絡会ルートなど）や、社会福祉協議会やボランティアセンターからの情報提
供、新聞・テレビ・ラジオ・CATV・防災無線などのメディアを通じて、被
災者に対して資料の取り扱いに関する情報を提供してきた。近年ではSNS（X
やFacebookなど）も活用が可能であるが、インフラが途絶している被災地
においては紙媒体のローカルメディアのほうが、情報が行き渡る場合もある。
特に、被災地の最前線で作業をする一般のボランティアの方々に「家族の思
い出の品」に関するものは、むやみに廃棄しないよう所蔵者に呼びかけても
らえるように、平時から社会福祉協議会やボランティアセンターにも周知が
必要になってくる。以前は、歴史資料ネットワークが被災地の行政宛てに資
料廃棄を防止するよう依頼するFAXを送信していたが、被災地への負担を
考慮し、ウェブサイト上での告知にとどめ、近年では被災地ないしは近辺の
史料ネットに対応を任せている。

　さて環境省では、災害時に発生する廃棄物を適正かつ円滑・迅速に処理す
るための応急対策などをとりまとめたものとして「災害廃棄物対策指針」を
策定している[4]。その中には、「思い出の品等」（アルバム、写真、位牌、賞状、
手帳、金庫、貴重品〈財布、通帳、印鑑、貴金属〉等）に対する対応として、「市
区町村は、災害廃棄物を撤去する場合は思い出の品や貴重品を取り扱う必要
があることを前提として、遺失物法等の関連法令での手続きや対応も確認の
上で、事前に取り扱いルールを定め、その内容の周知に努める。思い出の品
等の取り扱いルールとしては、思い出の品等の定義、持主の確認方法、回収
方法、保管方法、返却方法等が考えられる。」と記されている。貴重品は警
察に引き渡すため、それ以外の思い出の品については、廃棄に回さず、自治
体等で保管し、可能な限り所有者に引き渡すことが求められている（『災害

廃棄物管理ガイドブック』朝倉書店、2021 年）。この中では、歴史資料など
の資料が位置づけられていないため、今後は廃棄物資源循環学会などとも連
携し、歴史資料廃棄の問題についても取り扱うように提言する必要があるの
ではないだろうか。

　なお、兵庫県加西市の地域防災計画（令和 3 年度修正）「震災対策計画編」[5]
では「近隣に被災した文化財等がある場合、ごみの一時集積場等に文化財等
の集積場を設ける」とあり、レスキュー後の一時保管場所を被災地内で確保
するためのユニークな取り組みをしている。

3.2. 災害後や日常時の取り組み

　人口減少社会に向かう現在、さらには自治体合併に伴う文化財行政の縮小
や、郷土史団体の会員数減少、これまで地域史の担い手であった中学校社会
科教員や高等学校地歴科教員の多忙化による郷土史団体離れなど、平時から
地域の歴史資料保全に関与する人びとの減少傾向が指摘されている。

　このような状況の中で、地域や家に残る歴史資料や記録を、災害時ととも
に日常時から保持継承するために、また多様な人びとが資料に関心を持ち続
けていくために、大学としてどのような取り組みが可能となるだろうか。当
然のことながら、文化財関係者以外の人びとに理解を得ることが重要であろ
う。博物館学やアーカイブズ関連科目はもちろんのこと、初年時の共通教育
科目の中で、人文科学のみならず社会科学・自然科学・生命科学系の学部生
への教育においても、記録保存の意義を説くカリキュラム開発が求められよ
う（奥村弘・村井良介・木村修二編『地域歴史遺産と現代社会』神戸大学出
版会、2018 年）。また、神戸大学大学院人文学研究科地域連携センターでは
2002 年より地域住民と行政とで連携し、歴史文化を活かしたまちづくりを
進めている。災害に遭う以前に、普段から地域に残る資料や記録の保存につ
いて理解を求めていく活動を行っている（神戸大学大学院人文学研究科地域
連携センター編『「地域歴史遺産」の可能性』岩田書院、2013 年）。

　さて、歴史資料ネットワークでは、救済した資料について、仮目録を作成
した後、地域住民や所蔵者らの生活が復興した後に返却を行っている。その
際には、必ず資料の内容や保存の意義についての説明を行うようにしている。

例えば、2009 年台風 9 号による水損資料については、佐用町教育委員会や佐用郡地域史研究会のメンバーとともにレスキューや応急処置、読解を行った。同会のメンバーは、その後も独自で読解を進め資料の翻刻集も作成している（松下正和「2009 年台風 9 号被災資料の保全と活用：佐用郡地域史研究会・佐用町教育委員会との連携」『災害・復興と資料』(2)、2013 年）。また宍粟市閏賀地区自治会文書の場合は、歴史資料ネットワークのメンバー板垣貴志・吉原大志両氏が地区住民に対し、レスキューした自治会文書の解説と展示会を公民館で行い、その後も地域住民との共同研究も進めている（閏賀のあゆみ編纂委員会『閏賀のあゆみ―《記録と記憶》を未来につなぐ―』2018 年）。

　また歴史資料ネットワークの被災資料についての応急処置・整理・撮影ボランティアには、文化財に携わる学生・院生とともに、一般のシニア層の方々が多数参加している。都市部に拠点を置いていることもあり、シニア層のボランティアは阪神間を行き来する「ノマド」型の方々が多く、被災資料だけではなく、襖の下張りはがしや古文書読解、土器洗い・接合など、毛色の違うボランティアも複数経験している。このように多様な関心を持つ方々とも連携することで、史料ネット活動への参加を促していきたい。

おわりに

　災害時対応は、日頃からの調査研究、保全活動の実践、制度や人的なネットワークの構築が基礎となる。少子高齢化どころか人口減少社会に突入し、家じまい・村じまいが増えるなど社会変容も進み、近年の気候変動の関係で風水害が頻発し、また大規模な地震も多発する現在、端的に言えば、もはや個人レベルでの「現地保存主義」を住民（所蔵者や管理者）だけに強いるのは困難ではないだろうか。

　文化財保存活用大綱の指針に「地域社会総がかり」での文化財保存ということが謳われているが、単に人口減少により文化財に携わる人びとが少なくなるために、「地域社会総がかり」で残さざるを得ないという消極的な側面を強調するだけでは不十分であろう。遺跡は研究者だけのものではなく、多様な人びとの関与や意義付けによって守られるものであるという「パブリッ

ク・アーケオロジー」の議論がある（岡村勝行・松田陽編『入門パブリック・アーケオロジー』同成社、2012 年）。地域に残る歴史遺産もまた同様に、多様な人びとの関与や意義づけによって価値を増すものである。多様な人びとの関与によってプライベートな民間所在資料をいかに「公共財」として残すことができるのか、そのためには何が必要なのか。今後とも全国各地での実践にも学びつつ、地域住民を主体とした被災資料の救済と、それらの活用を見据えた地域歴史資料学を深化させ、広く文化財の保存や活用に関心と関与を持つ人びとを増やすことで文化財を意義づけ守るという意味での「地域総がかり」を実現し、そのことによりそこに住む人びととコミュニティーも維持存続するための制度やネットワークづくりを進めていきたい。

注

1　活動の詳細は、歴史資料ネットワークウェブサイト（http://siryo-net.jp/）を参照。（以下ウェブサイトはすべて 2024 年 1 月 23 日最終閲覧）

2　兵庫県教育委員会ウェブサイト「兵庫県文化財防災・災害マニュアル」（https://www2.hyogo-c.ed.jp/hpe/bunka/cont_cate/兵庫県文化財防災・災害対応マニュアル/）

3　文化庁ウェブサイト「各地方公共団体が作成した「文化財保存活用地域計画」」（https://www.bunka.go.jp/seisaku/bunkazai/bunkazai_hozon/92040101.html）

4　環境省ウェブサイト「災害廃棄物対策情報サイト」（http://kouikishori.env.go.jp/guidance/guideline/）

5　加西市ウェブサイト「加西市地域防災計画」（令和 3 年度修正）第 3 章災害応急対策計画（https://www.city.kasai.hyogo.jp/uploaded/attachment/16252.pdf）

参考文献

・高妻洋成・小谷竜介・建石徹編『入門大災害時代の文化財防災』（同成社、2023 年）
・天野真志・後藤真編『地域歴史文化継承ガイドブック』（文学通信、2022 年）
・（一社）廃棄物資源循環学会編『災害廃棄物管理ガイドブック』（朝倉書店、2021 年）
・正村美里「もの部会【報告】令和 2 年 7 月豪雨における被災アンケート実施と結果について」（『岐阜の博物館』187、岐阜県博物館協会、2020 年、p.3）

- 奥村弘・村井良介・木村修二編『地域歴史遺産と現代社会』(神戸大学出版会、2018 年)
- 佐用郡地域史研究会「襖の下張調査から知る郷土の歴史〜三日月藩久崎役所関係の手紙など」(『佐用郡地域史研究会紀要』6、同会、2018 年)
- 閏賀のあゆみ編纂委員会『閏賀のあゆみ―《記録と記憶》を未来につなぐ―』(2018 年)
- 奥村弘編『歴史文化を大災害から守る　地域歴史資料学の構築』(東京大学出版会、2014 年)
- 神戸大学大学院人文学研究科地域連携センター編『「地域歴史遺産」の可能性』(岩田書院、2013 年)
- 松下正和「2009 年台風 9 号被災資料の保全と活用：佐用郡地域史研究会・佐用町教育委員会との連携」(『災害・復興と資料』2、2013 年、pp.27-38)
- 奥村弘『大震災と歴史資料保存』(吉川弘文館、2012 年)
- 岡村勝行・松田陽編『入門パブリック・アーケオロジー』(同成社、2012 年)
- 松下正和・河野未央編『水損史料を救う　風水害からの歴史資料保全』(岩田書院、2009 年)
- 地方史研究協議会編『歴史資料の保存と地方史研究』(岩田書院、2009 年)
- 歴史資料ネットワーク編『歴史資料ネットワーク活動報告書』(2002 年)

第2部

資料救済・保存の考え方

第 3 章

紙資料の救済

▨　天野真志（国立歴史民俗博物館）

はじめに

　本章で対象とする紙資料とは、主に人びとが活動するなかで生成し蓄積した記録類を指す。文字記録が中心となるこれらの資料は、作成された時期や目的によってさまざまな紙が用いられており、古文書と呼ばれるような歴史的・文化的価値が認知されているものから、日常的なメモ、雑誌等に至るまで、多様かつ膨大な資料群として各所に伝えられている。

　紙資料は、博物館や図書館、文書館など公的機関に多く所蔵されてもいるが、その一方で個人宅などに保存・管理されているものも膨大に存在しており、その地域や家の成り立ちを伝える存在として継承されてきている。これらは、組織・団体が管理する記録類や個人の日記や書翰類、蔵書など多岐にわたるが、多くの場合が資料群として保存・管理されている。そのため、災害等の被害を受けた場合、大量の被災資料に対応することが想定され、特に水濡れ状態の紙資料を的確に状態を把握し、処置を施すことが求められる。

1. 被災紙資料の救出

　災害によって保管空間に損傷が生じた場合、容器に収められていない資料は散逸の危機が想定される。また、津波や豪雨などの影響で水濡れ被害が発生すると、水を含みやすい紙資料は腐敗やカビの発生により急速な劣化が進

行し、文字等資料情報の消失、さらには資料そのものの崩壊を引き起こしてしまう。

書翰や書類などの記録資料は、紐でくくられたり、封筒・袋などに収納されたりして、複数点をひとくくりで保管されていることがある。これらは資料が保管される段階で管理者が資料の時代や内容に即して整理した可能性を含んでおり、日常的な資料整理では、搬出の前に資料の保管状態、構造を記録する、いわゆる

津波によって水濡れ被害を受けた資料群
（2012 年 3 月 23 救出）

現状記録をとることが原則である。記録資料の整理・搬出においては、資料が整理・保管される空間自体が重要な情報であるとの認識の下、資料の形状や配列情報を保持した状態で整理することが基本とされる。

しかし、災害時においては、限られた時間のなかで速やかな搬出が求められるため、必ずしもこうした基本原則に沿った細密な現状記録が作成されるとは限らない。そのため、現場ではなるべく資料の搬出過程を写真や動画で記録し、後の整理作業における参考情報として保持しておくことが望ましい。また、紙資料の場合、現場作業の段階ではそれが歴史資料であるのか否かの判断を行うことは容易ではない。被災現場では水濡れや泥汚れなどによって資料情報を即座に把握できないことが想定される。より多くの資料を救済するためには、紙媒体のものはひとまず搬出し、応急措置の段階で内容を把握しながら選別することが必要となる。

紙資料を搬出する際は、濡れた状態で触れると損傷しやすいため、取り扱う際に破損や散逸を回避するよう注意する。紙資料の多くは家や組織によって蓄積される記録群であるため、一般的には一つのまとまりとして保管されている。また、それらが箱などの容器に収められていることも多い。搬出に際しては、極力そのまとまりを維持し、容器に収納されている場合は容器ごと搬出する。容器に収められていない場合は、まとまりごとにビニール袋や

段ボールなどに移して搬出する。その際、まとまりの秩序を維持した状態での搬出が理想であるが、限られた状況のなかで細密な秩序維持は困難をともなうため、写真や映像でおおよその現状を記録して容器に移し搬出する。

2. 状態の把握と一時保管

2.1. 状態の把握

　被災した紙資料に対応する上で、まず留意する必要があるのは、破損および水濡れの有無である。地震等の被害では断裂など破損の被害が懸念され、降雨や高潮・津波などで水濡れ被害が発生した場合も、同様に破損が発生することが想定される。加えて、水濡れ被害の場合、放置してしまうと腐敗やカビが進行し、歴史資料としての維持・継承ができなくなる事態になってしまう。そのため、搬出した資料の状態把握として、以下の点を把握する必要がある。

①資料の概数確認

・救出段階で資料の詳細な点数把握を行うのはほぼ不可能である。そのため、まずは作業工程の計画を目的とした概数把握を行う。紙資料の場合、容器に収められている場合が多く、基本的には容器ごとに搬出する。そうでない場合は段ボール等の容器に収納して搬出し、それらを「段ボール○○箱分」のように、容器を単位とした概数を把握する。あわせて、簿冊類や書籍、書翰・はがき、塗工紙など、搬出資料のおおよその形態を可能な範囲で把握する。

②水濡れの有無

・降雨・高潮・津波・河川のいずれによるものであるか、もしくは保管場所の湿気や漏水によるものなのか、水濡れの要因を把握する。降雨や湿気の場合は水そのものへの対処に注力できるが、河川や海からもたらされた水は、場所によっては水分以外の汚損物等が含まれることが想定され、その後の対応に際して乾燥以外の作業が必要になることがある。

・全体的に水濡れ状態にあるのか、部分的な被害にとどまるのか、水濡れの程度を把握する。また、水が滴るほどの濡れ具合であるのか、すでに

乾きつつあるのか、といった状態も把握しておく。

③被害程度

・水濡れ以外の被害として、カビ発生の有無、腐敗および臭気の有無、紙同士の固着の有無について確認する。ただし、この時点ではあくまで表面観察でわかる範囲の把握にとどめる。特に、カビや腐敗・臭気の確認に際しては、健康面への被害が懸念されるので無理に顔を近づけて確認することがないよう留意する。固着の確認についても、濡れた状態で資料を取り扱うのは破損の危険性が高まるため、無理に剝がすなどの作業を行わないよう注意を要する。

2.2. 搬出後の一時保管

　水濡れ状態の資料を常温で保管することは腐敗を進行させてしまうため、速やかに乾燥させることが理想的である。総数が100点未満など少数であれば、搬出直後より乾燥処置を施すことが可能かもしれないが、大量の水濡れ資料を取り扱う場合は、処置に向けた準備が必要になり、即時の対応が困難となる。そのため、処置に向けた準備を行う間、冷凍庫等を用いた冷凍保管が想定される。

　冷凍保管の利点は、生物被害を含む資料の腐敗・劣化を抑制することができる点にある。特に、台風が多発する時期は高温多湿の季節にあたるため、水濡れ状態の資料を取り扱うことは、急速な腐敗をもたらす危険性がきわめて高い。そのため、一時的に冷凍保管することで、気温や湿度が下がった季節に本格的な作業を実施するなど、作業時期の調整を行うことも可能となる。

水濡れ資料の冷凍保管

　冷凍の方法は、1点ごとにビニール袋に梱包して冷凍することが理想的であるが、状態が悪く、すぐには開披できない場合はひとまず固まりの状態でビニール袋に包み、冷凍しておく。大型の冷凍庫をすぐに確保するのは容易ではないため、被災対応を想定して、あらかじめ大型冷凍庫を保有する近隣施設を把握し、有事の際に協力してもらえるよう交渉しておくことが望ましい。

3.　被災紙資料の応急処置

　紙資料の応急処置に関しては、これまでに多くの災害対策時の実践例やそれらを踏まえたマニュアルが国内外で多数公開されており、一連の工程に関する詳細な技術が紹介されている。そのため、本章では具体的な技術の紹介よりも応急処置として求められる対応とその考え方を中心に確認しておきたい。

　被災紙資料の応急処置を行う場合、一つの到達点として現状記録が可能な状態、具体的には資料の点数が把握され、常温による保管・管理に大きな懸念がなくなった状態が想定される。そのためには、腐敗や破損、カビの進行といった、急速な劣化・消滅の危機が回避された状態に導くことが求められるが、基本的な作業として、乾燥作業、クリーニング・固着展開に大別される。

3.1. 乾燥作業の考え方

　水濡れ資料にとって第一に取り組むべき課題としては、乾燥作業が挙げられる。もっとも、対象となる資料の状態や規模、対応人数に応じてその方法は一様ではない。これまでの災害対応を通して多くの実践例が紹介されているが、方法や目的から整理すると、三つのパターンに分類することができよう。

　一つは送風乾燥である。この手段は、直射日光の当たらない空間に資料を広げ、自然風もしくはサーキュレーターなどで風を送って乾燥させる方法である。この方法は、数ある乾燥法のなかでもコスト面・技術面で用いやすい方法であるが、腐敗等のリスクを考えると、カビや汚損などが軽微であり、

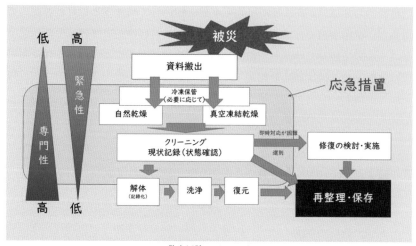

低 高

緊急性

専門性

高 低

被災

資料搬出

冷凍保管
（必要に応じて）

自然乾燥　　　　真空凍結乾燥

クリーニング
現状記録（状態確認）

応急措置

即時対応が困難

選別

修復の検討・実施

解体
（記録化）　→　洗浄　→　復元

再整理・保存

救出以降のイメージ

乾燥し始めている状態の資料への対応時に用いることが有効であろう。

　次に吸水乾燥が挙げられる。近年では具体的な工程も提案され、実践事例も多岐にわたるが、基本的な考え方としては、資料を吸水紙で包み、圧力を加えることで水分を絞り出すという点では共通している。この方法では、大量の水分を含む資料に対して有効であり、資料1点ごと、もしくは一つの固まり単位で吸水紙に包み、圧力を加えることで資料中の水分を効果的に取り出すことができる。

　大量の資料を取り扱う場合は、パウチに入れて掃除機などの吸引装置で脱気することで水分を絞り出す方法もある。

　吸水乾燥の場合、この方法のみで乾燥状態に導くことは相応の時間を要する。そのため、一般的には送風乾燥を行うための手段として吸水乾燥を施し、紙同士の固着をおおよそ開披できる状態まで導いた段階で送風乾燥に移行する流れが一般的である。

　三つ目の方法としてあげられるのが、真空凍結乾燥である。この方法は、真空凍結乾燥装置を用いた大規模な資料乾燥法であり、数千点以上におよぶ大量の水濡れ紙資料に対応する際に有効な手段である。国内では1992年に埼玉県草加市で発生した民家の火災とその消火活動によって水濡れ被害を受

送風乾燥（2018年7月30日、広島県立文書館）

吸水乾燥①：資料を吸水紙に包む（2018年12月11日、広島県立文書館）

吸水乾燥②：パウチにいれて脱気（2018年12月12日、広島県立文書館）

第2部

けた資料の乾燥に真空凍結乾燥法が導入された。その後大規模な水濡れ被害が発生した際にこの方法が用いられているが、装置を保有する施設との調整やコスト面での課題などもあり、必ずしもあらゆる場面で活用できるとは限らない。そのため、大規模災害を想定するなら、同装置を保有する近隣の博物館や研究機関等と事前に連携を図っておく必要があるだろう。

　以上のように、資料の乾燥についてはいくつかの方法があるが、特定の手法に固執せず、状況と目的に応じた技術の選択が求められる。その際の原則としては、手動での作業に際しては、熱を加えるなど資料にダメージを与えかねない方法は避け、急速な温度変化を伴わない対応が重要である。また、同じ紙資料でも塗工紙などは、完全に乾燥させてしまうと固着して剥がれなくなる恐れがあるため、吸水乾燥によっておおよその水分を取り除いた段階で塗工紙が含まれているかどうか資料の概要を把握しておくことが望ましい。

　いずれの方法にしても、特定の方法のみで乾燥状態まで導くことは難しい場合が多く、資料の状態や作業人員に応じていくつかの方法を組み合わせて対応することが必要となる。

　一例として、2018年に発生した西日本豪雨での対応を挙げると、広島県で発生した豪雨により、広島市内の民家から数千点の紙資料（帳簿・葉書・書翰・絵画など）が水濡れ被害を受ける。これらを受け入れた広島県立文書館では、以下の手順で乾燥作業を実施した。

乾燥方法の選択めやす

	送風乾燥	吸水乾燥	真空凍結乾燥
コスト	◎	○	△
作業効率	△	△	◎
汎用性	◎	○	△
想定される使用法	カビや汚損が少なく、水濡れが軽微な場合	多量の水分を含む場合に使用、送風乾燥のための一時的処置	大規模な被害時

①資料の分類

- まず、帳簿・冊子類、葉書、書翰、絵画など形態別に分類する。
- 形態別に分類した資料を、（a）大量に水を含むもの、腐敗の進行が甚だしいもの、（b）乾燥が進み始めているもの、（c）すでに乾燥しているもの、水濡れが確認されないもの、の3類型に分類する。

②分類した資料への処置

　（a）1点ごとにビニール袋に包み、段ボールに梱包して外に臭気や水分が
　　　出ない状態にして冷凍保管

　（b）棚を準備し、直射日光が当たらない風通しのよい場所で送風乾燥

2018 年西日本豪雨時における広島県立文書館での作業工程（天野等 2019 より）

(c) カビや汚損状況を確認しながらクリーニング。ここでは汚れを落とすことよりも後述の固着展開を中心に実施し、深部まで乾燥していることを確認する。

③冷凍資料の解凍・乾燥

・（a）については、対応した時期が夏期であったことを勘案し、腐敗の進行しにくい時期まで段ボールで17箱分を冷凍保管した。冬期になり乾燥作業を実施した。

・ビニール袋から冷凍状態にある資料を取り出し、1点ごとに吸水紙（このときは新聞紙）で梱包する。

・吸水紙に包んだ冷凍資料をパウチに詰め、脱気して経過を観察する。1〜2日程度で資料が常温に戻り始める。資料から出た水分を吸水紙が吸収していることを確認し、パウチから資料を取り出し吸水紙を取り替え、再度脱気する。

・上記の工程を数回繰り返して資料が開披可能な状態まで導き、最終的には送風乾燥に移行して乾燥させる。

　広島の事例では、広島県立文書館を拠点として広い空間が確保され、冷凍庫の手配や多くの作業協力者を得ることができたことにより、このような作業工程を構築することが可能となった。対応する場所によっては、電源やパウチなどが確保できないことも想定されるため、この通りの工程を経ることが困難な場合も想定される。例えば、パウチなどがない場合、資料を吸水紙にくるんで平らな場所に並べ、上にものをのせることでも脱水は可能である。基本的な考え方としては同様であり、資料に損傷を与えない方法によって脱水する方法を選択することが重要である。

3.2. クリーニングの目的

　乾燥工程を経た資料を一時保管可能な状態に導くために、クリーニングを施す必要がある。クリーニングに関しては、乾燥状態で行うドライ・クリーニングと、水を用いたウェット・クリーニングがある。資料に付着した汚損物を取り除くことがクリーニングの目的となるが、どの程度の処置を施すか

は重要な課題である。この点は応急処置の到達点にも関わる問題であるが、主に記録資料が中心となる紙資料の場合、この過程で行う作業として、資料の固着開披が挙げられる。

　水濡れに由来する紙同士の固着であれば、ヘラやピンセットによって慎重に固着部に隙間を作っていくことで開披することができる。その場合決して無理せず、破損の懸念が生じた場合は中断して別の箇所から開披を試みることが必要である。固着の要因が泥やカビに起因する場合、開披に際しては相当の困難が予想される。その場合はいったん作業を中断し、現状を記録化した後にカビや汚損物が飛散しないよう梱包し、一時保管に注力することで応急処置を終えることも一つの判断となる。この場合は、あくまで応急処置の段階ではすべての処置が完了しないことを念頭におき、修理計画に向けた手配を進めることが望ましい。

　乾燥処置まで施した資料には、被害状況に応じて泥汚れやカビなどが付着していることがある。そのため、カビについてはひとまずエタノールを含ませた布や紙でおさえることで表面に発生するカビの胞子を取り除くことが必要となる。また、泥汚れなども、資料の破損につながらない範囲で取り除くことが想定されるが、ドライ・クリーニングで除去できるものは限定的であり、刷毛などで払って除去した場合、汚れやカビが飛散する危険性が生じる。そのため、ドライ・クリーニングの段階ですべての汚損物を取り除くことは想定せず、固着を開披することを目的とした対応が重要であろう。その場合、作業者は健康被害対策に心がける必要がある。具体的には、カビ等を吸引しないよう防塵性能の高い産業用マスクの着用であり、高い粒子捕集効率を有するものが求められる。日本であれば厚生労働省が定めた国家検定規格に基づく DS2 マスクがそれに該当し、アメリカの規格では N95、ヨーロッパが定めた規格では FFFP2 がそれに相当する。

　固着の開披を中心に実施した場合でも、カビや汚損物はある程度飛散するため、作業に際しては十分な換気を行うことが重要である。また、空気清浄機などを設置して作業環境を清浄に保つ装備も必要となろう。

　紙資料の応急処置としては、基本的に資料の全体的な状態が把握できること、水濡れ由来による固着の開披が完了すること、一時保管に向けて臭気・

水濡れによって固着した資料
（サンプル）

カビによって固着した資料

カビ・汚損が他所に広がらないこと、が到達点として設定できる。その場合、固着を無理に開披しようとすると、大規模な破損が発生することもあるため、その後の簡易補修の見通しが立たない場合は固着への対応はいったんとどめるべきであろう。また、汚損物や臭気の除去を目的としたウエット・クリーニング（洗浄作業）を応急処置として実施することもある。ただし、水を用いた洗浄作業では、大半の場合で資料の解体が必要となるため、この場合も洗浄後の手当を行いうる技術と設備を保有していることが前提となる。これらを勘案して紙資料の応急処置を整理すると、一時保管に耐えうる状態に導く行為としての応急処置段階で、固着の開披や洗浄作業は必ずしも絶対条件ではなく、それらの作業に向けて技術的・施設的環境を整えるための前段階的処置として位置づける必要があろう。記録物の救済では、文字情報をいち早く読める状態に導くことに注力しがちであるが、長期的に見た場合、段階的・計画的に作業を進めていくことが資料の保存・継承にとって有効である。

おわりに

　紙資料は、全国各地に膨大な規模で残されており、資料救済時には大量に被災した状態で確認される。水や破損に対して脆弱な紙資料は、救出から乾燥段階にかけてきわめて迅速な対応が求められる。身近な記録物も含めて、多くの実践報告が紹介されているので、具体的な技法などはそれらを参照してもらいたい。ただし、作業工程を複雑化せず、応急処置の到達点を設定して対応することに留意する必要がある。そのためには、（1）資料を乾かす：緊急的な危機を脱する、（2）資料を開く：概要を把握する、（3）資料を管理する：本格的な対応に向けた検討を進める、という基本的な目的を念頭に置いて対応を進めることが重要であろう。その過程で具体的かつ簡易的な手当の考え方や方法については、山口悟史「紙製地域資料を遺す技術」（参考文献参照）が紹介しているので参照されたい。

参考文献

- 西向宏介・下向井祐子「広島県立文書館における「平成三〇年七月豪雨」被災文書のレスキューと保全活動」（『広島県立文書館紀要』15、2020 年）
- 増田勝彦「水害を受けた図書・文書の真空凍結乾燥」（『保存科学』31、1992 年）
- 山口悟史「紙製地域資料を遺す技術」（天野真志・後藤真編『地域歴史文化継承ガイドブック』文学通信、2022 年）
- 天野真志・吉川圭太・加藤昭恵・西向宏介・下向井祐子「西日本豪雨で水損被害を受けた文書資料乾燥法の検討」（文化財保存修復学会第四一回大会ポスター発表、2019 年）
- 独立行政法人国立文化財機構文化財防災センター編『浮遊カビ等からの人体の防護に関するマニュアル』https://ch-drm.nich.go.jp/facility/2022/03/post-49.html（2023 年 12 月 25 日最終閲覧）

第 **4** 章

写真資料の救済

▨　松下正和（神戸大学）

はじめに

　歴史資料ネットワークが保全対象としている歴史資料は、民間所在の未指定文化財である。阪神・淡路大震災以降に行われた、地域や家の歩みを示す古文書類のレスキューは、どちらかといえば旧家や自治会保管の地域の記録を対象とし、被災地復興の際に必要な歴史的・地理的背景を把握する意味合いが強かった。一方、写真資料は個人・家や地域の歩みを示すものとして、一般の家庭なども含めどこにでもあるものである。特に、2011 年の東日本大震災や紀伊半島大水害時における汚損写真レスキュー・洗浄の活動は、その担い手に多くの一般市民も参加することで、家や個人の歩みとしての記録や「思い出」レスキューの手段として、被災地ボランティアの中に一定のウェイトを占めるようになった。

　よって本章では、家族の記録のうちでも写真資料のレスキュー活動について述べる。デジタルカメラや携帯電話が普及して以降は、写真記録はデジタルデータとして各種記録媒体にデータが保存されている。そのためデジタルメディアも含めた救済や保存修復についても触れるべきではあるが、紙幅の都合もあり、本章で扱う写真資料とは、白黒・カラー写真プリント（印画紙）、ポケットアルバムや糊付き台紙アルバムに限定する。このような一般家庭で保管されている写真資料を前提として、その救出から乾燥・洗浄に至るまでの作業について記してみたい。

1. 写真資料の救出と一時保管

　風水害に遭うと資料が水損・汚損するのは当然のことであるが、地震発生後にも建物が被害を受けると雨漏りが生じ、またその後の降雨・降雪、津波により資料に水損が発生する。また地震は火災を伴うこともあるため焼損とともに、消火に伴う水損も発生する。つまり、いずれの場合においても災害による被災資料は水損を免れることができないことが多いため、ここでは写真資料が水損した場合の救出処置について述べる。

　東日本大震災の被災現場で見られたように、写真資料に限らないが、津波被災資料・洪水被災資料の場合は、そもそも元の場所から流されてしまい、自衛隊などによって集められることもあるものの、最悪のケースとしては流出し失われる可能性もある。流出を免れた場合であっても、銀塩紙焼き写真（一般の白黒・カラー写真）やネガは水に長時間浸かることによって画像層であるゼラチンやその内部の画像銀や色素が劣化し、画像そのものが消失・溶解していたり、変色・退色している事例が多い［**写真 1**］。特に夏場の高温多湿の被災地では腐敗が進みやすく、写真表面のゼラチン層の腐敗や、虫菌害といった生物被害に遭いやすい。洪水や津波の場合は、さらに生活排水や汚泥、海水の塩分などさまざまなものが写真表面に付着し、一層劣化が促進される。

　また写真は水損後の自然乾燥の過程で、救出する際には、写真相互が貼り付いたり、アルバム内でカビが生えたままになっていたり、アルバムの保護フィルムに画像層が貼り付いて画像イメージが崩れるケースもある［写真 2］。

写真 1　長期間の水損により
写真表面の画像層が溶けた写真

　写真資料の救済は、被災現場を巡回中にレスキューする事例よりも、相談や持ち込みにより処置することの方が多い。歴史資料ネットワークが主体となって対応したレスキュー現場、例えば兵庫県佐用町水害

（2009 年 8 月台風 9 号）の際には、新聞の記事で我々の被災資料保全活動を知った被災者から水損アルバムと固着した写真の束について相談があり、被災者宅にてアルバムの清掃（泥落とし）・乾燥・デジタルカメラ撮影による複製作成などの応急処置を行った。ただ水場も遠く、床が抜けて処置の場所もない

写真 2　津波被害でポケットアルバムの保護フィルムと固着した写真

中での作業は困難を極めた［写真 3］。2011年以降は可能な限り、被災現場で処置するのではなく、水場などが確保されている作業場にて処置を行うことにしている。

　先述のように濡れた状態のままでは写真表面の劣化が促進する。画像の損傷を少しでも食い止めるためには、写真資料にカビが発生しないように冷凍保管できる冷凍庫と一時保管場所を確保することが望ましい。冷凍保管ができない場合は、扇風機などを利用し、陰干しすることで可能な限り乾燥を進め、また一時保管場所では可能な限り温湿度を低く保てる環境を保持する。

写真 3　佐用町での汚損写真クリーニング（2009 年 10 月 12 日撮影）

　被災現場から持ち出す際には、被害状況の撮影などの簡単な現状記録を作成し、被害にあった写真資料の数量（アルバムの冊数など）を確認した後、所蔵者との間で借用証を取り交わすこととしている。ここで重要なのは、所蔵者との間で被災写真の処置について十分に意思疎通しておくことである。技術的な習熟度の異なるボランティアが主体となる作業であるため必ずしもすべての写真が元通りになるわけではないこと、プライベートな内容が大多数を占める写真資料が処置の段階で多数の作業者の目に触れることを、あらかじめ了解を得ておく必要がある。特に洗浄するか否かは、画像の残存度に

大きく影響を与える。被害の甚大な写真の場合、洗浄をすれば確実に画像層は流失する。しかし、汚損したまま放置すればいずれ虫菌害に遭い劣化はますます促進し、再び閲覧することはできない。所蔵者との間でそれぞれの処置に伴うメリット・デメリットについて理解を求める必要がある。

2. 被災写真資料の処置

　以下では、洪水や津波などで水損・汚損したカラー写真の処置方針について、平成 21 年（2009）台風 9 号（佐用町水害）の際の個人宅アルバム・写真処置、平成 26 年（2014）8 月豪雨の際に広島県立文書館で行われた作業や、平成 30 年（2018）7 月豪雨（西日本豪雨）の際に岐阜県博物館協会により関市文化財保護センター内で行われた作業などを参照して記してみたい。

　作業時の注意点としては、その他の水損資料の取り扱いと同様に、カビや泥・ほこりなどを吸わないことである。そのため防塵マスクやラテックスゴム手袋などの着用、作業後の手洗い・うがい、作業室内の換気にも注意するなど、ボランティア作業従事者の衛生面に配慮した。作業の使用する物品については下記を参照のこと［写真 4］。

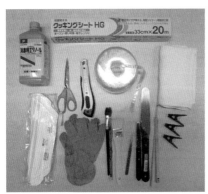

写真 4　被災写真資料処置に使用する
道具の一例

写真をアルバムから取り出す作業に必要なもの

・マスク，ゴム手袋（薄手のもの）
・へら（竹製，ゴム製），刷毛，ピンセット
・パレットナイフ，カッター，ハサミ，雑巾
・消毒用エタノール（70%），霧吹き
・新聞紙，キッチンペーパー（吸水用）
・クッキングシート，レーヨン紙（フラットニング用）
・記録用のデジタルカメラ，空気清浄機，除湿機など

写真の洗浄作業に必要なもの

・マスク，ゴム手袋（薄手のもの）
・洗浄用の水を入れるバット（洗い用とすすぎ用の 2 つを用意）
・毛先のやわらかい小筆
・水を切るスポンジマット，タオル，ラック・キッチンペーパーなど
・干すための洗濯バサミ，クリップ，洗濯ロープ，ビニール紐など
・新聞紙

広島県立文書館「土砂災害で被災したアルバム・写真への対処法（手引き）」より

　なお写真の被害状況によって必ずしもこの作業手順通りに行ったわけではない。また白黒写真や劣化のひどい写真の処置については、写真専門店による修復を勧めたい。

2.1. 現状記録とアルバムからの写真の取り出し

①アルバムへの付番と撮影

　写真資料の被害事例として、ポケットアルバムや糊付き台紙アルバムに写真が収められているケース、写真が束のまままとめられて固着しているケースが想定される。いずれにしても乾燥させる必要があるため、まずは写真を一枚ずつ分離することからはじめる。ただし、写真を分離する際には画像を損なうことがあるため、またどのような順番でどのページに貼られていたのかというまとまり情報も記録するために、必ずアルバムを解体したり写真の束を崩す前には、現状記録の写真をデジタルカメラで撮影する。

　アルバムごとに番号を付けて、開くところは全ページ撮影して記録しておく。特にポケットアルバムに記されているメモ、糊付き台紙に挟みこまれているメモ類は、その写真に関する情報を記していることが多いため写真とともに必ず記録する。

②アルバムの泥汚れの除去

　まずはアルバムの外側の汚れを除去する。表紙や裏表紙、小口についた泥は竹ヘラや刷毛、キッチンペーパーや雑巾などで落とす。可能であれば固く絞った雑巾により水拭きをしたり、消毒用エタノールをしみこませたキッチンペーパーなどで消毒も行う。その後アルバムを一ページずつ開いて、ページごとに泥汚れを除去する。

　ポケットアルバムや糊付き台紙の保護フィルムについた汚れも、竹ヘラや刷毛などで取り除く。ただし、保護フィルムと写真表面の間に水分がある場合は、フィルム面を強く押すことで画像が動いてしまうことがあるため清掃作業は慎重に行う。

③泥汚れ除去後の状況を撮影

　アルバムを一ページ開くごとにページ全体をデジタルカメラで撮影あるいはスキャナーでスキャンする。可能であれば、さらに写真一枚ごとを撮影す

るのが望ましい。保護フィルムを取り外したり、洗浄した際に画像が流れる
可能性があるためである。

④アルバムの乾燥

　アルバムは可能ならページを広げて立てた状態で乾燥させる。空気清浄機
や除湿機、換気扇を稼働させ、できるだけ直射日光の当たらない、温度・湿
度の低い、清潔な一時保管場所で乾燥するのが望ましい。

⑤写真の取り出し

　保護フィルム内に汚水が入っている場合など、被害が甚大な場合は、ポケッ
トアルバムや糊付き台紙アルバムアルバムから写真を取り出し乾燥させる。
写真の輪郭に沿って保護フィルムにカッターの刃を入れ、保護フィルムを取
り外す［写真5］。保護フィルムと写真の間に汚水が入って、無理に剥がすと
画像が壊れる場合や、保護フィルム面に画像が転写している場合には、写真
から保護フィルムを剥がさないままにしておく。糊付き台紙から写真を取り
上げる際にはパレットナイフや竹ヘラなどを用いて剥がすが、剥がれない場
合は、台紙を相剥ぎにして台紙の表裏を分離し、写真に台紙がついた状態で
取り外すこともある。

写真5　糊付き台紙からの写真の取り出し（2014年9月8日撮影）

2.2. 写真の洗浄と乾燥

　アルバムから取り出した汚損写真は、そのまま放置すると劣化が進行するため、洗浄し汚れを落とす必要がある。ただし、洗浄することで画像が流失することもあるため、洗浄する前には必ずデジタルカメラで写真を撮影するなど複製を作成する。写真を扱う際にも、ラテックスゴム手袋と防塵マスクを着用する。

①洗浄

　汚損写真を水を入れたトレイの中に漬ける。画像層は小筆や指の腹で軽くなぞりながら汚れを落としていく。その際には、写真の端や角の部分から水に漬けて、画像が流失しないかを確かめること、特に人物などの被写体は無理に洗浄しないことに注意する［写真6］。写真裏面も同様に洗浄する。その際には、表面の画像層を触らないように写真の両端を指で挟むなど、写真の持ち方にも注意が必要である。なお、写真の画像層がすでに溶けて、赤色や黄色などがマーブル状に見える場合は洗浄してはいけない［写真7］。

写真6　小筆による写真の洗浄

写真7　マーブル状になった写真表面

②すすぎ

　粗く洗浄した写真を、きれいな水を張ったすすぎ用のトレイに入れ、再び軽く洗浄する［写真8］。

③水切り

　すすいだ写真を新聞紙やキッチン

写真8　写真のすすぎ

タオルなど吸水紙の上で軽く水切りを行う。

④乾燥

洗濯ロープやネット
などに洗濯ばさみやク
リップで写真を吊るし
て干す。可能な限り写真
が貼られていたアルバ
ムや順番がわかるよう
に、最低限アルバムの番
号札やページの番号札
もあわせて付けておく
とよい［写真9］。乾燥場
所が限られている場合

写真9　写真の乾燥

は、新聞紙などの吸水紙の上に平置きで乾燥したり、スリット台の上で乾燥
することもある。乾燥後、写真がカールしている場合は、写真同士が再びくっ
つかないように、レーヨン紙やクッキングシートなどで写真を一枚ずつ挟み、
上から重石を載せて平らにする。

　乾燥後の写真は、粘つきがない場合は新しいポケットアルバムに入れて保
管する。もし乾燥後も粘つきがある場合は、写真同士の間にクッキングシー
トなどの間紙を挟んで保管する。

2.3. 写真を洗浄しない場合

　先にも述べたように、写真の画像層が溶けてマーブル状に見えている場合
は洗浄を行わない。また、アルバム被害がそれほどでもなく、写真表面に泥
汚れや臭いもなくきれいな場合は無理に洗浄せずにそのまま乾燥させる。ポ
ケットアルバムや糊付き台紙から外せるようであれば一枚ずつ乾燥すること
が望ましい。

　一般には写真の被写体を保持するため、可能な限り画像層を破壊しないよ
うな配慮が求められる。兵庫や岐阜の事例では洗浄は行わなかったが、一方
広島の事例では写真表面がマーブル状に残ることで災害の記憶がよみがえる

ために、画像が多少流失してもよいのできれいに洗浄してほしいという要望があった。このようにプライベートな写真資料は所蔵者の意向により処置方針が異なってくる。そのため作業前には所蔵者との間で処置方針についてあらかじめ合意を得ておくことが必要である。

2.4. 写真洗浄に伴う課題

　甚大な被害に遭った現物のアルバムや写真自体をどう保存するのかは難しい問題である。結婚式や誕生日アルバムなどはアルバムの表紙自体にもデコレーションが施されており、可能な限り元の形に近い形で残すように処置をしている。ただ、被災した写真資料は、水損を経ることにより劣化速度が増すために、現物自体を残すのが難しい場合が多い。そのため乾燥済みの被災写真とともに、スキャナやデジタルカメラ撮影した複製を作成し、DVD などに焼いたデジタルデータとしても提供している。さらには写真データを利用しデジタル上で復元している宮崎資料ネットワークのような例もある。

　また一般家庭で保管される写真は公的支援を受けにくく、基本的にはボランティアベースにならざるを得ず、その他の未指定文化財と同様の問題を抱えている。ただし、近年では被災写真の取り扱い情報の提供や、ポケットアルバムなど写真保存グッズの提供を行う企業もある。また、2018 年 7 月の西日本豪雨の際には、岐阜県博物館協会の「もの部会」が中心となって、関市内の汚損アルバムの処置が行われた。また岐阜県関市は被災者に配布した「被災者支援制度ガイドブック」内に、写真・アルバム洗浄の支援について掲載を行った。これによって、被災者が汚損アルバムの洗浄依頼窓口を知ることができた。このような取り組みは先進的なものであり、今後の被災地行政による被災写真資料対応のモデルケースとなる[1]。今後も、史料ネットや写真洗浄専門のボランティア団体や行政、企業などとの連携による救済活動が有効となるだろう。

おわりに

　2000 年代に入り、徐々にプリントされた写真を目にする機会も少なくなっ

ている現代だからこそ、デジタル化される以前のアルバムに収められている
プリント写真などが被災した場合の応急処置方法について周知する機会を設
けることが必要であろう。災害時にはフィルム関連の企業や、写真関連の学
会から救済に関するガイドラインの公開や支援もなされてきたが、各地の史
料ネットによる救済活動とともに、被災地発の写真洗浄ボランティアによる
実践的な活動[2]も重要である。

　人びとの「思い出」や「愛着」が詰まったものを救うことにより、被災地
の人びとの喪失感を少しでも和らげ日常性を取り戻すことにつなげることが
できるのではないか。また大切な家族や家を失うなど被害に遭った際に、家
族ゆかりのものが残ることによって、個人の精神的な復興を後押しする力に
なっていることはさまざまな被災現場で語られている。災害時における写真
レスキューの広がりを通じて、災害時のみならず日常時にも個人の記録を保
全することの重要性、ひいては家族や地域の歩みを残す私たちの被災資料保
全活動の意義が伝わることを期待したい。

注

1　なお関市は令和5年（2023）台風7号の際にも「被災者支援制度ガイドブック【初
　　版】」を作成し、被災古文書、写真等の応急処置支援を被災者に対して周知して
　　いる。

2　被災写真洗浄活動@流山のブログに写真洗浄ボランティア一覧（2023/9/20更新）
　　があり（https://ameblo.jp/sunnyblog/entry-12744745156.html）（以下ウェブサイト
　　は2024年1月23日最終閲覧）

参考文献

・ 山内利秋「台風被害にあった写真資料の保存と修復について」（吉備国際大学文化
　　財総合研究センター編『吉備国際大学文化財総合研究センター紀要　文化財情報学
　　研究』4、2007年3月、pp.123-128）、山内利秋「真空凍結乾燥法による写真資料の
　　保存処理について」（同、pp.129-134）
・ 大林賢太郎『写真保存の実務』（岩田書院、2010年）

- 大林賢太郎『劣化する戦後写真　写真の資料化と保存・活用』(岩田書院、2010 年)
- 板垣貴志・川内淳史編『阪神・淡路大震災像の形成と受容　震災資料の可能性』(岩田書院、2011 年)
- 動産文化財救出マニュアル編集委員会編『動産文化財救出マニュアル　思い出の品から美術工芸品まで』(クバプロ、2012 年)
- 吉川圭太・吉原大志「広島土砂災害による被災写真アルバムの保全活動」(『史料ネットニュースレター』77、2014 年 12 月、pp.9-10)
- 広島県立文書館ウェブサイト「保存管理講座〜文書・記録を残し伝えるために〜」内の広島県立文書館リーフレット「土砂災害で被災したアルバム・写真への対処法(手引き)」(2014 年 12 月)(https://www.pref.hiroshima.lg.jp/site/monjokan/sub19.html)
- RD3 プロジェクト『被災写真救済の手引き　津波・洪水などで水損した写真への対応マニュアル』(国書刊行会、2016 年)
- 正村美里「平成 30 年度もの部会事業「関市の水害における汚損アルバム写真等の洗浄ボランティアについて」の報告」(岐阜県博物館協会「こと部会」編『岐阜の博物館』183、岐阜県博物館協会、2018 年 9 月、p.3)
- 西日本豪雨災害「残す。」編集チーム編著『残す。西日本豪雨災害　私たちは真備に何を残そうとしたのか』(同、2021 年)
- 松下正和「史料ネットによる水損写真資料の保全・応急処置−「思い出」をレスキューするために」(『日本写真学会誌』84-2、2021 年、pp.72-79)

第2部

第 5 章

民具の救済

▨　日髙真吾 （国立民族学博物館）

はじめに

　文化財レスキューとは、自然災害により被災した美術工芸品を中心とする
文化財等を緊急に保全し、廃棄・散逸や盗難の被害から防ぐため、災害の規
模・内容に応じて文化庁が立ち上げる事業で行われる活動である[1]。この文
化財レスキューにおいて、数多くの支援要請が出される民具は、もともと同
じようなものが大量にあることで、その地域の生活文化を見渡すことができ
る文化財群である。このため、文化財レスキューの対象となる民具の数は膨
大なものとなる。一方、数多くの文化財レスキュー要請が出されるとはいえ、
そもそも民具が大切な文化財であるという理解が地域で得られているかとい
うと、残念ながらそうではなく、この点は矛盾がある。ただ、災害で地域そ
のものが消滅するという危機が現実的なものとなったとき、一つ言えること
は、被災者にとっての民具が先祖から受け継いだかけがえのない存在として
被災地や被災者自身のアイデンティティのよりどころとなるのではないだろ
うかということである。そして、日常、あるいは先祖の生活の記憶を表象す
る民具が残ることで、地域再生について考えるきっかけをあらためて地域全
体やそこに住む人びとに与える役割を民具が担うようになるのではないだろ
うか。本章では、そうした民具が被災した場合の救済の在り方について、東
日本大震災で行った民具の文化財レスキューを振り返る。なお、文化財レス
キュー事業では、活動の柱を救出・一時保管・応急措置としているが、本章

では具体的な処置事例を述べるので、応急措置は応急処置という表現を用いる。

1. 被災民具の救出活動

　東日本大震災で行った民具の救出活動では、まず、床面に散乱しているガラスの破片を取り除き、津波が運んできたヘドロをかきだしながら、埋もれている民具を探し出す作業からはじまった。装着しているゴーグルは汗ですぐに曇り、全身汗まみれとなりながらの捜索作業は、著しく体力を消耗するものであった［写真1］。また、どれが民具でどれががれきやごみなのかの判断がつかないものが多数でてくる。そもそも日常の生活の記憶をとどめることで文化財としての価値が見いだされる民具は、生活の場で使われていたものががれきやごみとなっている被災現場において、こうした事態が生じるのは、ある意味宿命なのかもしれない。そこで、がれきやごみなのか？　あるいは民具なのか？　という判断に迷った場合は、すべて救出の対象とすることとした。いったん廃棄されてしまったら、二度と取り戻すことはできないが、逆に、その後の整理作業で、これはがれきやごみだったという判断が確実にできた場合に廃棄すればよいのである。救出活動のような過酷な環境での作業は、作業者の判断はどうしても鈍ってしまう。だからこそ、「民具かもしれないから、まずは救出の対象としよう。」という心構えが必要となる。また、救出した民具の状態は、程度の違いはあるが、基本的にがれきなどから生じる砂埃(すなぼこり)による汚損［写真2］が多い。また、被災文化財自体の転倒や落下、収蔵棚の転倒による衝撃で破損し、原形をとどめていないものもある［写真3］。そうした状態の民具をがれきやごみのなかから見つけだすためには、救出活動を行う構成メンバーに日ごろからさまざまな文化財を見慣れている博物館・美術館の学芸員が加わることが望ましいと考える。

　次に、被災した民具の救出活動の体制について述べてみたい。救出活動はとにかく多くの人員を要する作業である。わが国は、阪神・淡路大震災以降、大きな災害に見舞われ、そのたびに文化財が被災し、官民を問わず多くの博物館・美術館の学芸員や文化財の保存機関の関係者が被災地に集結する体制

第
2
部

写真 1　被災した博物館での民具の救出活動
（2011 年 6 月和高智美氏撮影）

写真 2　被災後、砂埃で汚損した民具の事例
（2010 年 2 月橋本沙知氏撮影）

写真 3　破損して原形をととどめていない民具
（2011 年 6 月筆者撮影）

写真 4　救出作業の事前調査
（2011 年 6 月和高智美氏撮影）

写真 5　作業前ミーティング 2011 年 6 月
（河村友佳子氏撮影）

を整えてきた。そして、被災した文化財や博物館資料の救出を行い、大きな
成果を上げるという経験を重ねてきた。一方、実際に作業を行う作業チーム
の陣容は、全国各地からさまざまな専門性をもつ学芸員や研究者で構成され
る。そのため、作業に参加する者が自身の価値判断や専門性にとらわれると、
ばらばらの活動を展開することとなり、作業目標を達成できなくなってしま
う。そこで、救出現場全体を掌握し、作業計画を立て、作業者に指示を出す
作業責任者が必要となってくる。

　作業責任者の仕事は、救出現場の事前調査を行うことからはじまる［**写真
4**］。事前調査では、事故がおこらないよう、効率的な作業計画を立案してい
く。文化財レスキューが行われる時期は、被災地は復旧途中の段階であり、
道路交通網の多くも復旧していない。東日本大震災時の救出活動では、こう
した復旧途中の道路事情のなかで、現場までの移動には平常時では考えられ
ない移動時間の長さがかかり、3時間を要することがほとんどであった。こ
のことは、現地での作業時間を十分に確保できないことに直結する。そこで、
限られた少ない時間のなかで、どのように効果的な救出活動の成果をあげる
のかという計画を、事前調査で綿密に練る必要があった。

　次に、実際の作業では、作業責任者は、まず、作業チーム全員に作業目的、
計画を説明する作業前ミーティングを行う［**写真5**］。作業チーム全員が作業
目的や計画、さらにはその日の達成すべき作業目標を共有していないと効果
的な成果はまず得られない。そして、作業中のこまめな休憩や作業場の安全
確保に努め、けが人や病人をださず、事故が発生しない現場管理を実行しな
ければならない。特に、休憩の指示は徹底する必要がある。救出現場の過酷
な状況は前述した通りである。したがって、休憩をきちんととらなかった場
合は、脱水症状を起こしたり、熱中症になったりする危険性が高くなる。そ
の場合、どうなるのであろうか。結局、被災者の助けに頼ることになるので
ある。そうならないために、体を休め、頭の冷静さを取り戻すための休憩が
必要なのである。作業責任者はこのことを自覚するとともに、作業チーム全
体にこの意識を共有させることが大きな役割の一つとなる。例えば、筆者が
作業責任者を務めた東日本大震災での救出活動では、40分ごとに10分の休
憩をとることとした。その結果、けが人や病人をださずに、効果的な救出活

動を展開できたと考えている。

　最後に、作業責任者は、その日に実施した救出作業について、次の作業責任者に引き継ぐための日報を作成する役割がある。東日本大震災は、被災地の範囲が広大で、現場の状況によっては、作業責任者を交代することが求められる場合があった。こうした際、作業日報によってきちんと作業を引き継ぐ体制づくりを構築しておく必要がある。

2.　一時保管と整理・記録

　一時保管とは、救出作業の現場から文化財を移動させ［写真6］、安全な場所で一時的に保管する作業である［写真7］。ここでいう安全とは、雨や風がしのげるということはもちろん、施設を施錠し、管理するという防犯対策の面での安全性も条件に含まれる。

　一時保管の作業では、被災した博物館などの文化財収蔵施設の担当者が限られた時間のなかで立ち会うことになるため、文化財を一気に保管場所へ移送することが求められる。そして、限られた時間で大量の民具を一気に運び出すためには、「美術梱包」をしている余裕はない。そのため、脆弱なものは別として、ある程度強度のあるものは可能な限りトラックの荷台に積み重ねて移送する［写真8］。また、被災した民具の移送作業では、トラックの運転を専門とするドライバーではなく、筆者のようなトラックに不慣れな人間が不安定な道路状況のなか、事故を起こさないように50キロメートルから100キロメートルほど離れた目的地まで運転する。こうした過酷な条件のなか一人のドライバーで安全運転に努めるのは難しい。そこで、複数人のドライバーを確保した上で、交代しながら運転し、移動中の安全に留意することが必要であろう。

　救出から一時保管の作業は、時間的な制約のなか、迅速な動きが求められる。しかしながら、ここで忘れていけないのは、大量の民具を所定の場所から一時的にせよ移動させるということである。このときには、何を移動させたのかという情報を残すことが必須である。Aという施設の「○○という文化財○点」という情報がなければ、その後の活動において、救出した民具の

写真 6　一時保管場所への移送作業
（2011 年 6 月和高智美氏撮影）

写真 7　一時保管場所への仮置き作業
（2011 年 6 月筆者撮影）

写真 8　トラックに可能な限り積載した被災民
具（2011 年 7 月筆者撮影）

写真 9　テンバコを利用した資料整理
（2011 年 5 月筆者撮影）

写真 10　当面の使用が見送られた施設の一時保
管場所（2011 年 7 月筆者撮影）

点数を確認できなくなってしまう。そこで、一時保管の作業では、大まかで
はあっても全体の点数を確認するための「整理・記録」の作業が必要となる。
ただし、限られた時間で被災文化財を移送するという作業のなかで、完璧な
リストを作成することはできない。そこで、東日本大震災の際には、まずは
民具をまとめて入れるテンバコの箱数でカウントすることとした。この作業
では、テンバコに入れている民具の全体がわかるように1カットの写真を撮
影し、テンバコに付与した仮番号とともにその写真データを管理することと
した［写真9］。その後、民具の応急処置が行えるようになった際に、はじめ
て民具1点ごとの「整理・記録」の作業を行っていった。

　次に一時保管の環境について考えてみたい。被災現場にある民具は、災害
そのものの被害に加え、救出され、一時保管場所へ移動するまでにさらされ
た雨や風、粉塵などによって劣化が進行する。だからこそ、一刻も早く救出し、
一時保管し、応急処置を施すことが求められるのである。一方、一時保管の
場所では、温度湿度や光がコントロールされる博物館の収蔵庫の環境は望め
ないことはいうまでもない。また、大規模な災害時においては、さまざまな
施設が被災していることから、比較的環境のよい場所のほとんどが被災者の
避難所や救援物資の資材置き場などにあてられる。したがって、被災した民
具の一時保管場所として提供される場所は、避難所や資材置き場として利用
されなかった場所であったり、学校の空き教室や使用されていない施設のエ
ントランスホールであったりする場合が多い［写真10］。そのために、一時
保管場所の環境をどのように安定させるのかも重要な活動となる。災害時に
一時保管場所として提供される場所は、大きな窓や開口部があり、空調シス
テムはまず機能していない。そして、この大きな窓や開口部は、外気の影響
を受けやすい状況となっている。このことは、温度湿度の大きな変動を生み
出し、脆化した民具はこの温度湿度の変動で破損したり、変形したりする危
険が高まる。また、大きな窓や開口部の開閉のためのサッシが取り付けられ
ているレールなどの隙間は、そのわずかな隙間から室内に入ってくる埃によ
る汚損が懸念される。また、民具を食害する害虫の侵入を許し、生物被害が
発生しやすい環境となる。さらに、大きな窓から外光が入射することで、紫
外線の影響を受けやすくなるなどの劣化要因に民具がさらされてしまうこと

になる。

　そこで、こうした課題については、博物館環境に詳しい保存科学者との連携を推奨したい。保存科学は文化財の保存を学問的に考える研究分野であり、博物館環境もその対象となっている。特に、2009 年 4 月 30 日に公布された「博物館法施行規則の一部を改正する省令」において、学芸員養成課程で「博物館資料保存論」が必修科目（2012 年度に必修）となった前後に、博物館環境についてまとめられた保存科学の研究成果はさまざまな形で出版されている[2]。ここでは、温度湿度の管理や生物被害対策など、一時保管場所においても留意したい事項が整理されているので、そうした事項を参照しながら実施可能な環境整備を進めていく必要がある。

3. 被災民具の応急処置

　応急処置は、被災した文化財の劣化を食い止めるための作業である。地震や水害などによる文化財の被災状態は、ほこりや汚泥、砂などがこびりついた表面の汚損が最初に観察される。また、災害そのものの衝撃や、棚からの転倒、落下の衝撃による破損も確認される。このうち表面を汚損するほこりや汚泥、砂などは、湿気を呼び込む作用もあることから、カビの発生を促進させる要因ともなる。さらには、これらの汚れは、民具そのものの取り扱いを困難にし、整理作業などの活動を著しく阻害する要因ともなる。したがって、応急処置で最初に行うべきは、被災した民具を汚損している物質を除去するための洗浄作業となる ［写真 11］。なお、応急処置で行う洗浄作業は、必要最小限にとどめておきたい。少しでも多くの被災した文化財を救出するためには、救出した民具 1 点ごとに関わる時間をいかに少なくするかということも重要な要素となる。あまりにも丁寧な作業はかえって、応急処置の点数を制限してしまうことにもなるので、作業責任者は応急処置の程度をしっかり見極めながら、作業全体を監督することが必要となる。そこで、筆者は応急処置として洗浄作業を行う場合は、大、中、小の三種類の刷毛、大、小2 種類のブラシ、それに筆一種類で構成した 6 種類の洗浄キット ［写真 12］を作業者に渡すことにした。もちろん、被災状況によっては、この種類が少

写真 11　被災民具の応急処置
（2011 年 8 月筆者撮影）

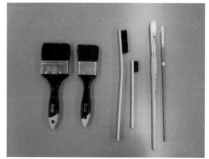

写真 12　洗浄セット

なくなることもある。そして、この洗浄キットで落とせる範囲の汚れだけを洗浄対象とし、それ以上の洗浄作業はあえておこなわないというルールで臨んだ。日ごろ、博物館資料や文化財に携わっている学芸員や保存修復の専門家は、このような応急処置としての洗浄作業に物足りなさを感じることもあるかもしれない。しかし、本格的な洗浄あるいは破損個所の接着復元といった専門的な技術を要する作業は、この次に行われる保存・修復活動で行うものと割り切ってもらうことにしている。

　次に東日本大震災で実施した具体的な応急処置の活動を紹介する。東日本大震災で被災した民具を汚損しているものは海砂であった。そして、この砂は、乾燥すれば、刷毛などによる払い落としの作業で十分に除去できるものであった。そこで、被災した多くの民具については、水は極力用いず、払い落としの作業で対応することとして、前述したように洗浄キットで除去できるところまで実施するというきわめて明快な判断基準で洗浄作業に臨んだ。

　また、東日本大震災は、筆者が経験したことのない津波による被災であった。そこで、被災した民具の大きな劣化要因として問題視されるものに、海水に含まれている塩分があった。この問題については、実際の文化財レスキューの応急処置の現場のなかで、出土遺物や自然史関係、古文書などの文化財は、塩分除去のための脱塩処理が施され、この処理に関する情報についても講習会が開催されたり、WEB 上でその方法論が公開されたりしていた。筆者自身も東日本大震災で被災した民具に対して、脱塩処理が必要になるか

もしれないという考えはあった。しかし、海水に飲み込まれた期間が限定的な津波被害によって、浸透した塩分を除去するための脱塩処理を優先的に行うべきかについては、慎重に判断すべきと考えた。

　民具は他の文化財に比べて、平常時の状態は安定しているものが多い。それは、日常生活や生業のなかで比較的最近まで使用されてきたものであることが大きな要因となっている。また、美術工芸品のように観賞するためではなく、使うために製作されたものでもあることから、必然的にある程度の耐久性を備えたものとなっている。したがって、通常、筆者が民具の保存修復で脱塩処理が必要と判断するものは、常時、塩水にさらされてきた漁撈用具や高濃度の塩分にさらされる製塩用具、あるいは醤油醸造用具が中心となる。

　実際に東日本大震災で被災した民具の状態を観察したところ、2011年段階においては、塩分に起因する劣化を示しているものはなかった。むしろ、脱塩処理を行った場合の問題の方が大きいと感じた。それは、脱塩処理を行う環境である。民具はさまざまな形状や大きさがあり、その素材は木材を中心としつつ、金属や紙、漆塗りなども含まれており、多様な素材で構成されている。また、大量の資料群をまとめて扱うこととなる。したがって、民具の脱塩処理では、複数の構成素材の状態を注意深く観察しながら行わなければならない。また、大量に処理できる大きな水槽［写真13］、もしくは大量の水槽［写真14］を用意する必要がある。つまり、脱塩処理を行うという判断をする際は、こうした作業環境を整えることが求められるのである。また、木材を脱塩液に浸漬するということは、当然、処理後の乾燥作業が必要とな

写真13　大型資料の脱塩槽
（2012年8月筆者撮影）

写真14　資料に応じた複数の脱塩槽
（2012年8月筆者撮影）

る。大量に水を含んだ木材は一気に乾燥させると木材の収縮、変形、あるいは亀裂のような破損を引き起こしてしまう。したがって、一度、脱塩処理を実施した場合、ゆっくりと乾燥させる場所が一定期間必要になってくるのである。また、金属部分は水に浸漬することで錆が発生するため、錆止め処理をする場所が必要となる。こうした点から、被災現場からやっとの思いで救出し、あまり広くないスペースに仮置きすることが求められた一時保管場所で、ここにあげたような脱塩処理に関する問題は解決できないと筆者は考えた。

　そこで、東日本大震災で被災した民具については、基本的に脱塩処理を行ない判断をし、より緊急的に実施しなければならない対応として、資料に付着した津波による砂やヘドロの除去を中心とした洗浄作業を優先的に行うこととした。ただし、塩分に関する問題を棚上げにしたわけではない。2011年は洗浄作業に専念した後、2012年2月からは脱塩に関する予備実験を実施し、翌3月から本格的な脱塩処理について宮城県を中心に技術指導を行った［写真15］[3]。

　最後に、繰り返しにはなるが、被災した民具の応急処置の手順と考え方について、以下に簡単にまとめる。被災した民具の応急処置として実施する洗浄作業では、まず水を使わず、洗浄道具で落とせるだけの汚れを落としていくことを基本としたい。しかし、泥が固着して簡単には落とせなくなっているものや、複雑な形状で隙間に泥や砂が詰まっている民具については、水槽に溜めた水のなかに浸け込んだり［写真16］、流水したりしながら汚れを除去する方法［写真17］を選択する。ただし、水を使った洗浄作業を行う場合は、作業場に水洗した民具を乾燥させる場所を整えておく必要がある。湿気が高い、あるいは乾燥させる場所がないという作業環境で水洗作業を行うとカビが発生し、その対応に時間を取られてしまうこととなる。このため、実施の判断は注意が

写真15　脱塩処理の技術指導
（2014年和高智美氏撮影）

写真16　水槽への浸け込みによる洗浄作業　　　　　写真17　流水による洗浄作業
（2011年5月河村友佳子氏撮影）　　　　　　　　　（2011年5月河村友佳子氏撮影）

必要である。

　なお、応急処置の考え方として留意すべきことは、応急処置は自身のもっ
ている技術を披露する作業ではないということである。まずは、より多くの
民具を取り扱える程度にまで安定させることを優先させなければならない。
それには、どのような作業を行うべきか、そして、次に行われる作業にどの
ように引き継いでいくのかを意識しながら、洗浄作業をはじめとする応急処
置を行っていってほしい。

おわりに

　ここでは、被災直後の民具の対応について、文化財レスキューの活動の柱
である救出、一時保管、応急処置についての考え方を東日本大震災の経験を
もとに述べてきた。ただし、この作業だけで民具が地域の文化財として継承
されるものへと再生できるわけではない。この後に行われる作業が重要と
なってくる。

　その作業とは、本格的な修復が必要と判断された被災文化財について専門
家が行う保存修復［写真18］、そして、復旧した博物館などで民具を安全に
保管する恒久保管の活動へと展開する［写真19］。次に、これまでの文化財
レスキュー活動で得られた知見や恒久保管の場となる博物館などで行われる
専門的な研究活動を取りまとめ、その成果を公開する研究・活用という活動

写真 18　専門家による被災した民具の保存修復
（2010 年 6 月橋本沙知氏撮影）

写真 19　被災文化財の恒久保管
（2010 年 11 月筆者撮影）

写真 20　被災民具を対象とした企画展「歴史と
文化を救う」の開催（2010 年 7 月筆者撮影）

写真 21　文化財防災についての地域住民との
意見交換会（2010 年 11 月）

へとつなげていく［写真 20］。そして、研究・活用という活動を通じて、地域住民に対して、その民具が地域のアイデンティティであることをしっかりと理解してもらうために、博物館という機能を存分に生かしながら働きかける工夫が求められる。その上で、次の災害に備えた防災の在り方を地域ぐるみで考えていく活動へと展開させていく［写真 21］ことで、民具が地域の文化財として継承されるものへと再生できるのではないかと考える。

参考文献

1　文化財防災センター「文化財レスキューについて」

https://ch-drm.nich.go.jp/disaster_response/rescue.html（2023 年 7 月 21 日アクセス）

2   村上隆「博物館の展示環境」岡田文男責任編集 京都造形芸術大学編『文化財のための保存科学入門』（角川書店、2002 年、pp.314-325）

三浦定俊「収蔵庫内の保管環境」岡田文男責任編集 京都造形芸術大学編『前掲書』（角川書店、2002 年、pp.326-33）

三浦定俊・佐野千絵・木川りか『文化財保存環境学』（朝倉書店、2004 年）

独立行政法人東京文化財研究所編『文化財の保存環境』（中央公論美術出版、2011 年）

石崎武志編『博物館資料保存論』（講談社、2012 年）

本田光子・森田稔編『博物館資料保存論』（放送大学教育振興会、2012 年）

稲村哲也・本田光子編著『博物館資料保存論【新訂】』（放送大学教育振興会、2019 年）

3   日髙真吾『災害と文化財―ある文化財科学者の視点から』（千里文化財団、2015 年）

第 **6** 章

美術資料の救済

▨　大林賢太郎（京都芸術大学）

はじめに

　「美術品」とは、書画、彫刻、工芸品等のなかで芸術的な評価を得たもの、言い換えれば一定の商品的価値を持つものを指すことになるが、その定義はもともと厳密なものではない。たしかに文化財として公的に認められたものはわかりやすいが、それだけを残していければよいということでもない。未指定の文化遺産でも、所有者の思いのこもったものを伝承するなかで、歴史的な価値や美術工芸としての評価が付与されていく事例もある。また、版画や写真などの複製可能なもののなかでも美術品として高く評価されているものもある。被災時にそれを基準に仕訳（トリアージ）することは現実的にも難しいので、美術品たり得るものとして「美術資料」と呼称して曖昧にひとくくりにして述べていくこととする（美術資料という用語は、作品の制作背景や来歴などを伝える「作品とは別の紙資料など」を指す場合もあるが、本章では制作物そのものを指す用語としてあえてこれを使用する）。

　また、本章では、こうした美術資料のなかで、装潢文化財を中心に取り上げる。彫刻、工芸品、あるいは絵画でも油画等の洋画に関しては、素材・構造も違うので、将来的にそれぞれの専門家の稿を待ちたいと思う。

1. 日本の書画の素材構造

1.1. 装丁のある書画（装潢文化財）

　装潢文化財は指定・未指定を限らない用語で、原理的には装丁をともなった書画を指す。つまり絹・紙に書画が書（描）かれたものが作品の実体（＝本紙と呼ぶ）であるが、それを補強するために裏打ちが施され、用途に応じた道具としての形態、つまり間仕切りの形として屏風や襖や衝立、読むための形として巻子や冊子、鑑賞するための形として掛軸や画帖や額に仕立てられる。これらの形態においては、本紙は装丁（裏打ちやそれぞれのパーツ）と糊付けされて一体化していることが最大の特徴と言える。言い換えると、この形の作品の本格修理では、本紙を装丁から分離して本紙修理を行った後、裏打ちを行ってそれぞれの装丁の形に仕立ててはじめて修理が完了する。長く伝承されてきた書画の場合、修理は何度も繰り返されて今に至っているはずだが、装丁は修理の際に新調改装されて元のものが伝わっていないことが圧倒的に多い。装丁は本紙を引き立てる衣裳のようなものと考えられており、古くなって汚くなれば着替える、つまり新調することが当たり前で、装丁自体を修理までして再使用することは稀であった。これこそが日本における書画の伝承の特徴的なあり方である。美術資料では、未表装のものも含まれることがある。

1.2. 本紙修理

　本紙の基底材は絹もしくは紙で、数の上では圧倒的に紙が多いが、作品としての格は絹の方が高い。この基底材の上に書であれば墨で、絵画であれば絵具で表現がなされている。基底材と色材（墨や絵具）は基本的に何らかの接着剤で固定されており、その接着力が維持されることが必須である。本紙修理の目的は、基底材の平面性を維持し、表現である色材と基底材の接着力を維持し、表現（墨や絵具の色や質感など）を明瞭に読み取れるように表面の異物を除去したりすることである。基底材の平面性を維持するためには欠失部に補填を行って1枚のシートの状態に戻すことも必要であるし、基底材だけで形を維持できない場合は裏打ちによる補強が必須になる。絵具の接着

強度を確実なものにするためには剝落止めが必要であり、色を明瞭にするためには汚れやシミを除去軽減させるクリーニングが欠かせない。

1.3. 装丁仕立て

　本紙修理の後、裏打ちから装丁の組み立て工程とするが、絹本の場合などでは裏打ちを打ち替える（＝旧裏打紙を除去して新しい裏打紙で打ち直す）ことが、修理のなかで最も重要な工程で、特に最初の裏打ち、つまり本紙に直接接着する肌裏打ちを本紙修理に含める考え方もある。その後、それぞれの形態に組み立てるが、形態による差が大きいので、代表例として掛軸と屏風の構造と工程を示す［図1・2］。

1. 修理前調査
2. 解体（絹本の場合は肌裏を残して）
3. クリーニング
4. 剝落止め
5. 肌上げ（旧補絹／補紙の除去）
6. 補絹／補紙
7. 肌裏打
8. 裂地調整
9. 増裏打
10. 折れ伏せ
11. 付け廻し
12. 中裏打
13. 総裏打
14. 仮張り
15. 補彩
16. 仕上げ
17. 作業報告書

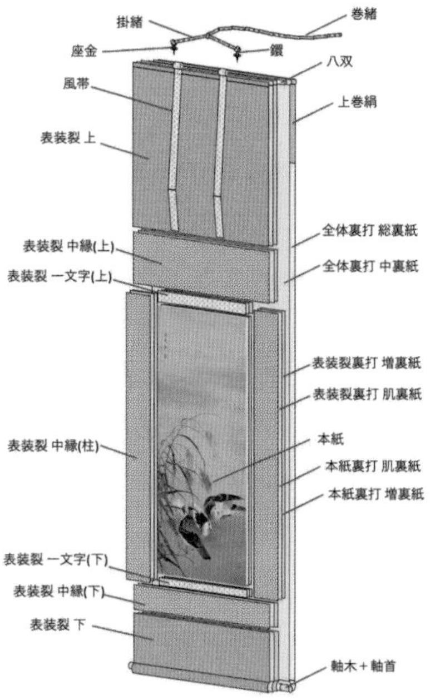

図1　掛軸の構造

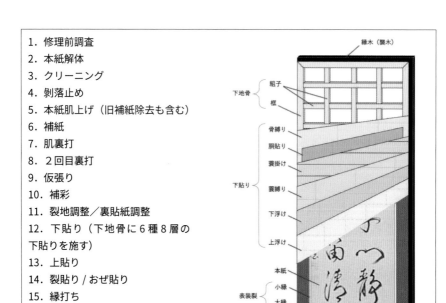

1. 修理前調査
2. 本紙解体
3. クリーニング
4. 剝落止め
5. 本紙肌上げ（旧補紙除去も含む）
6. 補紙
7. 肌裏打
8. 2回目裏打
9. 仮張り
10. 補彩
11. 裂地調整／裏貼紙調整
12. 下貼り（下地骨に6種8層の下貼りを施す）
13. 上貼り
14. 裂貼り / おぜ貼り
15. 縁打ち
16. 報告書

図2　屏風の修理工程

　これらは一般的な工程を順番に並べたもので、作品の素材や劣化状態などによっては画面に表打ちをして肌裏紙を除去する「乾式肌上げ法」が採用されるとさらに工程が増えたり、順番が入れ替わったりする。また、剝落止めは絵具の状態などによっては修理前半に行うだけでなく水を使った作業の後で再度行うこともある。修理中、修理後においても記録を取ったり写真撮影を行ったりするがここでは省略している。

　いずれの形態でも装丁仕立てに関しては専門家でない限り、たとえマニュアル等があってもハードルが高いのは明白である。ましてや、本紙修理においては、素材・構造を把握した上で、その劣化・損傷の程度を見極めて適切な処置（修理）を行うことは、経験の積み重ね抜きで行えるとは思えない。さらには文化財レベルでの長期保存を達成するには、装丁仕立ての専門家である表装技術者のなかでも文化財修理の原理原則にのっとった修理仕様を設計、施工できる業者／技術者によるしかないのが現状であるが、その数は限

られている。こうした専門家が、被災時のレスキュー、応急処置、本格修理まで関わることができれば理想的であるが、こうした知識経験を持ち、技術をもった専門家は、日本ではそのほとんどが民間組織／人であることも含めて、災害時から現場に投入することはかなり難しいと言える。だからといって、後回しにすればするほど、美術品としての評価を得る可能性を保持したまま伝承できる可能性は限りなくゼロに近づいてしまう。本章では、それを回避するために、被災時に現場でするべきこと、できることを検討していく。

2. 美術資料の被災

修理技術者の立場からいうと、被災の種類が違っても、本紙の状態、劣化損傷の種類と程度が重要であるが、本章ではまず被災の種類ごとの特徴的な劣化、損傷を挙げていくことにする。

2.1. 地震災害

地震による被災では、主に高所からの落下や建造物倒壊による圧潰等を原因とする物理的な劣化・損傷が想定される。本紙の突き傷、断裂、欠失、擦れ、さらには装丁構造（掛軸、屏風、襖等）の破損が主なものである。しかしながら、地震による被害は被災時のものにとどまらない。被災したことでインフラが失われて温湿度管理ができなくなってカビなどの生物被害が発生

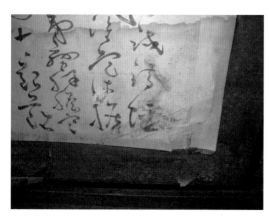

写真 1　突き傷・擦り傷（大船渡市 C 家襖）

したり、建造物が被害を受けた場合は雨漏りや貯水タンクの水漏れによる水損が発生したりすることも少なくない。

2.2. 洪水、津波（高潮）、土砂災害

　こうした災害による劣化・損傷は水損の一部としてまとめられるが、雨漏りや水漏れとは違って、美術資料そのものが、建物ごと流されたり、あるいは屋外に流されたりして行方不明となり消失してしまうこともある。また、日本の書画は紙や絹が基底材であり、色材の固着剤のほとんどが水溶性の接着剤であること、装丁（裏打ちを含む）の多くの部分が水溶性の小麦澱粉糊で接着することで仕立てられていることなどから、水への浸漬は大きなダ

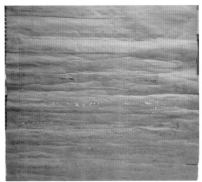

写真2　絵具層の一部の総裏への貼り付き（長野市長明寺）
掛軸の裏側（総裏紙）に絵具が付着している。当然、画面側に残っている絵具も
膠着力が低下しているので、剥離剥落する恐れがある。

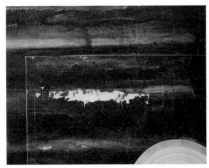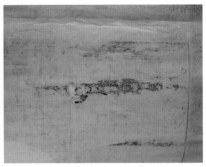

表　　　　　　　　　　　　　　　　　裏
写真3　本紙料紙の一部の総裏への貼り付き（長野市長明寺）
掛軸の裏側（総裏紙）に本紙料紙が貼り付いている。

メージを与える。しかも、それが長時間にわたることでダメージがより拡大していく。絵具層の剥離剥落が進行し、基底材が紙の場合は水素結合が解除されたりして脆弱化する。掛軸が巻いた状態で水損を受けると画面と総裏紙が貼り付き、絵具層の一部が総裏に付着してしまうことがある［写真 2］。絵具層だけでなく本紙料紙自体が総裏に付着して画面が欠失してしまうこともある［写真 3］。屏風の場合でも畳んだ状態で水損を受けると画面同士が貼り付くこともある。

　水損といっても単なる水であることは稀で、雨漏りの場合でも屋根から被災資料に伝わる経路にあるさまざまな異物を溶かして含んだ汚水であり、洪水や津波や土砂災害では言うまでもなく周囲の環境にあるさまざまなものが溶け混じった汚水である。また、被災資料にかかった水が純粋な水であったとしても、作品自体の表面や内部に存在する埃等の異物や劣化生成物等が溶け出して汚水となる。こうした汚水によって、画面に汚れが固着［写真 4］

修理前　　　　クリーニング後
写真 4-1　汚れ（泥）固着
（大船渡市 S 家掛軸まくり）

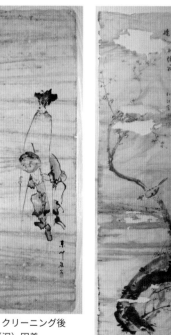

写真 4-2　断裂・欠失（大船渡市 S 家掛軸まくり）
巻いた状態で津波で被災し、泥が付着した状態で長期間経過した。その部分の料紙が腐朽したことで断裂、欠失が生じており、クリーニングを行っても完全には除去できない。

クリーニング後

第2部

83

したり、汚水の色のシミとなったり、不均等に乾燥した場合には乾燥の瞬間の境界線で際付いたり［写真5］する。

美術資料を汚損するのは、外からの汚水が原因とは限らない。美術資料自体に水に弱い色材などが使われている場合は、水に濡れることで表現以外の場所に移動すると、もともとが本紙の構成要素であっても視覚的な損傷とな

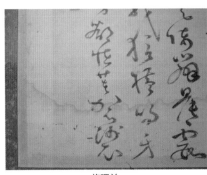 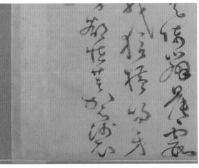

修理前　　　　　　　　　　　　　　　　　修理後
写真5　シミ（際付き）（大船渡市 C 家襖）
海水を吸い上げ、乾燥する境目で汚れが定着するため濃い色になり輪染み（際付き）が生じる。

写真6　染料系絵具の滲み（大船渡市 S 家浮世絵）
明治期の浮世絵で使用された洋紅や合成染料のなかには水に弱いものが多く、
重ねて保管されていたために水濡によって移動して汚損を拡げた。

る。例えば染料系の絵具が使われていたり［写真6］、水性のインクで文字が書かれていたり、掛軸の表装裂を染めた染料の定着ができていなかった場合［写真7］等も本紙の他の部分を視覚的に損傷させる。

　水損はほとんどの場合、被災後にさらに生物被害を生じる。最も普遍的な

 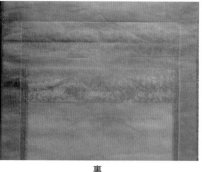

表　　　　　　　　　　　　　　　　　　裏

写真7　表装裂の染料移動（長野市長明寺）
掛軸が巻いた状態で保管されていたが、表装裂（中廻）の紫色の染料が洪水による水濡れによって内側2周目の途中まで移動して本紙を汚損している。

ものがカビによる被害である。それは、単に見栄えが悪くなるだけでなく、菌糸の成長によって色材層や基底材の物質そのものが破壊されたり、成長する過程で別の濃い色素を産生［写真8］して視覚的な損傷を与えたりする。また、浸漬時間が長くなると、菌糸が密集してできる菌核が形成され、基底材自体を破壊して発芽することもある［写真9］。

　海水に浸漬した場合は、別の形の劣化を引き起こす。塩水も周囲の環境が一定湿度以下になると水分が蒸発して乾燥するが、塩分は基底材中に残る。塩分は環境湿度が一定以上に達した時点で潮解（物質が水蒸気を取り込んで自発的に水溶液となる現象）を生じるた

写真8　色素産生カビによる着色
（大船渡市S家巻子）

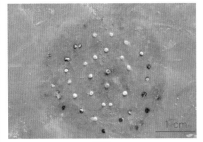

屏風

掛軸

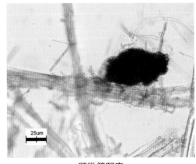

顕微鏡写真

写真9　菌核（大船渡市S家）
低温で長時間濡れた状態が続くと菌糸が密集して菌核と呼ばれる塊が生じる。発芽の際に本紙料紙を突き破って表面に白と黒の斑点状の突起が生じる。一般的にはキャベツなどの農作物で見られるが、条件が揃うと美術資料でも起こる。

冊子小口

冊子表面

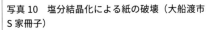

写真10　塩分結晶化による紙の破壊（大船渡市S家冊子）
紙中の塩分が潮解と乾燥を、何らかの条件下で繰り返すと結晶が集合した塊が生じる。これによって、紙の繊維同士の結合が一部では破壊される様子が見受けられるので、基底材の強度低下を招くと考えられる（美術資料ではないが、同様のことが起こる可能性は否定できないので掲載した）。

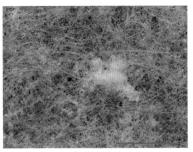

顕微鏡写真

め、乾燥していても、降雨などで高湿度になると直接水がかからなくても濡れた状態に近づく。これを繰り返していくと、結果的に濡れた状態の時間が長くなるので、劣化も進むと考えられる。また、このように塩分が潮解と乾燥を繰り返すうちに一箇所に集中して結晶の塊のようなものを形成する事例［写真10］もあり、そういう意味でも塩分の除去が必要である。

2.3. 火災

　火災による災害では、焼損によって焼失してしまうことが多いが、幸いに焼け残る場合もある。基底材の紙は高熱によって炭化する［写真11］が、経年で黒ずんだ銀は逆に還元されて制作当初の白色に戻る場合もある。また、火災による被災時には消火活動で水を被る場合があり、高温の影響を受けていない場合は水損と何ら変わらない場合もあり得る。また、近年では消火剤もさまざまなものが使われているが、化学消火剤による美術資料への影響などについては、不明である部分もあると思われる。

写真11　焼け経（泉福寺経）
紙が焦げて炭化すると脆くなり、曲げるだけで割れや剥落が生じるので、画面を養生して表面コーティングや裏打ちによる補強が必要。

3. 被災時の安定化処置

　上述したように、装丁を伴った書画が被災した場合、本来の伝承できる形

＝表装仕立てまでを完了するには相応の修復期間が必要で、被災直後に短期間で行えるものではない。また、解体すること自体、その美術資料の本紙の素材構造や状態、装丁の構造などを理解した上で行う必要があり、やはり専門家の関与がなければ難しい。そういう意味で、当初から専門家が関われるかどうかが一番の問題である。関われる場合はその専門家が修理完了までの全体の行程を考え、その場ではどこまでの処置をするのかを判断することが望ましい。そうではない場合は、専門家による修理が行われるまでの間、安定した状態を保つことを目標とすると考えるべきである。とはいえ、資料の種類や素材構造、被災の種類や程度、状態によって千差万別である。被災現場では難しいとはいえ、その最初のタイミングから専門家のアドバイスを求めることが、修理後の仕上がりに直結し、伝承していくべき価値を残せるかどうかにも関わってくる。

　安定化処置は、被災現場でのレスキュー活動から始まる。

3.1. 現状把握（被災現場での判断）

　被災現場において、判断しなければならないのは、まずレスキュー対象かどうかからである。美術品として残すかどうか＝レスキューして移動するかどうかを（できれば所有者に確認を取って）判断する。安定化処置が必要かどうかもこの時点で判断し、必要なら、処置ができる場所への移動を前提にレスキューを行う。安定化処置が必要なタイミング（至急か、後でもよいのか）の判断も、移動先等の決定を左右する場合がある。もう一つ重要なのは、そのまま移動することができる状態かどうかという判断である。その上でレスキューを行って、一時保管場所での保管方法について指示を行い、早急に処置が必要なら作業者への指示、あるいは専門家への打診などを行う必要がある。

3.2. 保管処置方針の確認（一時保管場所／処置作業場での調査と処置）

　レスキューしたものを一時保管場所に運んでも、そこでどのように保管するのか、どういった処置がどの段階で必要かを改めて確認する必要がある。この時点で専門家に直接見てもらえるとよいが、それが難しい場合は、専門

家に相談するための情報を集めなくてはならない。必要最小限の情報の例を
以下に整理しておく。

・被災資料の状態

　まず、全体としてどういう状況かということを本紙だけでなく装丁も含め
て把握する必要がある。物理的損傷を生じているのか、浸水被害を受けたの
か（濡れた状態のままか、すでに乾いているのか）。現状で持ち上げたり移
動できたりする状況か。また、美術資料では保存箱に入っていたり、包材で
包まれていたりするので、それが機能しているか、却って本紙にダメージを
与えているかなどについても確認する。その上で、以下の重要な項目を確認
する。

・カビによる被害 ［写真8］

　コロニーが生じていたり、色素を産生していたりすれば肉眼で観察でき
る。美術資料の場合、基底材自体や接着剤等、カビの生育に必要な養分が存
在するので一定の温度で湿度が上がれば必ず発生し、特に浸水した場合はそ
れが真水でも海水でも乾燥する段階で発生する可能性が高い。カビによる被
害は視覚的なものだけでなく物理的にも基底材や接着剤の強度低下を起こす
ので、これ以上繁殖させないためにも殺菌処置が必要である。ただし、菌自
体はどこにでも存在し、処置後にも発生する可能性が高い。処置をすれば終
わりではなく、その後の保管環境も同時に考慮する必要がある。

・劣化を促進する（可能性のある）物質の付着、含浸

　被災時に本紙（基底材や絵具層）の表面に異物が付着する場合や、含浸し
て内部で定着する場合がある。特に浸水による含浸では、先述したようにさ
まざまな有機物、無機物が本紙中に残されることになり、ゆくゆくは劣化を
促進する可能性が高い。安定化処置で最も必要な処置は洗浄作業であると
いっても過言ではない。塩分の除去は金属素材の場合は必須であるが、紙の
場合でも条件次第では劣化させることがわかったので、水洗による除去は必
須である ［写真11］。

・絵具層の劣化損傷

　顔料は膠などの固着剤で基底材（紙や絹、木等）に接着された構造であるが、
軸装（掛軸や巻子）屛風などで向かい側に貼り付いていたり、移動したりし

89

ていれば比較的容易に肉眼観察で確認できるが、単純に強度が低下しただけではわかり難い場合もある。特に浸水した場合、時間が長ければ固着剤の接着力が低下し、乾燥後見た目は同じでも少しの物理的な力が加わっただけで剝離剝落する可能性が大きくなる。こうした場合は触診などが必要であるが、経験がなければ難しい。その上で、処置方法を選択するが、これは、その後の本格修理とも深く関係するので、専門家からの指示を受けることが望ましい。染料系の色材（インク等も含む）は浸水すると滲む可能性が高いが、横だけでなく裏側や接している別の紙やものにも移動することがある。これは肉眼で確認できる［写真6］。

・基底材の劣化損傷

　被災によって物理的な損傷を受けた場合は視覚的にわかり易いが、強度低下等の劣化については見ただけではわかりづらい。触診による判断が可能な場合もあるが、いずれにしても経験に依存するといってもよい。

・装丁の劣化損傷

　装丁は破損している場合は取り替えることを前提としてよい。ただ、この段階で、考える必要があるのは、この装丁の存在によって本紙がダメージを受ける可能性がある場合である。何の処置もせずに保管できるケースではさほど問題にならなくとも、安定化処置で水洗などの処置をする際に邪魔になる場合もある。例えば表装裂に使われている染料が水で動く場合は先に外しておく必要がある［写真7］。あるいは、異物の除去をする場合やカビの処置をする場合でも、裏打紙があると完全に除去をすることが難しくなったり、時間が掛かったりする可能性がある。そういった場合は、トータルでの本紙強度を勘案して必要に応じて裏打紙を除去しておく方がよい。

　美術資料の種類によっては、あるいは被災の種別によっては、これ以外の劣化・損傷が生じていることもあるが、当然、個別に見極め対応する必要がある。

3.3. 安定化処置の考え方

　美術資料の場合は、最終的には専門の修理工房に搬入して本格修理を行わなければ、美術資料として伝承することにはならない。ここでいう安定化処

置は、本格処置までの間、現状を維持し、劣化の進行を止めたり、遅らせたりする目的で行われる。あるいは、時期が未定の本格修理を待って処置するより、今処置をする方がより高い効果が見込める場合の処置と言える。当然、それぞれの本紙の素材構造や装丁の状態、劣化損傷の程度、被災後の経過時間などに応じて違ってくるが、書画などの美術資料の場合は、劣化の進行を抑制するために何をすべきかというだけでなく、表現をいかに維持するかということも考える必要がある。

　物理的な損傷のみの場合は、保管環境が必要十分な条件を満たしていれば、触らずに梱包するなどしてそのまま置いておくことが可能な場合もある。

　浸水被害を受けた場合は乾燥させることが、劣化の進行を止め、カビの繁殖を防ぐために必要な処置ではあるが、美術資料の場合は、基底材の上に膠によって接着された絵具層があり、多種の素材が澱粉糊（でんぷんのり）によって貼り合わされた構造の装丁を伴っていることが多い。こういう構成であるがゆえに、ただ乾かせばよいというわけではない。形態や構造を壊さないように乾燥させる必要があるが、それこそがきわめて難しい。

　また、洪水、津波、あるいはその他の自然災害による水損の場合は、基本的に多くの水溶性、非水溶性の異物が含まれており、それらを本紙の中外に残しておくと劣化を加速する可能性が高い。特に冷凍保管でもしない限りはカビによる被害を免れ得ない。従って、できる限りそれらを除去しておくことが本格修理を待つ前提としても必要である。装丁（表装）は本紙を支える構造となっている一方で、劣化を促進する可能性のある異物が残った状態で本紙に接しているため、水洗作業をより難しくする場合が多い。また、裏打紙は本紙と一体になっていることで、裏打紙を含めた厚さの紙を水洗乾燥させるのと同じことになり、より多くの水を使ってより時間の掛かる作業となり、本紙に掛かる負担も増える。そういう意味においては、装丁を取り外して本紙だけにすることも、安定化処置の一環として有効である。

　浸水した冊子などの資料を乾燥させる方法として真空凍結乾燥がある。水洗して濡れたままの資料を凍結させて真空中で乾燥させることで、ページ同士が水素結合で貼り付くことを防ぐことができる。一方で、澱粉糊などの接着が解除されるため、美術資料でこの方法を採用できるのは、限られた条件

の場合だけで、特に絵具が使われていない場合に限られる。しかし、被災時にはカビの被害を食い止めるためにどうしてもせざるを得ない場合もあり得る。

　そして、美術資料としての表現を維持するには基底材と絵具層の構造が維持されていなくてはならない。しかしながら、水洗などの処置に耐えうるか、あるいはそういった処置を行った後の強度が十分かは、よほど低下していなければ専門家でも難しい。とはいえ、この判断を怠ると、美術資料として残したことにはならなくなる可能性がある。絵具の固着力を上げる剝落止め処置も専門家が行う方が確実であるが、どうしても難しい場合は養生紙を貼り付ける処置が可能な場合もある。いずれにしてもこの部分は専門家の指示に従って行うことが望ましい。

　安定化処置の先には、できるだけ早い時期に本格的な修理が行われるのが望ましい。被災時には複数の、というより大量の美術資料が現出するので、それを一気に修理すると言うことは現実的には不可能である。被災後時間をある程度経て冷静に考えることができるようになってから、被災によって減じた美術的な価値と伝承してきたことの意味などを天秤に掛け、さらには費用のことも含めて、修理の優先順位を決めて行っていくことが望ましい。

4．安定化処置事例（大船渡市 C 家の襖）

4.1. 初動調査

　現地での調査は被災後 2 カ月たった 5 月 6 日に実施できた。当日、襖の損傷状態を確認するなかで本紙が濡れた状態であることに驚いたが、後にそれは本紙中に残った塩分の潮解現象によるものであると判明する［写真 12］。この塩分を除去しない限り、雨が降って湿度が上がるたびに濡れた状態になり、天候が回復すると乾燥することを繰り返すことがわかった。この繰り返しによって劣化が進むことは明ら

写真 12　現地調査

かであり、最低でも塩分を除去する安定化処置が必要であると判断した。安定化処置をどこで行うかを検討したが、現地では襖を処置できる作業台や噴霧器等の器材、吸い取り紙等の資材など必要なものを揃えることは難しいということで移送して処置を行うことにした。

4.2. レスキュー

　襖自体を取り外して移送しようと試みたが、地震の影響で鴨居に上からの荷重がかかり取り外すことができなかったため、急遽、本紙だけを取り外して作業可能な場所に移送することにした。本紙の周囲には無地の台紙が取り付けられてすべての本紙を同サイズに調整した上で、その周囲に表装紙である砂子紙がめぐらされた形であった。この砂子紙のところで本紙をくり抜いて、下貼り層の浮けの層（図 2 下貼り構造図参照）ごと竹ベラで外すことにした［写真 13］。

写真 13　本紙取り外し作業

4.3. 安定化処置

4.3.1. 調査

　京都に到着した本紙を、安定化処置の方針を定めるためにさらに調査した。

・本紙の状態

　本紙の一部は被災時に津波で流されてきた何かがぶつかって破れた箇所がある。また、下部 1/3 程度まで津波による汚水に浸水したことでその境目にかなり濃い茶色の際付きが生じており、鑑賞を著しく妨げている。詳細に観察してみると、本紙の周囲の金砂子の表装紙に近い部分では緑色の変色が認められた。これは金砂子の素材が本物の金箔ではなく、真鍮箔であったことで、それが濡れたことによって緑青サビが生じたものと分かった。

京都へ移送して安定化処置を行うことにしたのは、津波による汚水に含まれる塩分が本紙中に残っているからである。環境の湿度が上がると潮解して再度濡れた状態になってしまい、乾燥と濡れを繰り返すことで、物理的な劣化が進んだり、カビによる被害が生じたりする恐れがある。それを止めておかなければ修理までの間、安定した状態を維持できないからであった。言い換えると、処置として最重要なのは水洗処置であり、基本的には本紙がそれに耐えうるかを検討する事が必要であった。

　色材である墨に関しては特に被害にあっても滲んだり転写したりして動いている痕跡はなかった。紙に関しては、江戸時代の文人（儒学者）の書に多い、竹紙か宣紙（実際は竹紙）であると思われたが、襖という装丁の宿命的な特徴である常に外気に曝され光が当たる条件から、紙の表面はすでに劣化が進んでいた。

・装丁

　移動時に本紙部分をくり抜いて取り外したが、周囲には真鍮砂子の表装紙の一部が接がれた状態である。本紙の裏に裏打ちが何層あるのかについては解体してみなければわからないものの、欠失箇所が旧修理ですでに繕われていたり、断裂（亀裂）箇所が接がれていたりすることから旧修理で少なくとも裏打ちが１層は施されていることはわかった。また、現地で取り外す際に竹ベラで外すことができたことから下貼り層の浮けの層が本紙側に１層残っている。つまり、最低でも２層の本紙以外の紙層があることがわかっている。

・旧修理

　欠失箇所の一部では旧修理で補紙（繕い）が施されているが、簀目の方向が本紙と一致していないために視覚的な違和感を感じさせる箇所もあった。

4.3.2. 処置方針決定

　調査の結果を踏まえて安定化処置の方針を立てた。

　最優先事項は、塩分の除去であり、水洗処置である。一般的な装潢文化財の作品の修理の際の水洗処置と同じ方法、つまり10枚程度重ねた吸取紙の上に本紙を置き、画面側から浄水（金属イオンや異物を除去した濾過水）を噴霧して、重力と紙の毛細管現象を使って下の吸取紙に吸収させることで、本紙上や中に含まれる異物を溶かしだしたり（水溶性の物質の場合）移動さ

せたり（繊維の隙間を通り抜けるほど小さな非水溶性物質の場合）して除去する方法である。その処置を行う上で本紙に与える負担を最小に減らし、効果を最大とするために何をしなくてはならないのかを検討した。

・本紙以外のものを除去するかどうかの検討

まず、前項で挙げたように、真鍮箔砂子の表装紙は水洗（乾燥）時に本紙にサビ由来の緑青色の変色物質が移動する可能性があるので、事前に除去が必要である。また、本紙以外にも 2 層の下貼り紙（浮け紙）や裏打紙があると、その中に含まれる塩分も含めて除去しなくてはならなくなるため、必要以上に洗浄水の量を増やす必要があり、処置時間も長くなることから本紙への負担が過剰にかかる恐れがある。これらも除去しておく方が良いと判断した。もともと大きさの違う本紙のサイズを揃えるために周囲に台紙（足し紙）が浸けられていたが、よほど傷んでいる場合を除いて、そこまでを本紙と定義して取り外さず処置を行うことにした。

・本紙が水洗に耐え得るかの検討

本紙の表現が墨書であり、墨以外には落款の朱が表現の主体である。これらは水に対してある程度の耐性があることが知られているが、パッチテスト（濡れた吸取紙の小片を置いて移動しないかを確認するテスト）を行って移動しないことを確かめた。

4.4. 安定化処置

4.4.1. 表装紙除去

本紙の周囲に残っている表装紙は継目に少量の水を与えて接着剤である糊を緩めて除去した。

4.4.2. 旧下貼り紙（浮け紙）、旧裏打紙除去

旧浮け紙は作業台の上で裏側を上に向けて置き、浄水を噴霧して除去を行った [写真 14]。旧裏打ち紙も同様にして除去を行った。除去を始めたところ、裏打紙は 2 層あることがわかった。本紙が短い繊維の紙ですでにかなり劣化（強度低下）していること、亀裂部は裏打紙があることでつながっていること、欠失部には補紙が施されて 1 層目の裏打紙（肌裏紙）がそれを支える形であることから、この肌裏紙の除去は非常に困難であると感じた。こ

の肌裏紙を除去するためには、その場で欠失部の旧補紙を除去して新しい補紙を補填し、新しい肌裏紙を打つ（接着する）、つまり本格修理を行う必要があることになるので、この1層目の裏打紙（肌裏紙）は残して水洗処置を行うという判断をした。

写真 14　裏打紙除去作業

4.4.3. 水洗処置

　肌裏紙だけを残した本紙を重ねた吸取紙の上に置いて浄水を噴霧して水洗処置を行った［写真 15］。津波による塩水を含んだ部分はなかなか水が浸透しなかったが、時間をかけると徐々に浸透し、噴霧を数回繰り返しては本紙の直下の吸取紙に含まれる水の塩分の濃度を計測し、ほぼゼロなったところで水洗を終了した［写真 16］。

　この水洗で浸水した部分との境目に生じていた茶色の際付きもかなり軽減されほとんど気にならなくなった。

写真 16　塩分濃度測定
塩分が除去できたかどうか、表層の吸取紙に含まれている塩分濃度を測定して判断した。

写真 15　水洗処置
本紙に負担を掛けないように、上から浄水を噴霧して浸透させ、下に敷いた吸い取り紙に吸収させて除去した。

4.4.4. 乾燥

　水洗が完了した本紙を毛布の上に置いて自然乾燥させた。裏打紙を残した状態でもあり、本紙がしっかりしていたことから、乾燥による暴れはほとんどなかった。

4.4.5. 保管

　乾燥後は、色材が剥落する恐れもないことから本紙を重ねて巻いて保管した。

写真 17　乾燥
急激に乾燥させると輪染みなどが生じるので、毛布の上でゆっくり全体的に乾燥させた。

第2部

　以上が、被災後 2011 年度に行った安定化処置に至る経緯と処置内容である。こういった処置は現地でも条件が揃えばできないことはないと思う反面、やはり設備が整っている慣れた環境で状態を確認しながら処置する方が格段に安心できると感じた。特に、この事例では対象が墨書であったが、もし絵具（色材）による表現のある美術資料に対して現地で処置を行う必要があったらどうしただろうと考える。

　（本美術資料に関しては、その後 2014 年度に、京都造形芸術大学の特別研究費や東北大学災害科学国際研究所、特定非営利活動法人文化財保存支援機構からの援助もあり、最終的な修理まで行うことができた ➡コラム参照）。

おわりに

　最初に現状の課題について考えてみたい。こうした美術資料を修理（処置）できるのは現代では工房などにいる技術者以外には、数える程しかいない。被災時にこうした民間の専門家に関わってもらえるような仕組みを整えたり、専門家と協議を行える知識と経験を持ち、場合によっては応急処置を行える人材を養成したりすることが必要だと感じる。本格的な修理は無理でも、応急的な安定処置を担える人材はいずれにしても必要であろう。とはい

本格修理

　安定化処置から３年後に予算が付いたことで、本格修理を行うことができた。
　安定化処置の際に判断したように、旧肌裏紙を本紙に負担を与えずに除去することは難しいことを再度確認した。旧肌裏紙も本紙の一部として残し、旧補紙は紙の向きが斜めになっていたりして違和感を生じていたため、すべて除去して本紙に似寄りの補修紙で新しく補填し、さらに２層目の裏打ちを施した。下地骨は歪みもなくしっかりしていたため元のものを使用し、６種８層の下貼りを新たに施して本紙を貼り込んだ。表装紙（台紙）には真鍮箔砂子が使用されており、それが水損したことで青い銅サビの色が本紙を汚損していたため、本金砂子の表装紙を新調した。引手は元のものを使い、縁木は黒漆塗縁木を新調して仕立てた。現地で敷居、鴨居、柱の傾き等に合わせて調整して納めた。

肌裏打ち　　　　　　　下貼り（胴貼り）　　　　表装紙貼り込み

次の間（修理前）

補修紙（修理前）

補修紙（修理後）　　　　　　次の間（修理後）

え、すぐには解決できそうもないので、当面は、専門家を紹介してくれる窓口に頼ることになるだろう。現在、独立行政法人国立文化財機構のなかに文化財防災センターができてそういった相談もできるが、文化財としての対応となる。民間では歴史資料ネットワーク（史料ネット）でも対応はしているが、美術資料に関しては NPO 文化財保存支援機構の方が直接専門家が対応してくれる。それ以外にも文化財保存修復学会にも専門家が所属しており紹介してもらうことが可能である。

　最後に、筆者がいくつかの被災資料の修理（処置）に携わって感じたことを述べて締めくくりたい。被災した美術資料の修理では、実際には被災したことによる損傷というより、長年放置された経年による劣化損傷に対する処置の比重が大きいことが多いと感じる。つまり、修理が必要な段階に至っていたのに放置されていたのが、被災がきっかけで修理が始められたという皮肉な現実に直面するのである。たしかに、被災した際の処置や修理について考え、備えておくことが重要なのは当然であるが、こうした美術資料（未指定の美術品）の場合は、美術的な価値を維持することが重要であり、メンテナンスを行いながら、日常的に守っていくにはどうしたらよいかということが根底にあるのではないだろうか。

参考文献

・ 津波により被災した文化財の保存修復技術の構築と専門機関の連携に関するプロジェクト実行委員会・赤沼英男・鈴木まほろ編『安定化処理 ～大津波被災文化財保存修復技術連携プロジェクト～』（津波により被災した文化財の保存修復技術の構築と専門機関の連携に関するプロジェクト実行委員会・日本博物館協会・ICOM 日本委員会、2018 年（増補版））

・ 動産文化財救出マニュアル編集委員会『動産文化財救出マニュアル　思い出の品から美術工芸品まで』（クバプロ、2012 年）

・ 大津波被災資料連携プロジェクト安定化処置（動画）
　https://www.j-muse.or.jp/06others/stabilization.php 　（2024 年 1 月 23 日最終閲覧）

第3部

資料救済への備え方

第 **7** 章

救出のシミュレーション：行動計画

▨　山内利秋（九州保健福祉大学）

はじめに

　日本各地で毎年のように災害が発生し、被災する文化財が後を絶たない。災害が文化財に対して破壊や汚損といった直接的な被害をもたらしている状況はもちろん、まだ直接的でなくとも文化財を保管・内包してきた施設が被災し、いち早くレスキューしなければならない場合もあるだろう。言うまでもなく文化財を災害時に放置するのは滅失・棄損のリスクが高いわけであって、そのためには災害発生後のある時点で比較的安全な場所へ移動させる必要性がある。ここで重要となってくるのが、ある地域で被災した文化財をレスキューする役割を担おうとする人びとが、災害後のどのタイミングで作業を遂行するかであり、さらにはどのような人員や装備の準備が必要であるかを知っているかどうかであろう。

　現代の行政施策では地域防災計画をはじめさまざまな自然災害リスクに対応した計画・マニュアルが作成され、状況に応じてその都度改変がなされている。例えば被害予測・減災の観点から作成されている「ハザードマップ」、避難経路と避難場所の確認といった避難行動を整備した「避難計画」、避難所の準備から閉鎖までを定めた「避難所運営手引き・マニュアル」、災害時に発生したゴミ処理を遂行するための「災害廃棄物処理計画」や、さらに被災者の思い入れのある所有物を廃棄物として処理せずに被災者へ返還することを目的とした「思い出の品取り扱いマニュアル」といったように、過去の

災害で生じたさまざまな課題を検討し、同様な事態が発生した際にも対応できるよう明文化されている。

　博物館・文化財保護分野に限ってみれば災害発生時の行動がいまだ指定文化財の状況確認のみにとどまっている事例や、担当職員が限られることもあってBCP（Business Continuity Plan: 事業継続計画）が構築されていない事例も見受けられる。大きな災害を経験した自治体では行政施策のさまざまな分野で高いリスクを想定したマニュアルやハンドブック・ガイドライン等が整備されていると考えられるものの、時間が経過して担当者が代わる等によってノウハウが継承されなくなるケースも想定しておかなければならない。

　このように博物館・文化財保護の分野でも災害に備えた運営計画を継続的に構築・検討していくべき必要性が高い。そこで、災害を想定した資料レスキューに関するシミュレーションを通じて、特に市町村クラスの自治体における防減災マネジメントを構築し、自治体や民間団体等の関係機関での合意形成を目指していく活動について考えてみる。

1. 災害に備えたシミュレーション

　災害を想定して準備されているさまざまな計画・マニュアルは、実際に災害が発生した際に記載された通りに遂行できるかというと恐らくそうはいかない場合が多いだろう。しかし、完璧ではなくともさまざまな条件を想定して可能な限りの行動を模索・構築していく作業を通じてしか、災害時にリアクションは起こせない。こうしたことから、災害発生時に活動の中核となる自治体や以前から防災教育が行われている学校や企業はもちろん、住民による自治防災組織においても防災マニュアル策定が進められている。

　博物館や文化財の保存に関与する立場（行政・民間を問わず）でも、「備える」必要性は確実に存在する。

　愛知県立美術館では災害発生時に予期されるさまざまなシチュエーション下で実践的な対応が行えるように想定された「シミュレーションミーティング」が行われ、対応方針の見直しが繰り返し行われている[1]。

　神奈川県博物館協会では毎年「総合防災計画活動」を実施しており、この

活動では県内複数のブロック単位での情報集約を行う遠隔情報伝達訓練等が行われ、あらかじめ決めていた幹事館園が事故にあった際にもバックアップできる体制を構築していくなど、さまざまな条件が設定されている[2]。また、担当者を変えながら継続的な防災訓練研修を行うことによってノウハウが継承される仕組みを構築している。

　こうした活動は博物館に限らず、『文化財保存活用大綱』が各都道府県で出そろったことによって、文化財保護行政においても広く行われるようになりつつある。実際、群馬県では『文化財防災ガイドライン』の「災害に備えた取組　防災計画の作成」のなかで「災害時のタイムラインを作成する」という記述がある。タイムラインは国交省をはじめとする省庁で防減災行動に関わる防災行動計画として策定されるものであるが[3]、群馬県では文化財所有者・管理団体用にフローチャートをもとに個別のタイムライン策定を促しており、住民単位での行動計画であるマイ・タイムラインに近い。

　鹿児島県では『文化財保存活用大綱』の「防災・防犯・災害発生時の対応」のなかに、「水害を想定した資料レスキューの知識や技術を学ぶオンラインワークショップ等の情報提供」という記載がある。文化財防災や被災資料取り扱いに関わるワークショップが各所で実施されているが、オンライン化が進んだ現在では遠隔地間での開催も普通に行えるようになった。

　災害に直接関わる市町村クラスの自治体において、文化財の災害時対応の近年の課題として考えておく必要があるのは、職員削減や充足率低下によるマンパワー不足や世代交代も含めた異動によって知識・技術が継承されなくなる可能性である。小規模自治体では専門職員が補充されず一般事務職員を担当職に充てる事例も散見され、災害対応はおろか文化財保護や博物館での専門業務の低下も懸念されざるを得ない。災害時には自治体間の広域連携、資料ネットやヘリテージマネージャーといった民間団体とも連携した調整能力も求められる。市町村では博物館と文化財保護を兼務で担当している場合も多いが、レスキューに際しては博物館という特定の公的施設を対象とした場合と地域コミュニティ全体に広く分布する文化財に関与する場合とでは条件が異なる等、さまざまなケースに応じていかなければならない。また、地域の郷土史研究団体等の高齢化による縮退、学校教員の多忙化や異動の多さ

から地域資料と向き合いにくくなった現状もあり、地元で期待できる新たな市民ボランティアを開拓・育成していくことも求められる。

こうしたことから災害時における文化財―資料のレスキュー、広く「文化財をまもる」ことについての諸活動を、自治体職員のみならず活動諸団体をも含めた合意形成を目指す取り組みとして検討していかなければならない。

そこで、宮崎・鹿児島の資料ネットでは、災害を想定したシミュレーション訓練であるDIG（Disaster Imagination Game）を博物館・文化財保護分野での、被災資料レスキューの実施を想定して、タイムライン上で変化していく情報・人員・装備、資料退避施設等の整備、外部団体との連携、安全管理を含めてノウハウの理解を目指したワークショップとして実施している［図］。もともとはマンパワー不足が想定される地方の資料ネット間での連携を想定した運用訓練として考案したが、準備から実施・評価まで自治体担当者とともに確認していく過程で、対象となる自治体において必要な災害時の体制や問題点を関係者が把握・理解・共有しやすいことが確認された。これまでの参加者からは「災害に対する準備の不足」や「さまざまな立場の協力の重要性」等についての理解が確認され、災害時の文化財マネジメントにつ

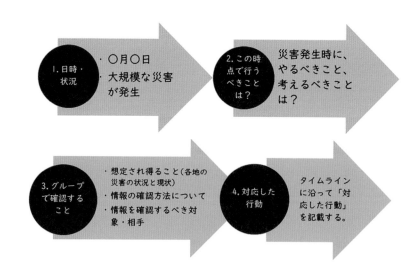

図　災害を想定した資料レスキューの DIG

ながる課題もみえてきた。

1.1. DIG をやってみる

　DIG は、もともと自衛隊の指揮所演習をベースに、1997 年に防衛庁防衛研究所（当時）と三重県が災害時における自治体のシミュレーションとして開発されたものである[4]。

　基本的にはある時点で災害が発生し、刻々と変化していく状況に応じてどのように対処していくかを検討し、災害に備えていくことを目的としている。応用の幅が広く、現在は全国の自治体やボランティア団体等市民団体の防災研修で実施されていることも多い。筆者らはこれを気象予報士・防災士といった方々のアドバイスを受けて文化財レスキュー用に応用し、改良を加えながらプログラムを組み立てている。もともとは宮崎・鹿児島という南九州の隣接する 2 県における災害時の資料ネット間の協力関係を確認・強化していく目的からはじめたのだが、自治体の文化財保護担当や博物館学芸員、生涯学習機関職員等にも行っている。

　我々の行っている DIG には、大きく＜準備＞・＜実施＞・＜評価＞の三つの段階がある。以下、それぞれ具体的な手順を見ていきたい。

1.2. 準備

　準備段階ではワークショップの目的、実施時期、対象、どんな災害を対象とするか等を決定し、これに応じた準備を行っていく。ワークショップではミッションを「災害によって被災した場所にある資料を安全なところへ運び出す」というシンプルな内容としているが、これは他のミッションに変更することももちろん可能である。ワークショップの実施時期は、気象災害が発生しやすい季節や過去に地震・津波等が実際に発生した時期を踏まえて企画するのがより効果的であろう。

　設定としては、対象とする自治体・地域で過去に発生した最大級の災害を想定する。ハザードマップや各種地形図を参考とするのはもちろんだが、タイムラインを設定するには災害の時間軸上の経過を理解しなくてはならない［表］。気象災害や地震の場合は気象庁から発生からの経緯経過が公開されて

表　過去の台風災害をベースに作成した資料レスキュータイムライン

（宮崎県高鍋町での事例から）

【前提】

　1983年9月19日、トラック島上空に弱い熱帯低気圧が発生し、西北西に進みながら発達し、21日にはグアム島南南西の会場で台風10号となった。急速に発達しながら23日には沖縄南東1,000kmの海上で中心気圧885hpa、最大風速55m/sの猛烈な台風に成長した。台風は26日から27日にかけて、東シナ海北部で向きを北から北よりに変え、次第に弱まりながらも東進し、28日10時20分頃長崎市附近に上陸した。九州上陸後は速度を速めて東に進み、九州中部を横断して28日には高知県宿毛市附近で温帯低気圧になった。その後、この低気圧はスピードを上げて本州の南海上を東進し、29日9時には関東地方の東約450kmの会場に進んだ。

　台風の北上に伴って日本の南海上に停滞していた秋雨前線が25日から活発となり、九州から関東地方の太平洋側を中心に強い雨が降り始めた。26〜27日にかけて九州と四国を中心に大雨となり、28日は台風の通過により四国から関東までの広範囲での大雨となった。現在の気象用語で言う線状降水帯が各地で発生していた可能性がある。

　この台風に伴う被害は38府県に及び、浸水や山・がけくずれ等によるもののほか、用水等の増水による学童の水死事故が目立った。大小河川の氾濫や増水が多く、交通機関の被害も少なくなかった。

【被害】

　宮崎県地域では当初は台風の直撃。

　26日には日南市・串間市で豪雨、そして27日には宮崎市と児湯郡を中心に中小河川の氾濫が相次ぎ、浸水被害が続出した。高鍋町では同日午前3時から4時にかけて85mmの強烈な雨が降り、宮田川沿いの地区で河川が氾濫した。氾濫は宮田川左岸の塩田樋門から分流する塩田川方面に広がり、特に水門を閉じたことから塩田川の水が行き詰り、用水路や排水路へ水が逆流して町の中心部が浸水した。松原町、旭通、十日町、筏地区等での床上浸水は136世帯、床下浸水は445世帯、一部破損が3世帯であった。降りはじめの25日から28日午前6時までの雨量は494mmにまで達した。

　宮田川から塩田川方面へ逆流して市街地が内水氾濫となる被害はたびたびあり、2018年9月の台風24号でも発生している。

日付	時間	1983年の気象状況をもとにしたタイムライン	状況	この時点で行うべきことはなにか？	グループで確認すること	準備する参考資料
9月25日〜28日		25日から大型台風接近によって宮崎県内全域で夜半より雨が続く	松原町、旭通、十日町、筏地区等での床上浸水は136世帯、床下浸水は445世帯、一部破損が3世帯			
		26日、串間・日南市で大雨				
		27日、宮崎市・児湯郡を中心に豪雨となる				
		台風は長崎市付近に上陸後、通過				
		高鍋町で25日〜18日の総雨量が472ミリに達する				
		災害対策本部を設置して、警戒にあたった。				
		日豊線が早朝から不通となり、運休が相次いだ。高速道路も、九州自動車道・宮崎自動車道が、上下線とも通行止めになった。				
9月29日		公共機関は停止しているところが多い。JR九州によると、鹿児島県内の路線はすべて止まり、とくに日豊線はがけ崩れなどで寸断された状態。全県で、6、7両合わせて80,000人に影響する見込み。	台風が通過し被害の全貌が把握されてくる。宮田川から塩田川にかけての水門を閉じたことによって内水氾濫が発生。市内の複数の歴史的建物や公共施設が水に浸かるという情報があり、市文化財課職員が確認に行く。⇒図書館敷地にある旧明倫堂書庫等の2軒の蔵、社会福祉協議会が管理している歴史的建造物（登録有形文化財、旧鈴木馬佐也別邸）	● 状況確認・情報伝達において実施するべきことは？ ● この期間に準備すること、想定されることは？	● 状況確認の手段・対象、関係諸機関とのやり取りはどうするべきか。 ● 資料の所在に関する情報を、どの範囲の人にまで周知させるべきか。	● 洪水ハザードマップ・土砂災害等防災マップ

		が水に浸かっていたことが確認／内部にある歴史資料が被害を受けている可能性が推測された。	●この段階での情報集約はどうするか？ ●人員・資材の確保や分担（どんな人？なにが必要？）		
9月30日	災害粗大ごみの受付開始 ボランティアセンター開設	災害粗大ごみの受付の開始とボランティアセンターの開設により、被災地で片付け作業が一斉に始まる。			
10月1日		自治体職員は避難所運営が優先されるため、文化財に関わる作業は後日となった。ただ、旧鈴木馬佐也別邸に関しては社会福祉協議会が管轄しているため、後片付けについては登録有形文化財であることから必ず教育委員会と調整する旨申し出た。 社会福祉協議会からは、建物の清掃、特に畳の除去、軒下等に溜まっている汚泥の除去と乾燥を早めに行いたい旨要望。			
10月3日		資料については、被災個所から外へ運び出す計画をたてる。搬出場所は総合体育館弓道場となった。			
10月5日	JR九州が5日午前まで全線運休。県内で停電や電話が不通の地域がのこる。また、九州自動車道や国道の一部区間で通行止めのまま。県道などを含めた幹線道路の通行止めや片側通行が多数。	現地での資料レスキューのタイミングを見極めつつ、被害情報の把握を行う。	●現地の安全性についてどのように確認するか ●移動ルートはどう確認するか ●人員への諸注意はどうするか ●移動ルートは再検討の必要はないか	●鹿児島・宮崎・延岡方面や、児湯郡周辺からの移動ルート図があると便利	
		蔵については図書館職員によって、管理できる時間帯は扉を開いた状態にし、室内を乾燥するようにした。その際、資料が水損している状況が確認された。			
10月6日		旧鈴木馬佐也別邸の内部状況について、社会福祉協議会から、フスマが水に浸かり一部破損しており中に文字のかかれた紙が貼ってあることが確認された旨、社会教育課に連絡。			
		資料が水で濡れており、これに対する処置を想定した準備。			
		宮崎県教育委員会、技術・物資支援のため宮崎歴史資料ネットワークとも調整。			
10月8日	8:00	高鍋町歴史総合資料館前にレスキュー活動に参加可能な町職員と宮崎県・資料ネットメンバーが集合。役割分担を確認して現地へ移動（自動車・リヤカー）。	●現地への移動、現地到着時に行うべきことは？		

第3部

109

	9:00		レスキュー活動開始。資料の水損被害が予想より大きい。	●記録作成時に必要なことは？
	10:30		●記録調書作成可能な場合は記録作成を実施し、その後資料搬出。記録作成困難な場合は状況写真のみ撮影し、資料搬出。 ●部分的に汚泥した資料を確認、また、比較的程度が軽い資料もある等状態はさまざま。 ⇒泥が付着したまま乾燥がはじまっているもの、悪臭・カビが発生し細菌による資料劣化がはじまっている記録資料類（写真など）を確認。 ●現場からの移動・仮梱包作業に困難が認められ、15:00頃になると作業者にも疲労が。搬出した資料を駐車場へ。駐車場にて仮梱包等、自動車へ積載作業。	●作業終了時・運搬・保管時に行うべきことは？
	16:00		現地での作業終了。	
	17:00		資料を搬送、一時保管場所へ。	

いる。国交省地方整備局に属する各地の河川国道事務所では一級河川整備に関わる情報が公開されており、過去の災害発生個所や水位上昇の記録、災害となった直接的な原因等が確認できる。また、自治体の情報としては自治体誌のみならず災害記録誌が刊行されている場合には大いに参考となるし、危機管理担当課の協力が得られれば地域の災害時の自治体対応を記録したタイムラインに関する情報を提供してもらえる場合もある。昭和期等少し古い時期の災害となると自治体でも記録が少なくなってくるが、過去の広報や当時の新聞の情報が活用できる。ただし、南海トラフ地震クラスとなると現代の水準で活用可能な過去の記録が限られてくるので、シナリオを検討する際には注意しなければならない。過去の記録は災害発生のみならず、当時の自治体・コミュニティがどのように対応していったかについても理解できるが、シナリオとしてタイムラインを設定する場合には、少し古い時代の事例となると現在の行政の災害対策のように整備されていないので、そのまま当てはめず部分的にでも現状に置き換えて検討する。

　タイムラインとともに資料レスキュー体制を検討していく。被災リスクの高い資料所在場所のチェック、レスキューに関わる人材の確保や連絡体制、機材や資料移動後の一時保管場所等の設定であるが、この段階で当該地域の

資料レスキュー体制がどの程度整備されているかを再認識することとなる。特に平成大合併後は、現在は同一自治体であっても、本庁と支所等かつての自治体域での土地感覚や地域コミュニティの把握の差が残っていることもよくあり、資料レスキューに関わる諸状況の確認の必要性を再認識する事も多い。

1.3. 実施

　ワークショップを実施する場合、参加者は 1 グループ 4 〜 7 人が手頃な人数である。ワークショップに慣れていないグループは手順がわからない場合もあるので、その際にはテーブルファシリテーター[5]を配置すると進行がスムーズになる。

　対象となる場所の地図（A1 版等に大きく拡大）・ハザードマップ（A3 版程度）、過去の災害に関する記録、ペン（はっきりと文字が読める水性と油性の細書）、付箋紙（四角いタイプでできれば強粘着、最低 2 色はほしい）、A3 サイズの厚めの出力用紙でプリントした付箋紙を貼り付ける台紙（後述）、透明の書き込みができるシート（ライティングシート、ホワイトボードシート等）、プロジェクター（可能ならば 2 台）と PC を設置する。プロジェクターからは一方はパワーポイントによるタイムラインを、さらにもう一方には対象となるポイントを押さえたハザードマップ（国土交通省「重ねるハザードマップ」が便利、ネットワーク接続する必要がある）を投影する。机を配置し、その上に拡大した地図・ハザードマップ・付箋紙を貼り付ける台紙を設置する。地図には透明のシートを上から重ねて書き込みできるようにしておくと便利である。さらにタイムラインを表にして各テーブルに配布しておくと、参加者が再確認しやすい。

　全体を統括するメインファシリテーターとともに、アドバイザーとして保存科学や保存修復の専門家がいると、資料保存についての幅広い知見と、より説得力のある解説が提供可能となる。この際にレスキュー時に必要となるヘルメット、マスク（DS2/N95 相当）、防塵メガネ、ニトリル手袋等を提示できるようにしておく。

　メインファシリテーターはワークショップの内容について説明し、タイム

ラインに沿ってシナリオを展開していく。災害発生時の状況、被害と対応、被災エリアと道路の復旧状況等を確認しながら、一方で資料が被災してレスキューが必要であることを述べ、実施のための準備、実際のレスキュー、搬出して仮置き場に据え置くまでの流れを話していく。

　その間、参加者に対して設問を出すが、筆者らは下記の三つの内容を問題文としている。

> 設問1：状況確認・情報伝達において実施するべきことは？
> 　　　　この期間に準備すること、想定されることは？
> 設問2：現地への移動、現地到着時に行うべきことは？
> 設問3：記録作成時に必要なことは？
> 　　　　作業終了時・運搬・保管時に行うべきことは？

　このように「自分たちがなすべき、対応した行動」について検討してもらい、付箋紙に記述した上でA3サイズの質問用紙に貼ってもらう［写真1］。設問内容は必要に応じて変更するのも可能であろう。各設問には、15分程度の考える時間を設け、参加者は自分の考えたアイデアを付箋紙に書き出す。この際、付箋紙1枚につき必ず1項目の文章として記述してもらうようにする。複数の項目が記載されてしまうと後で分類が難しくなるので注意する。付箋への記載は参加者個々人による作業である。次はそれをグループで内容から分類し、台紙に張りなおしていく。この分類作業を通して他者との意見交換を行い、自分の考え方を再確認する。所定の15分が過ぎた後、アドバイザーからそれぞれの設問に対して解説を入れる。保存科学等の専門家を確保できない場合にはメインファシリテーターが解説を行うこととなるが、この場合にもあらかじめ専門家からアドバイスを受けておくのがよいだろう。解説の際、あくまでも「正解」はなく、さまざまな考え方を提示していくのを目的とする点は話しておく必要がある。

　タイムライン終了後に、各グループでの発表を行う。これによってこの日のワークショップを振り返り、学習内容の定着がはかられる。ここまでかかる時間はスタートから休憩をはさんで2時間半から3時間程度が見込まれ

写真 1　付箋に書いたアイデアを台紙に貼り付けていく

る。一連のプログラムはオンラインによっても可能であるが、その際には"miro"等のオンラインホワイトボードを使用すると効果的である。オンラインでの開催は、地域を飛び越えた幅広い参加を可能とする。

1.4. 評価

　ワークショップ終了後、参加者にはアンケートを記載してもらう。参加したワークショップを通して理解できたことや、課題として考えていくべきことについて挙げてもらい結果をフィードバックしていく。
　以下、質問の例を挙げておく。

・このワークショップで、あなたが最もよく理解できたことは何でしょうか。一つだけ選んで下さい。
　　資料保全活動の作業がどういった流れで行われるか／資料保全活動にあたっての必要な準備と、準備の何ができていて、何ができていないか／資

料保全を行う上で必要な知識と技術／人口減少・高齢化・空き家の増加といった地域社会の現状／民間（ここでは資料保全に関わる活動）組織間や行政との連携の難しさと重要性

・ ワークショップの内容について、最もわかりにくく感じたことは何でしょうか。

被害を想定する手段やどんな情報を収集する必要があるかがわからない／どんな手順で資料保全作業を行うのかがわからない／どんな装備・道具が資料保全で必要なのかがわからない／土地勘がなく地理的なイメージがわかない／わかりにくく感じたことは特にない

・ このワークショップの意義について最も感じたことは何ですか。次の八つの選択肢のなかから強く思うことを二つまで選んで下さい。

災害から文化財・博物館資料をまもることが地域社会の維持・継続にもつながると感じた／災害から文化財・博物館資料をまもることが将来の大規模災害に備えることにもつながっている／資料は博物館などの機関だけでなく、個々人が所蔵しているケースが多く、これらを守ることが所有者だけでなく地域社会にとっても重要であると感じた／地域の歴史・文化をまもるためにはさまざまな立場の人の協力が必要であると感じた／災害においては、隣接する地域間での連携をはかることが極めて重要であると感じた／将来の災害に備えるためには、若い世代が関与していくことが必要だと感じた／活動の意義はなんとなく理解できるものの、細かい作業や役割といった点で今一つ理解できなかった／活動の意義やさまざまな役割の重要性を全く理解できなかった

2. 今後の展開

　全国の自治体で『文化財保存活用地域計画』が策定されつつあり、災害を想定した文化財の保存についても記述されている事例も多い。次にはこの課題を実践する上での実施計画が必要となってくるわけだが、事前防災はもちろん、災害時に関わるマネジメントの構築はきわめて重要であり、シミュレーションはこのマネジメント構築の一プロセスでもある［写真 2］。また、今回

写真 2　宮崎県高鍋町でのワークショップの様子

紹介したシミュレーションを実施してから実際の被災資料のハンドリングを伴うアクティビティを加味することによって、より効果の高いものも目指せるであろう。

　東日本大震災での災害対応の教訓として「備えていたことしか、役には立たなかった」、「備えていただけでは、十分ではなかった」という言葉がある[6]。完璧にはならずとも、災害に対して一定のリアクションを可能とするための活動が望まれる。

注

1　副田一穂「シミュレーションミーティングと防災訓練」（『平成 26 年度地域と共働した美術館・歴史博物館創造活動支援事業「みんなでまもるミュージアム」報告書』「みんなでまもるミュージアム」事業実行委員会、2015 年、pp.169-173）

2　神奈川県博物館協会総合防災計画推進委員会「神奈川県博物館協会総合防災計画活動報告」（『神奈川県博物館協会会報』第 88 号、2017 年、pp.62-79）

3　タイムラインの定義としては、次のものがある。「災害の発生を前提に、防災関

係機関が連携して災害時に発生する状況を予め想定し共有した上で、「いつ」、「誰が」、「何をするか」に着目して、防災行動とその実施主体を時系列で整理した計画をいう。」（国土交通省 水災害に関する防災・減災対策本部防災行動計画ワーキング・グループ『タイムライン（防災行動 計画）策定・活用指針』）

4　平野昌「災害救援時における新しいボランティアのあり方と災害図上訓練DIG」（『近代消防』36-3、1998年、pp.148-152）

　三重県地域振興部消防防災課「市民啓発型の災害図上訓練DIGの概要と課題」（『消防科学と情報』No.63、2001年、pp.44-48）

　小村隆史「DIG（Disaster Imagination Game）－「納得して地域と付き合う」ためのワークショップ型災害図上訓練のすすめ－」（『消防防災』2004年秋季号、2004年、pp.92-102）

5　ファシリテーターにはワークショップの会場全体を統括するフロアーファシリテーターと、小グループの「班」の進行をともに考えるテーブルファシリテーターの二つの種類があり、特にテーブルファシリテーターの一番大きな仕事は、ワークショップの「場づくり」「雰囲気づくり」とされる（阪神・淡路大震災記念 人と防災未来センター『災害ボランティア　実践ワークショップガイド』2006年、p.19）

6　国土交通省東北地方整備局『東日本大震災の実体験に基づく災害初動期指揮心得』（2013年）

第 8 章

救済方法のシミュレーション：
災害対策の実務を考える

▨　天野真志（国立歴史民俗博物館）

第
3
部

はじめに

　資料救済に向けた取り組みを推進する上で、担い手の養成は大きな課題となる。第 2 部で紹介してきたように、災害時にはさまざまな資料の救済と応急処置が要請されるが、各地の被災現場で一連の作業を統括し実践するのは、博物館・図書館・文書館等職員が中心であり、必ずしも資料の保存や修復に関する専門的知見・技術を保有しているとは限らない。災害発生時には、多様な情報が錯綜するなかで的確な状況判断と迅速な作業工程の策定が求められ、災害対策の人材育成を考えるためには救出から応急処置、さらにはその後の恒久的保存に向けた調整に至る一連の作業立案を担いうる考え方や具体的な技術選択の対応力を養成するトレーニングが必要となる。

　こうした課題に対し、災害対策を想定したワークショップが開催されている。その内容は多岐にわたるが、近年の傾向を概観すると、おおよそ次の 3 系統に分類できる。

　まず、啓発型ワークショップである。この系統は、主に各地の「資料ネット」や博物館などが主体となって実施するもので、対象を特定せず、具体的な実践方法を紹介することで資料救済の活動を周知し、資料保存・継承に向けた担い手の拡大を目指すという目的が看取される。この活動のなかでは、身近

な生活用具などを用いた水濡れ資料の吸水乾燥などを紹介し、資料保存という取り組みの重要性を共有することに重点を置いている。

　次に、技術訓練型ワークショップである。ここでは主に、資料の修理や保存に関わる技術者が対象として想定され、被災資料の応急処置やその後の本格修理に向けた技術習得や開発など、専門家の養成を目的としたワークショップとして理解される。

　3点目が行動計画型ワークショップである。詳細は第7章の山内論考を参照されたいが、特定の地域を想定し、その地域の多様な関係者との机上訓練により災害時の連絡体制や現地への移動、搬出計画を検討するものである［図1］。

　これらのワークショップは、資料救済時の行動を理解する上で有効であるが、災害時に資料救済を現場で担う実務者として求められるのは、直面した被災状況を把握して救済から一時保管に至る作業工程を検討することであり、外部の各種専門家との交渉やボランティア等の調整に至る、現場運営における総合的なマネジメントである。特に、作業工程に関しては、対象となる資料の観察とそれに基づく工程の策定が重要な課題であり、多様な技術や知識のなかから状況に応じた最適な方法を選択することが必要となる。そ

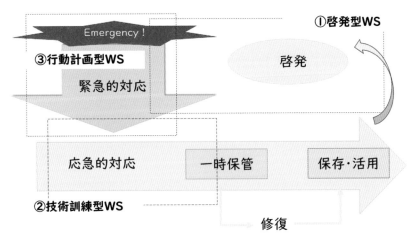

図1　災害対策を想定したワークショップの傾向

のためには、作業の全容を把握することに加え、資料への注目点を理解して
具体的な対策をシミュレーションすることが重要であり、その意味でワーク
ショップを通した訓練と検討が効果的である。そうした場を設定する際、参
加者に実際の作業工程を検討する段階から追体験させ、おのおのが考案した
工程の何が有効であり、どの点に問題があったのかなど、失敗も含めた体験
の場を提供することで、災害対策の考え方や具体的な行動イメージを共有す
ることができると考える。

　以上の問題意識に基づき、本章では資料救済を想定したワークショップに
ついて、資料救済のトータルマネジメントのスキルアップに向けた取り組み
について、その目的と方法を紹介する。

1.　目的

　筆者はこれまで、自治体職員や博物館学芸員、大学教職員・学生など、資
料救済の現場作業を担いうる人びとを主な対象としてワークショップを実施
してきた。そこでの課題設定は、被災資料、特に困難な対応が求められる水
濡れ資料の対応を想定した救済後の具体的な対応を検討するものである。こ
こでは、一方的に考え方や技術を紹介するのではなく、参加者相互で具体的
に検討し、試行錯誤する場の設定を目指した。

　このワークショップでは、救済以降の応急処置から、一時保管に至る一連
の作業工程について、何を、どこまで、どのように取り組むべきかを実践的
に検討するものである。特に重視するのは、被災した資料に直面した際の資
料観察とそれに基づく対処とその考え方である。自然災害が多発するなかで
災害対応事例が蓄積され、それらの経験を通して多くの報告書やマニュアル
が公開されている。これらを読むことで、災害対応未経験者でも対策のイメー
ジをつかむことは可能である。その一方で、摂取した一連の知識を実践に結
びつけるには、作業の全容を把握した上で、得た知識や技術がどの段階で必
要になるのか、具体的にどのような状態の資料に対して有効であるのかを理
解することが必要となる。ワークショップでは参加者自らが資料の観察と対
応の検討を行う。さらに、その結果を参加者相互で議論しながら実践を試み、

これらの課題と向き合うことで、必要な技術を得るだけでなく、災害対策のマネジメント力を向上させることを目指している。

2. 準備

2.1. サンプル・道具の準備

　このワークショップでは、被災資料の応急処置を疑似体験するため、まず検討対象となる被災資料を準備する。もっとも、実物の被災資料を取り扱うのは困難であるため、サンプル資料の準備が必要となる。ここでは、紙資料の救済を想定したサンプルについて紹介する。

　紙資料の救済として想定するのは、日本各地の博物館や図書館、文書館、さらには個人宅などに多く残される江戸時代以降の古文書群である。和紙、具体的には楮紙を準備して帳簿や書翰・書付に模した束を作成し、これらを疑似的に被災させる。サンプル資料を「被災」させるために、汚損をイメージさせるための紅茶や緑茶の茶葉（ないしは使用済みコーヒー豆）とぬるま湯とともに資料をビニール袋に入れ、常温にて一晩置いて汚損・劣化を促す。汚損を表現するために泥を混ぜるという選択肢もあるが、会場の環境や健康面を勘案した場合、極力安全なものを準備することを推奨する［図2・3・4］。

　その他準備品は、なるべく日常的に利用しているものに限定する。例えば、吸水紙であれば新聞紙やキッチンペーパーなど、道具についてはピンセットや刷毛といった、ホームセンター等で誰でも入手可能なもののみを準備し

図2　作成した古文書群のサンプル

図3　茶葉等と混ぜてぬるま湯に浸した状態

ておく。また、場合によっては参加
者に対し、資料救済に必要と考えら
れるものを持参するよう促してもよ
い。この際のポイントは、「資料救済」
などと漠然とした言葉でのみ伝える
ことである。この呼びかけは、「資
料救済」という行為を参加者が具体
的にどのような作業として理解し、
そのためにいかなる道具が必要と考
えているかを把握することにもつながる。

図 4　疑似被災状態のサンプル

　ワークショップ全体を統括するファシリテーターには、過去に災害現場の
差配経験のある人物、もしくは保存科学や修復に関する専門家が望ましいが、
アドバイザーとしてこれらの意見を得ることができればこれに代えることも
可能だろう。

2.2. 課題設定

　基本的には資料の救済直後からの対応を想定した課題を設定する。救済に
向けた検討については、行動計画の机上訓練として第 7 章の山内が紹介する
ものがあり、こうしたシミュレーションと連続的に実施することで全容をイ
メージすることが可能となろう。

　想定する災害については、ワークショップ参加者の主要な活動地域の地理
的環境に沿った設定が望ましい。例えば、近隣に大きな川が流れている場合
は河川氾濫を想定したもの、沿岸部であれば高潮や津波を想定したもの、山
沿いであれば豪雨による土砂崩れを想定したものなどである。その地域で発
生した過去の災害を踏まえた被害を想定すると、より具体的なイメージを共
有することが可能となるだろう。

　参加者は、災害時に救済された資料に対応する現場担当者である設定とし、
準備したサンプル被災資料群を各自に渡してその対応を検討させるものとす
る。検討項目としては、①資料観察、②到達点の設定、③作業工程の 3 点で
ある。

第3部

①資料観察

・スクリーンに投影した被災資料群の画像および配布したサンプル資料群を観察し、資料の劣化や破損に関わるリスクを検討してまず対処すべき作業を判断する。

・そのリスクに対処する上で、作業環境・健康双方の面で留意すべき点を検討する。

②到達点の設定

・応急処置の範疇で作業工程を策定するために、具体的に資料をいかなる状態に導くことを目指すのかを検討する。また、応急処置を終えた資料を一時保管するにあたり、留意すべき点を検討する。

③作業工程

・①と②を実践するための具体的な作業工程を検討する。

　以上について、まずは各参加者が誰とも相談せずに単独で検討する。その後、3〜5名程度でグループディスカッションを実施し、おのおのが検討した内容を議論してグループとしての作業工程を策定する［図5・6］。

3. 実践

　このワークショップでは、3〜5名をグループとして実施する。前述の課題設定を説明の後、単独で10分間検討した後にグループで20分議論を行い、各自が導き出した工程に基づき作業を実施させる。なお、ここまでの段階でファシリテーターは議論に参加せず、あくまで参加者のみで検討と実践を行う［図7・8］。

　一連の検討と実践を終えた後、各グループから検討内容を発表し、ワークショップ全体での検討に入る。検討では、各グループからの発表に対してファシリテーターが、検討項目に対する評価点と課題、改善に向けた提案をコメントする。ファシリテーターは、以下の点に重点を置いてコメントを付す。

　まず資料観察の妥当性である。被災した季節と救出までに要している時間、

設問 1．膨大な水濡れ資料の対応を求められたあなたは、まず資料のどんなリスクに注目しますか？

①資料に発生したカビ
②資料に付着した泥汚れ
③腐敗などから生じる臭気
④資料が吸収した水分
⑤その他：

設問 2．1 で注目したリスクを踏まえ、あなたはどのような作業目標を設定しますか？
①「レスキュー」の到達点：何をどこまで対応する？

②一時保管（仮置き）にむけての留意点

設問 3．2 の目標を達成するためにどのような方法が想定されますか？
　　　　　具体的な作業手順を検討してください。

図 5　検討用に用いるテキストイメージ

【グループ意見取りまとめ用】

設問１　膨大な水濡れ資料の対応を求められたあなたは、まず資料のどんなリスクに注目しますか？

設問２　１で注目したリスクを踏まえ、あなたはどのような作業目標を設定しますか？

設問３　２の目標を達成するためにどのような方法が想定されますか？ 具体的な作業手順を検討してください。

図6　検討用に用いるテキストイメージ

図 7　ワークショップの様子
（2023 年 5 月 20 日　福島大学）

図 8　ワークショップの様子
（2023 年 11 月 27 日　埼玉県）

第
3
部

資料群としての規模や対象とされる資料の性質を踏まえ、参加者が被災状況を具体的に想定できているかがポイントとなる。その際、画像やサンプルでは追体験できない被害状況、特に臭気やカビのリスクを説明し、資料に対するアプローチだけでなく、そのための事前準備として健康被害対策や搬出先の環境対策などに留意する必要性を伝えることが重要となる。

　到達点の設定と作業工程については、応急処置という段階があくまで一時的な措置であるという前提に立ち、現場作業として無理なく策定できているかを判断する。参加者に救済活動の経験者がいる場合は、その経験や実績を尊重しつつ、状況に応じてさまざまな意見や方法も踏まえて総合的に検討する必要性を伝え、特定の考え方に固執せずに対応することの重要性をコメントすることもある。

　それぞれの意見を踏まえてコメントした後、ファシリテーターは、全体の議論を総括するかたちで、救出から応急処置に至る工程の基本的な考え方を解説する。これらの考え方について、筆者が実施するワークショップでは、本書第 1 部および第 2 部の内容を前提としている。その考え方に基づき、あらためて各参加者が実施した作業内容を検討し、より安全で効果的な工程を確認した上で、サンプルを用いてその方法を実践する。最後に、ワークショップ中で実践した作業が、災害対策全体のなかでどの段階に位置するものかを確認し、ワークショップを終了する。

おわりに～失敗を経験して検証する～

　本ワークショップの目的は、参加者が主体的に検討・議論を行い、被災資料救済の作業工程の策定やそのための技術選択に関する考え方を習得することにある。筆者が実施するワークショップでは、一方的な講義形式に終始せず、参加者が保有している知識や技術が実際の作業現場でどのような役割を果たせるのか確認することに重点を置く。その際、検討・実践の過程でサンプル資料を破損させてしまうことも想定されるが、むしろ失敗を体験することでその原因を自らで検証し、相互議論によって解決策を検討することが可能となる。実際の現場では体験しえない失敗を経験し、そこから教訓を得ることは、ワークショップにおける重要な機会でもあるだろう。

　資料救済に関するマネジメント力の習得に関して、将来的には、一連の作業を運営する能力を身につけるカリキュラムが大学教育や博物館学芸員、自治体関係職員の研修等で整備されることが理想であろう。また、紙資料に限定されない多様な資料群を想定した総合的な対応力の習得も求められるが、これらの課題に向き合いながら、今後も資料救済トレーニングのあり方を議論していくことが必要となる。

参考文献

・ 天野真志「資料保存の担い手と技術をつなぐ」（天野・後藤真編『地域歴史文化継承ガイドブック』文学通信、2022 年）
・ 天野真志「紙媒体資料の救済を想定したシミュレーションワークショップの検討と実践」（文化財保存修復学会第 45 回大会ポスター発表、2023 年 6 月 25 日）
・ 高妻洋成・小谷竜介・建石徹編『入門　大災害時代の文化財防災』（同成社、2023 年）
・ 松下正和・河野未央編『水損史料を救う』（岩田書院、2009 年）

第 9 章

地域とのコミュニケーション

▨ 阿部浩一（福島大学）

はじめに

　本章の課題は、地域歴史文化の災害対策、資料救済において求められる、地域とのコミュニケーションの問題について論じることにある。検討対象とするのは、主に民間所在の歴史資料の救済と保全に取り組んでいる資料ネットであるが、その説明は第1部に委ねたい。被災地での資料救済活動にあたる場合、調査研究等で馴染みある地域であることは稀で、災害を機に初めて訪れるケースが大半である。そうした状況下で、外部からの専門家が自治体の文化財担当者、地元の郷土史家、所蔵者、住民と現場で初めて顔を合わせ、資料救済活動を円滑に進めていくためには、地域とのコミュニケーションが重要な鍵となることは言うまでもない。さらに、災害前から地域内外の人びとを結びつける場が用意されていれば、より一層効果的な活動ができて、豊かな成果が得られることは確実である。

　ただし、「地域とのコミュニケーション」と一口に言っても、多様なコミュケーションの核となる人と人との意思疎通のあるべき姿を普遍化することはきわめて困難であり、モデル化・マニュアル化するにも不向きである。全国に約30ある資料ネットのなかには豊富な実践例を有し、顕著な成果をあげているところもあるが、本章では紙幅の関係もあり、筆者が代表を務める「ふくしま歴史資料保存ネットワーク（ふくしま史料ネット）」と、全国初の市民主体の資料ネットで、筆者も幹事の一人である「そうま歴史資料保存ネットワーク（そうまネッ

ト）」を例に話を進めることをあらかじめお断りしておきたい。

1. ふくしま史料ネットの発足と直面した課題

　ふくしま史料ネットは、㈶福島県文化振興事業団（以下事業団、現在は公益財団法人福島県文化振興財団）が 2005 年に設立したふくしま文化遺産保存ネットワークを発展的に解消し、事業団・福島県立博物館・福島県史学会・福島大学を呼びかけ人として、専門家・行政・市民の連絡体として 2010 年11 月に発足した。各方面との連携・調整にあたった事業団の本間宏の構想は、未指定を含めた包括的な歴史文化遺産の把握・保全のため、市民ボランティアの参加が不可欠であり、所蔵者との信頼関係を構築していくためにも行政の文化財担当者の参画も推奨され、それによって市町村を越えた横につないだ連携も可能だというものであった。

　しかし、発足からわずか 4 カ月後、2011 年 3 月に東日本大震災・福島第一原発事故が発生した。ふくしま史料ネットは 4 月になってようやく代表・事務局の態勢を整え、支援を求める自治体・個人の資料救出に取り組んだ。6 月までに 25 件の調査・救出にあたる実績をあげたが、直面した課題は多岐にわたった。主なものとして、

①レスキューのための所在情報のデータ不足：所在目録などは整備されておらず、1980 年に福島県教育委員会が編纂した『福島県古文書所在確認調査報告』を手掛かりに、あとは個人で持ち寄るしかなかった

②ふくしま史料ネットへの自治体の不参加：現状でもメール配信という一方通行の関係にとどまっている

③地域コミュニティとのコミュニケーション不足：史料ネットの存在の周知が不徹底で、救出すべき資料があっても、レスキューを求める情報が史料ネットにまで伝わりにくい状況は変わっていない

④市民ボランティアの不在：防犯の観点から、被災地の情報は関係者間にとどめられ、救出活動は呼びかけ人機関のなかから動ける者を中心に進めざるを得ず、ボランティア募集は限定的にならざるを得なかった

　⑤連絡体であるがゆえの課題：救出した資料の管理責任を負えず、一時保
　　管場所や作業場所の確保も困難であった

といった点があげられる。本章のテーマと関わらせれば、「地域とのコミュ
ニケーション」が不足したまま、活動はスタートしていった。

　2012年5月に福島県被災文化財等救援本部が発足し、夏から旧警戒区域
の双葉・大熊・富岡町の資料館でのレスキュー活動が始まると、関係者の目
は旧警戒区域に向けられていった。連絡体にすぎないふくしま史料ネットは
何ら関わることはできなかった。筆者も福島大学の一員として旧警戒区域外
の一時保管場所での作業に従事したように、呼びかけ人はそれぞれの本務先
の立場で文化財レスキューに注力したが、一方で民間所在のレスキュー案件
がみられなくなり、ともすればふくしま史料ネットの存在感が希薄になりつ
つあった。連絡体にすぎないがゆえに直面した課題といえる。

2.　ふくしま史料ネットの展開

　2012年7月に代表となった筆者は、呼びかけ人の連絡体としてのふくし
ま史料ネットを基本としつつも、実質的な活動の軸を大学に移し、学生を中
心に日常的な活動を継続することで、直面した課題の克服に努めていった。

　①データ不足については、研究補助者の助力を得て、県内の所蔵者リスト
をできるところから順次 Excel で整理し、必要に応じて検索・抽出できるか
たちを整えた。その結果、2021年の福島県沖地震で震度6強の被害が出た
新地町では、『新地町史』などの所蔵者リスト（個人情報に厳しくなかった
当時は、所蔵者の居住地が字名まで掲載されている）と古い住宅地図を突き
合わせてリストアップし、宮城歴史資料保存ネットワーク（宮城資料ネット）
と連携して現地での所在調査に取り組んだ。その過程で、リストには漏れて
いた商家の蔵3棟の資料レスキューを実現できた。現地に行かないと本当の
情報はつかめないという好例でもある。

　②ふくしま史料ネットへの自治体の不参加の状況は今もって変わっていな
い。自治体間のネットワークは、2020年3月の福島県文化財保存活用大綱

の策定にともなって結ばれた、福島県と59市町村との「福島県内における文化財に係る災害時等の相互応援に関する協定」によって実現した。同年11月にはふくしま史料ネットなど関係4団体と「福島県内における文化財に係る災害時の応援活動支援に関する協定」が結ばれ、年1回程度の連絡会議を通じて情報交換や研修などが行われている。ふくしま史料ネットは連絡会議の場を通じて間接的に自治体と連携をとることになり、遅まきながら発足当初の構想の第一歩を踏み出したことになる。しかし、救出対象は災害時に自治体の管理する文化財に限定され、日常的な搬出活動の相互支援は想定されておらず、民間所在の未指定文化財の救出には適用されないなど、課題も多い。

　なお、富岡町と福島大学が協定を結び、役場内のプロジェクトチームが寄贈・寄託を受けて救出した資料の保全・記録整理を支援する関係を続けているが、ふくしま史料ネットは集中作業時に市民ボランティアの募集をかけるなどの支援を行っている。

　③地域コミュニティとのコミュニケーション不足については、学生たちの教育活動のなかでその解消を試みた。県北の国見町では文化財担当者、郷土史研究会、町内会と連携し、被災資料調査を行った。その結果、『国見町史』等で把握していなかった多数の未紹介資料を確認する成果を上げた。その成果をベースに、地域住民に学びながら学生目線で地域の文化財を再発見し、

写真1　国見町貝田地区まるごと博物館

資料保全につなげる「地域まるごと博物館」活動を展開していった［写真1］。この活動は伊達市梁川に舞台を移し、郷土史研究会やNPOの協力と指導のもとに学生たちの調査研究が進められた。コロナ禍にあっても、大学のある金谷川地区で

地域住民と連携し、観音信仰と和算の歴史の調査研究に取り組んだ。いずれも地域コミュニティをよく知る郷土史家や地元住民の理解と協力があったからこそ成し得たものである。学生たちの調査成果はリーフレットにまとめられ、地域理解の深化やまちあるき・観光などにも役立てられている。

　④市民ボランティアの不在については、日常的な活動の軸を大学に移したことで、発足当初の市民ボランティア参加の構想からは後退を余儀なくされた。それでも古文書学実習という資料整理の場を夜間に開講し、仕事帰りの社会人でも参加できる工夫を凝らした。関心ある近隣住民が史料ネットの呼びかけに応じてボランティアで集まり、学生とともに古文書の撮影や目録作成に取り組んだ。ときには自ら保全した資料を持ち込んで記録撮影する様子も見られた。2014 年からは 8 月に毎年 2 日間の夏季集中作業を企画し、県内外から広く市民ボランティアが集まる恒例行事となっている。

　大学での活動への参加の有無にかかわらず、市民ボランティアの地域の資料に対する関心はきわめて高い。2019 年の令和元年東日本台風で甚大な被害を受けた本宮市立歴史民俗資料館では、水損資料の保全作業に市民ボランティアが毎回のように集まった［写真 2］。その多くは文化財講座受講者や市民サークルなどに参加するシルバー人材である。そうした市民と日常的につながっている担当者の能力と人柄には一目置くべきものがあった。どの地域コミュニティにも人と人をつなぎ、事業を円滑に進めていく能力にたけたコーディネーターがいるものだが、こうしたキーマンといかに連携できるかが、地域とのコミュニケーション、ネットワークづくりにあたっての成功の鍵と言えるだろう。

　そして⑤連絡体であるがゆえの課題であるが、一時保管場所・作

写真 2　本宮市での水損資料の保全活動

業場所の不足という問題は、福島大学うつくしまふくしま未来支援センターの発足（現在は福島大学地域未来デザインセンターに発展解消）とセンター棟の完成（現在は食農学類棟に転用）、歴史資料担当の設置と資料保管室の確保によって解消された。現在は行政政策学類棟内に保管場所を移し、実習室などで保全作業を継続している。

　ふくしま史料ネットは今もって法人格を持たず、連絡体としての体裁をとる任意団体のままである。それでも今日まで変わらず活動を維持できているのは、皮肉にもこの 12 年間、ふくしまが常に災害とともにあったからでもある。原発被災地での資料保全活動は「現在進行形」という言葉で表されるが、その対応策を審議する福島県被災文化財等救援本部の会議は、福島県立博物館、福島県立美術館、福島県文化財センター白河館（まほろん）、福島県歴史資料館、福島大学、ふくしま史料ネットが顔を合わせ、継続的に情報・意見交換をする場であった。2019 年の令和元年東日本台風では、県の構想する相互応援協定が前倒しで実施され、関係機関からも公務で支援に駆けつけた。そのなかにはふくしま史料ネットの呼びかけ人の機関も含まれているが、公務では所属機関の立場で、ボランティアで来るときはふくしま史料ネットの一員として参加しているという心強い言葉が随所で聞かれた。連絡体としてのふくしま史料ネットのあり方を再確認する機会でもあった。専門家どうしの連携は 2021・2022 年の福島県沖地震でのレスキューにおいても機能し、多様な専門分野の目によって資料保全がはかられた。

　このように振り返ってみると、発足当初の本間の描いた構想とはだいぶ異なるかたちになってしまったが、それでも当初抱えていた課題については一定の解決の筋道を立てられたと自負している。ふくしまの官学産民を結ぶ包括的な文化財ネットワークづくりは道半ばであり、そのためにも資料救出・資料保全の現場で生まれた自治体・地域コミュニティ・所蔵者との縁を一つ一つ大切にし、着実に積み上げていく必要がある。とはいえ、これだけ広範囲に繰り返し災害が起こり、資料の救出と保全に走り回っていると、結果として中途半端に手を付けたまま放置状態になってしまっている案件が少なくないことも認めざるを得ない。資料救出活動と並行して、外部からの継続的支援だけでなく、地域コミュニティのなかで資料保全活動を長期的に継続で

きるような基盤づくりや、専門家でなくてもできる手法の定着を図っていくことが、次なる課題である。

3. 市民ネットとしてのそうま歴史資料保存ネットワークの発足

　資料ネットが一般に大学や博物館、自治体を中心とするネットワークであるのに対し、そうま歴史資料保存ネットワーク（そうまネット）は市民主体で組織・運営される全国初の資料ネットである［写真3］。

　そうまネットは2022年9月に発足し、日本画家の鈴木龍郎を代表に、相馬市民・出身者を中心に構成されている。鈴木は東京を拠点に創作活動に取り組んでいるが、東日本大震災を機に出身地相馬の支援に取り組むようになったという。相馬市内の実家は旧中村藩の武家屋敷地にあり、昭和初期に建てられた和洋折衷の建物である。東日本大震災の揺れにも耐えたが、2021年の福島県沖地震で柱に亀裂が入り、修復と耐震工事を考えていた矢先に、2022年の福島県沖地震で被災し、家屋が傾いた。特に相馬家当主を迎えるために作られた大玄関が瓦屋根の重みで崩れ落ちてしまった光景は衝撃的であった。

　ふくしま史料ネットは宮城資料ネットと連携し、2021年の新地町に引き続き、2022年は南相馬市鹿島区で資料所蔵者の聞き取り調査を進めていた。そうした折、相馬市に取材に訪れていたNHK関係者からの情報提供を受けて、筆者は鈴木と連絡を取ることができた。

　鈴木は被災者である傍ら、近隣で古い建造物が被災し、歴史資料が廃棄され、伝統工芸が存続の危機にある光

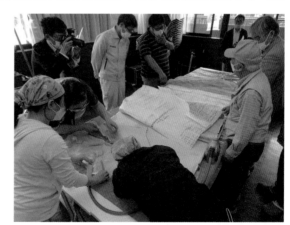

写真3　鈴木龍郎邸から救出された襖の下張り文書の保全活動

景を目のあたりにし、相馬の歴史と伝統文化の消滅に強い危機感を抱いていた。鈴木の同級生で福島県民俗学会会長の岩崎真幸、相馬商工会議所会頭で建設業を営む草野清貴も、災害のたびに家屋が解体されて更地が広がり、城下町の歴史的景観が失われていくのを強く危惧していた。こうして地元有志とふくしま・宮城ネット関係者が一堂に会し、資料救出のためにも情報を集める受け皿づくりが必要との共通認識からネットワークの立ち上げが提案され、草野の提案で「そうま歴史資料保存ネットワーク」と命名された。その後、鈴木宅の資料レスキューなどと並行して、組織づくりのためのメンバーの人選が用意周到に進められ、地震から半年後の2022年9月にそうまネットが正式に旗揚げした。

　そうまネットは連絡体としての性格を基本としつつも、その役員構成は相馬在住者と出身者で固められ、そこにふくしま・宮城ネットが関わる体裁をとっている。幹事は相馬商工会議所会頭、相馬郷土研究会会長・会員、馬城会（相馬高校同窓会）会長、福島県民俗学会会長、仙台福島県人会会長、ジャーナリスト、税理士、東北学院大学教員、福島大学教員で構成される産学民のネットワークで、相馬高校教員が事務局長を務めている。その核にあるのは、相馬高校の同窓生と関係者の結びつきである。鈴木の談によれば、事務局長で相馬高校教員の武内義明と相談し、相馬高校関係者から人選を進めたという。相馬高校は1898（明治31）年に福島県第四尋常中学校として開校された歴史を持つ伝統校で（旧制中学の時代に建てられた相馬高校講堂は登録有形文化財である）、地元を始め各界に多くの人材を輩出している。地域密着型のネットワークにとって、伝統校の同窓会組織を母体に持つことは大きな強みである。外部から地域とのコミュニケーションを図る上でも、既存のネットワークの存在はきわめてありがたい。わずか1年のうちに活動を軌道に乗せ、次々と実績をあげることのできた秘訣は、まさにこの点に求められよう。同窓会のネットワークに着目した鈴木らの慧眼に敬意を表するものである。

　地元密着型の市民ネットのメリットとして、救出すべき資料の所在情報を集めやすいこと、急な要請にも柔軟に対応できることがあげられる。市内の老舗料理店で地震被害と店主の急逝により休業と店舗解体が決まると、郷土研究会のメンバーを中心に歴史資料と店主の絵画作品の保全が行われた。そ

の熱意は、初めてのシンポジウム開催にあわせて企画された救出資料の展示会でも遺憾なく発揮された。

　そうまネットの幹事に同窓生のジャーナリストを迎えていることも特徴的である。寺島秀弥は WEB ニュースサイトの TOHOKU360 で綿密な取材に基づく活動記事を配信している。専任のジャーナリストを抱える資料ネットは稀であろう。そうまネットの活動が全国に配信される形で目に見えるのも、そうまネットの強みである。

　そうまネットはこのように多くの強みを持っているが、弱みもある。一般に同窓会組織は昔を懐かしむ高齢者層が中心であり、そうまネット関係者も同様に高齢者が多いため、例えば現場での力仕事には不向きである。蔵 1 棟を片付ける資料救済活動の経験もなければ、人手も足りず、資料保全のノウハウも専門的知識も持ち合わせていない。そこはふくしま・宮城ネット代表が幹事を務めていることで、ネットワークがもつ経験とノウハウを提供し、専門家や学生・卒業生さらに市民ボランティアに呼びかけて作業従事者を確保し、支援できる体制が整っている。

　こうして発足 1 周年の 2023 年 9 月、そうまネットの成果と課題を相馬市民および全国の関係者と共有すべく、相馬高校を会場にシンポジウムが開催された。当日は予想以上の参加者が集まり、新出資料の報告や展示への反響も大きかった。そこでも確認された当面の課題は、救出資料の長期的な保管場所の確保と、市民参加の裾野を広げるための仕掛けづくりである。そして行政との連携は目下最大の難題である。長期的には、市民ネットという画期的な取り組みを維持していくための組織固めと人材の確保、そして市民が地域の歴史を自らの手で護っていく文化の定着である。市民自らの手で運営されるそうまネットの先駆的試みが大いなる刺激となり、全国各地に同様の試みが波及していくことを期待している。

おわりに

　地域歴史文化の災害対策、資料救済において求められる地域とのコミュニケーションという所与の課題に応えるものとならなかったことをお詫びしな

第3部

ければならないが、いくつかの手掛かりは示せたように思う。地域コミュニティには地域歴史文化に心を寄せ、資料の所在に精通し、その滅失に危機感を持って立ち上がろうとする人が必ずいて、しかも地域でのコーディネーターになりうる資質を持ち合わせていることが多い。地域における資料救済さらに防災対策の実を挙げるには、こうした地域コミュニティのキーマンとの連携を大切にし、そこから住民たちとの連携の輪を広げていくことが肝要である。郷土史研究会、町内会、市民サークル、同窓会といった既存のネットワークとの結びつきもきわめて有効である。行政間のネットワーク構築はこれからというところも多いだろうが、そこに資料ネットが参画する機会を得られれば、被災資料情報の共有と応援体制の整備が一気に進展することも期待できる。資料ネットに求められる役割は、専門家どうしの連携を密にした上で、既存の多様なネットワークをフラットな関係でつなげる連絡体としての役割を果たすことであろう。それこそが改正文化財保護法の概要で示された、本当の意味での「未指定を含めた文化財の地域社会総がかりでの継承」につながっていくに違いない。

参考文献

・ 阿部浩一・福島大学うつくしまふくしま未来支援センター編『ふくしま再生と歴史・文化遺産』（山川出版社、2013 年）
・ 阿部浩一「ふくしまの現場から振り返る 11 年－できたこと、できなかったこと－」（『史学』92-1・2、2023 年）
・ 寺島英弥「福島県沖地震　相馬で文化財級の民家が全壊「貴重な遺産、生かしたい」」、TOHOKU360、https://tohoku360.com/316-soma/（2023 年 9 月 12 日最終閲覧）
・ 福島県被災文化財等救援本部編集『福島県被災文化財等救援本部活動報告書』（2023 年）
・ そうま歴史資料保存ネットワーク『そうまの歴史を守る・つたえる　2023 報告書』（2024 年）

第 10 章

歴史資料保存活動と「専門知」

▨ 市沢　哲 （神戸大学）

はじめに

　本章では、これまで本書で述べてきた、災害の際に歴史資料を保全するための「知識」「方法」「活動」の意味を問い直す。その際、現代社会における専門知（専門的知識）をめぐる問題を意識して議論を進める。なぜならば、歴史資料保全の活動は、専門知と市民知、市民社会と交差するところで実を結ぶと考えられるからである。専門知をめぐる問題に向きあうためにも、上述の「知識」「方法」「活動」が持つ可能性について考えることにしたい。

1. 専門知の現在

　2021 年に刊行され、同年に人文科学系の賞として権威あるサントリー学芸賞（社会・風俗部門）を授与された竹倉史人氏の『土偶を読む—130 年間解かれなかった縄文神話の謎』[1] をめぐるやりとりは、現代社会における専門知のあり方を考える上で注目すべき出来事である。すでにこの本については、『土偶を読むを読む』[2] で多角的に論じられているが、今一度本章の関心に沿ってこの本がもたらした問題について見直しておきたい。

　周知の通り、『土偶を読む』は、考古学の専門的研究者ではない竹倉氏が、考古学者に全く相手にされなかったという自説をまとめた本である。『土偶を読むを読む』で菅豊氏が述べられているように、『土偶を読む』は主たる

内容において考古学の専門的研究を正面から批判しているわけではなく、竹倉氏の土偶解釈が開陳された本であった。しかし、具体的内容を越えて、この本は専門知批判の書と受け止められたのである[3]。

　菅豊氏も指摘しているように、そのことをよく表しているのが、『朝日新聞 GLOVE ＋』の対談記事「『土偶を読む』の裏テーマは専門知への疑問 「素人」と揶揄する風潮に危機感」[4] である。記事のタイトルが語るように、竹倉氏の著書は「専門知への疑問」を呈した本、「素人」軽視を批判した本として評価されたのである。

　竹倉氏は次のように述べる。

　「土偶を読む」をこのようなかたちで世に問うことになった背景には、実は、3.11 の原発の問題をきっかけに生まれた専門知に対する不信感があります。

　市民がいくら原発の危険性を指摘しても、専門家たちはそれを「素人の意見」としてまともに取り合おうとはしなかった。しかし、絶対安全と言われていた原発はあっけないくらい簡単にメルトダウンにいたった。

　専門知も専門家も間違いなく必要です。でも、専門知がわれわれの生活を向上させる実践知に還元されず、既得権益として密室の中で独占されている。このような専門知のあり方が色んな分野で残っている。

　専門知がいかに実践知のほうに開かれていくか。リベラルアーツ教育のような形で専門知が一般の人に開かれ、ネットワーキングされ、実践知になり、市民に還元されていく。そういう動きが今後加速するといいなという思いがあります。

　僕の研究内容や「土偶を読む」について、すでに色んなジャンルの人が意見を表明しています。この本がそういう議論の着火剤になり、専門家だけでなくいろんな人の意見が交わされ、そこからどの土偶論が最も合理的なのか、広く討議されていくことを願っています。

ここでは専門知の閉鎖的で特権的なあり方が批判されているが、このよう

な専門知批判そのものは決して目新しいものではないだろう。これまでもしばしば言われてきた「専門バカ」批判の一つのバリエーションといえる。また、福島の原子力発電所問題を取り上げて、専門知は市民の意見を無視して原子力発電所を設置したと述べているが、福島についていえば、専門知のなかにもその危険性を主張した意見があったことを全く無視している[5]。竹倉氏の専門知に対する理解は粗雑なものであるといわれても仕方がない。目新しくもなく、かつ粗雑な専門知批判が声高になされ、それをマスコミが大きく取り上げたことは、現在の社会における専門知に対する風当たりの強さを示している。

また、対談のなかで中島岳志（なかじまたけし）氏は、次のように述べている。

　　僕の師匠の西部邁（にしべすすむ）が「世の中のエコノミストがことごとく間違えるのは、経済を知らないからじゃない、経済しか知らないからだ」とよく言っていて、複合的にいろんなことを考えなければいけない、と教えられました。竹倉さんの本を読んでいて、そのことを思いました。
　　古代について考えるには考古学だけで迫ることはできません。哲学、思想、人類学、いろいろな英知を集結しながら古代と向きあうことによって、私たちの未来も広がっていくと思うのです。そのような古代との向きあい方が、今、縄文を考える際に重要なことだと思います。

考古学だけでなく、あらゆる英知を結集して縄文時代を研究すべきであるという中島氏の意見は、至極まっとうである。しかし、このまっとうな意見が、専門知を粗雑に批判する言説と、知的な媒体において結びつくのも、考えさせられる現象である。

2.「生活」と専門知

ひるがえって歴史資料を保全する現場に立って考えてみよう。歴史資料の保全の場でも、専門知問題が起こることがあるのではないだろうか。

例えば、住む人がいない、住む人がいなくなる住居をボランティアが清掃、

整理し、新しい住人に引き渡す「おくりいえプロジェクト」活動を行っているやまだのりこ氏へのインタビュー[6]で、次のような話を聞いた。ある旧家の「おくりいえ」を行おうとした際、家屋に大量の古文書が残されていることがわかった。研究者を現場に呼んだところ、調査が必要なので現状変更しないように（つまり手を付けないように）と言われた。しかしその後、研究者の調査はなかなか進まず、結果的に「おくりいえ」は停滞してしまったという。

　上記の場合は、研究者のスケジュール感と「おくりいえ」を行う市民の生活感覚が整合しなかったところに問題が生じたと考えられる。このようなギャップについて、心理学者の東畑開人氏は職場のなかに離婚を機に調子を崩した仲間がいた場合を事例に、次のように述べている。

　　例えば、先の離婚の彼が、しばらくたっても回復しなかったらどうか。仕事が滞り、不機嫌が続く。いつもイライラしていて、周りに当たることもある。すると、世間知は彼を持て余し始める。彼は理解できない存在になり、厄介者扱いされるようになる。孤立していく。

　　そういうとき、専門知が解毒剤になる。「うつ病じゃないか？」。誰かが言いだす。それが視界を少し変える。仕事の滞りやイライラがうつの症状に見えてくる。すると、周囲は彼に医療機関の受診を勧めたり、特別扱いしたりできるようになる。

　　この素人判断こそが、心のサポーターに生えたささやかな毛だ。うまく専門家につながれば、そこで適切な理解を得ることができるし、すると彼の不機嫌さが悲鳴であったことがわかる。「厄介者」はケアすべき人に変わる。

　　これが心のサポーターの背景にある「メンタルヘルス・ファーストエイド」の思想だ。心のサポーターとは、専門知を浅く学ぶことで、とりあえずの応急処置や専門家につなぐことを身につけた素人なのである。専門知が世間知の限界を補う。

　　ただし、専門知がときに暴力になることも忘れてはならない。「うつ病だ」「不安障害だ」と名指しされることで、本来だったら周りから見

守られながら取り組むはずだった人生の課題が、心理学や医学の問題にされる。すると、人はまた別の意味で孤立してしまう。それくらい専門知にはパワーがある。

　心理士をしていると思う。私たちは大学院で山ほど専門知を学ぶが、それらは世間知抜きでは運用できない。世間知によってクライアントの生きている日常を想像できないと、支援は専門知の押し付けになり、非現実的になってしまう。だから、心理士もまた、プライベートでは専門家の帽子を脱ぎ、自分の人生をきちんと生きるのが大切だ。そうやって世間と人生の苦しみを知ることが、専門知を解毒するのに役立つ。[7]

　専門知は、本来なら生活のなかで解決すべき問題を、生活から切り離してしまう一面を持っているという警鐘は、生活のなかで守り伝えられてきた歴史資料を取り扱う際に、しっかりと想起されるべきであろう。

　また、生活と専門知の関係を考える際には、安東量子氏らによる福島県いわき市末続地区での活動も大きな示唆を与えてくれる[8]。福島原子力発電所のメルトダウンがもたらした放射線量をめぐる生活不安のなかで、専門家たちが自説に基づいてさまざまな安全基準を示したり、行政が納得できる説明もないままいったん示した基準を撤回したりした。そのため地域は混乱し、住民同士の意見対立も激しくなった。もちろん専門家に対する不信感も高まった。生活の基盤が動揺するなかで、安東氏は住民自らが放射線量を測定し、生活環境への信頼を取り戻す活動を行った。また、一貫してこの活動に関わり続け、測定値に基づいて専門的助言を行う専門家がこの活動を支えた。安東氏らの活動は、生活環境への信頼——そこには良好な人間関係も含まれる——の再建に向けて、専門知を生活に結びつけた、希有な事例である。

　東畑氏の指摘や安東氏の活動は、生活と専門知が取り結ぶ関係を考える際に大きな示唆となる。これらを踏まえて、あらためて本書で述べられてきた「知識」「方法」「活動」の意味について考えてみよう。

3. 歴史資料の保全活動が目指すもの

　本書で語られてきた「知識」「方法」「活動」は、市民を含むさまざまなアクターと協働した、実際の災害時の歴史資料救出や被災した資料の修復を通じて生まれてきたという特徴がある。そこでは専門知を共有していく、生活の問題と専門知をすりあわせていくことが不可避的に意識されざるを得ない。そういう本質を持っていることをまずは押さえておきたい。

　ではその「すりあわせ」を実現するためには、どのような前提に立った、どのような方法があるのだろうか。少し視野を広げてみよう。2022年に刊行された『「専門家」とは誰か』[9] は、この問題に正面から向き合っている。

　同書が前提としているのは、実際の生活の場、そこで生じる解決すべき課題に接続される場合に露わになる、専門的知識のある種の非柔軟性である。例えば隠岐さや香氏は、専門家が呼び出され意見を求められる場は、科学・技術・社会・政治・経済・行政の規則といった多種多様な要素が交錯する「ハイブリッド・フォーラム」（ミッシェル・カロン）であり、そこに呼び出された専門家は、それぞれの個人の専門研究から逸脱することが求められると指摘している。具体的な問題はしばしば学際的で、判断を下すことに対して強い時間的制約が課されることが多いからである[10]。

　また、神里達博氏は「諮問と答申」の「軛」、という問題を指摘している。行政が専門家の集まる審議会に諮問を行う。諮問された問題にはその時点の研究では答えられないものもある。しかし、「わからない」と答えるだけでは審議会は役割を果たせない。そこで、できる限りの評価を答申する。これを受けた行政が、そもそも限界があるその答申から都合のよい部分を「つまみぐい」する。というのがその「軛」である。神里氏はこの「軛」の背後には「行政機構の一部である事務局が審議会のアジェンダを決め、専門家を集め、事務局主導で審議会を運営する」構造があると指摘している[11]。

　では、本来的には限定的な性質を持つ専門知を、現実の問題に即して応用的に使おうとする場合、どのような手立てが取られるべきだろうか。この点について『「専門家」とは誰か』に収録された諸論文は、共通して次のような提起を行っている。

　一つ目は、当該の問題に関わる狭義の専門家以外のアクターも、解決のための協議に関わるべきだという考え方である。神里氏は、先ほどの「軛」対策として、エリック・マイルストンの提言を引きつつ、専門家がリスク評価を行う審議会の前段階に、何を専門家にアセスメントしてもらうか、その際にどういう範囲の専門家を集めるか（例えば自然科学だけでなく、人文社会系の専門家や、地域社会の住民代表など）、どれぐらいの期間で答えを出すかを議論する「社会的フレーミング」の段階を置くべきことを提言する。

　このような専門家、非専門家（他の分野の専門家を含む）による議論の場の重要性については、菅豊氏も「知のガバナンス」として論じている。菅氏によれば、「専門家と多様な非専門家がネットワーク化し、多元的な観点から知識の品質管理を行い、多元的な知識のあり方を理解し合う」知の「品質管理」のあり方が、「知のガバナンス」であるという[12]。

　歴史資料の保全の場合を考えると、そもそも歴史資料にはオーナーや研究者だけでなく、さまざまなアクターが関わっている。神戸大学地域連携センター刊行の『Link』では、歴史研究者ではないが、歴史表象や歴史資料に関わる人びとを「歴史研究の隣人」と呼び、インタビューを重ねてきた。家屋の整理を代行する業者の方[13]、古書店の店主[14]、一般向けの新書などで歴史研究の成果を発信する編集者[15]、先の「おくりいえプロジェクト」代表[16]、新聞の文化欄で歴史関係の記事を書く新聞記者[17]といった方々から話を聞いた。話を聞くなかで、研究者は歴史資料を扱うアクターの一人にすぎないことがよくわかった。

　二つ目は、専門知と社会をつなぐファシリテーター、「媒介の専門家」[18]、「ある専門分野の、実践についての知識を欠いた、言語についての専門知」[19]の役割の重要性である。マスコミと科学技術分野の研究者の間の情報流通を円滑化する SMS（サイエンス・メディア・センター）は、このような媒介的役割を果たす組織として設立されたという[20]。さらに、専門知と専門知を結びつけ、他の専門領域で起こっていることを伝える「文化の翻訳家」[21]も必要である。

　三つ目は、対象に巻き込まれる、参与する研究の活性化である。対象を観察者である自分から切り離して「客観的」に見つめるのではなく、対象に入

り込むことで、観察者であった自分を変えていくような研究が求められる[22]。このような研究のあり方は、「よそ者」が当事者である地域の人びととともに開発に参加し、自分を新たな当事者へと変えていく、中村尚司氏が唱える参加型開発論[23]と課題を共有している。

　以上のような専門知をめぐる課題（専門知側が持つ知識の射程、時間的感覚と、求める側とのギャップ）とそれに対する処方箋（①多様なアクターの参加、②専門知と社会、専門知と専門知をつなぐ媒介、③対象のなかに入り込む研究）は、歴史資料の救出、保全の場にもぴったりと当てはまるといっていいだろう。救出と保全はさまざまなアクターの協働なくして実現しないし、現場に臨む研究者は専門知と社会を結ぶ立場に立たざるを得ない。同時に対象となるさまざまな歴史資料の専門家、保存科学の専門家、行政、災害復興に関わる専門家等との相互理解をはからねばならない。さらに、資料を守り伝えてきた人びとや場に深くコミットすることなしに、資料が持つ意味を十分に後世に伝えていくことなどできないだろう。

　歴史資料の救出、保全に関わる「知識」「方法」「活動」は、専門知をめぐる問題と深く関わり、問題を乗り越えていく実践という意味を持っている。繰り返しになるが、そもそもこれらは、現場での実践を通して生み出され、新たな現場に持ち込まれて反省的に作り直されてきた来歴を持つ。このプロセス自体が、先に述べた処方箋①〜③の実践ではなかっただろうか。

むすびにかえて

　以上、専門知をめぐる問題を通して、歴史資料の保全に関する「方法」「知識」「活動」の意味を問うてきた。歴史資料問題は、歴史学、歴史研究の問題であることに立ち返ったとき、当然パブリック・ヒストリーの問題についても触れなくてはならないであろう。

　パブリック・ヒストリーについて整理した岡本充弘氏によると、パブリック・ヒストリーは多義的な内容を含むが、「基本的には『パブリックに対する』（to the public）歴史と『パブリックの中』（in the public）にある歴史」に区別できるという。前者は博物館などの社会教育機関、遺跡や遺物、さらには小説、

映画、漫画など、専門的な作り手から生み出される歴史である。対して後者は一般の人びとが作り出す習俗、伝承、記憶などを基礎にした歴史で、かつては専門的研究の埒外におかれていた。そして、この両者を、対立的に考えるのではなく、両者の相互性を重視する議論が盛んになっているという[24]。

　このような整理を参考にすると、歴史資料の保全は、「パブリックに対する」（to the public）歴史、「パブリックの中」（in the public）にある歴史の、双方にまたがる活動であると言える。さらに、時々の場面場面で専門家に限らず、市民を含むさまざまなアクターとの協働がつくられることに注目するならば、歴史資料の保全は、歴史資料にさまざまな関心やスキルに基づいて関わり合う新しい public をつくり出す働き（make the public）であるとも言えるのである[25]。

　現代社会は、誰でも自由に世間に向かって歴史について発信できる時代である。そのようななかで、自分の願望を歴史に仮託するような言説もままみられる。ときには自分が唱える正しい説を専門家たちは知りながら隠蔽しているという陰謀論もある。このような時代にあって、専門家を含めて、歴史を語る資料を残そうという大きな目標で一致し、そのための手立てを考えたり、救出、修復された資料について意見を交わしたりする Public な空間はきわめて重要な場になるだろう。

　以上、先学の引用に終始したが、歴史資料救出の「知識」「方法」「活動」は直接の目的を達成するためだけでなく、専門的研究と市民知、社会を結びつける性質を持つ営みである。今後その意味が一層深められることを期待したい。

注

1　竹倉史人『土偶を読む―130 年間解かれなかった縄文神話の謎』（晶文社、2021 年）。

2　縄文 ZINE 編『土偶を読むを読む』（文学通信、2023 年）。

3　菅豊「知の『鑑定人』―専門知批判は専門知否定であってはならない」（同上）。

4　The Asahi Shimbun Glove ＋の該当記事は、https://globe.asahi.com/article/14400149 から読むことができる（2024 年 2 月 15 日段階）。

5 添田孝史『原発と大津波　警告を葬った人々』（岩波新書、2014 年）、同書は専門知をとりまく諸々の力学を考える上で示唆にとむ。

6 インタビューシリーズ「歴史研究の隣人たち」第 2 回第 2 部一級建築士やまだのりこ氏（神戸大学大学院人文学研究科地域連携センター発行『Link』13 号、2021 年）。『Link』は神戸大学附属図書館の H.P. の「学術成果リポジトリ Kernel」から閲覧可能である。

7 『朝日新聞』社会季評（2021 年 6 月 17 日朝刊）。

8 安東量子『海を撃つ―福島・広島・ベラルーシにて』（みすず書房、2019 年）、『スティーブ＆ボニー―砂漠のゲンシリョクムラ・イン・アメリカ』（晶文社、2022 年）。

9 村上陽一郎編『「専門家」とは誰か』（晶文社、2022 年）。

10 隠岐さや香「科学と『専門家』をめぐる諸概念の歴史」（同上）、74 頁。

11 神里達博「リスク時代における行政と専門家―英国ＢＳＥ問題から」（同上）、引用は 163 頁。

12 菅氏前掲論文、419 頁。

13 インタビューシリーズ「歴史研究の隣人たち」（第 1 回）「家じまいアドバイザー」屋宜明彦氏（『Link』11 号、2019 年）。

14 同上（第 3 回）書肆つづらや店主原智子氏（『Link』14 号、2022 年）。

15 同上（第 2 回）第 1 部新書編集者山崎比呂志氏（『Link』13 号、 2021 年）。

16 注 6。

17 インタビューシリーズ第 4 回として、『Link』15 号に掲載の予定。

18 小林傳司「社会と科学をつなぐ新しい『専門家』」（村上編『専門家とは誰か』）、226 頁。

19 鈴木哲也「運動としての専門知」（同上）、250 頁。

20 瀬川至朗「ジャーナリストと専門家は協働できるか」（同上）、125 頁～。

21 注 18 小林論文。加えて、藤垣裕子氏はヨーロッパで議論されている「責任ある研究とイノベーション」（RRI）が社会の諸アクターの協業を掲げていることを引きながら、そのためには「隣の領域に口出しすることや、往復による柔軟性は不可欠である」と指摘している（同書所収、藤垣裕子「隣の領域に口出しするということ」、引用は 50 頁）。

22 注 19 鈴木論文。

23　中村尚司「当事者性の探求と参加型開発―スリランカにみる大学の社会貢献活動」（斎藤文彦編『参加型開発―貧しい人々が主役になる開発に向けて』日本評論社、2002 年）。

24　岡本充弘「パブリックヒストリー研究序説」（『東洋大学人間科学総合研究所紀要』第 22 号、2020 年）。

25　なお、このような「公共」（Public）の考え方については、斎藤純一『公共性』（岩波書店、2000 年）参照。

第3部

おわりに

▨ 松下正和・天野真志

　本書は、科学研究費補助金特別推進研究「地域歴史資料学を機軸とした災害列島における地域存続のための地域歴史文化の創成」（課題番号19H05457、代表：奥村弘）A班「地域歴史資料継承領域」による成果の一部である。この共同研究メンバーは、1995年の阪神・淡路大震災以降全国各地で頻発する自然災害に対し、各地域における多様な歴史資料の救済・保存・継承に取り組んでいる。さらに、その過程で直面した課題の検討を通して、地域社会における歴史文化の継承基盤を見出すことを実践的に進めてきた。各執筆者は現在もそれぞれに活動を推進しているが、本書にはそれらの成果を通して見出された歴史資料救済・継承の理念が凝縮されている。

　地域のなかで歴史資料を継承するために、資料そのものを守ることは当然の課題である。そのために、被災した資料を迅速かつ適切な手段により処置を施すことが求められるが、全国各地に点在する膨大な資料に対処することは容易ではない。これまでの取り組みを概観すると、被災地の対応には保存・修復の専門家ではない自治体職員や地域住民等が主体となることが多い。近年はさまざまな機会でこれまでの災害対応事例が紹介されており、それらに接することで活動のイメージをつかむことは可能である。反面、被災の状況は発生した時期や歴史的・地理的背景、災害規模・種類によって異なるし、活動主体の構成に応じて対象となる資料も多様である。災害対応は、特定の技法やマニュアルにとどまらない取り組みが重要であるが、その実践は決して容易ではない。本書を企画するにあたり執筆者間で議論を重ね、各章では方法論や実践事例の紹介に終始せず、それぞれの資料を救済するための考え方を提示することとした。資料を救い出し、当面の危機を脱する段階とはどのような状態なのか、その目的に向けた留意点とポイントを整理してさまざ

まな現場対応に参照してもらいたいという目的が本書の大きな目的である。

　資料をとりまく人びととの関係は、資料保存・継承を考える上で不可欠な要素である。特に各地域に伝来する多様な資料は、その地域で生活する人びとと密接な関わりを持ちながら伝えられてきた。地域の資料と向きあうことは、その地域のさまざまな来歴や人びととの対話を要請する。そのなかで歴史文化の専門家がいかなるかたちで関わっていくのか、対話を通した歴史文化継承のあり方が必要となるだろう。近年の地域資料救済において、「資料ネット」活動に象徴される多様な専門家が地域社会と対話することを、本書のなかで市沢哲は"make the public"と表現している。活動を通した新たな関係性のなかで、こうした公共空間が形成されるとすれば、資料保存という取り組みは、モノを救い出すことにとどまらない持続的役割が求められることになるだろう。そのための取り組みは各地で積極的に進められているが、今後もさらなる展開が期待される。特に、我々の実践や検討は、国際的にどのような取り組みとして理解されるのか、本書を企画するなかで議論となった。そこで日本語版とともに英語版を掲載し、Webでの発信とあわせて多くの人びとの目に触れてほしいと考えた。英訳に際しては、根本峻瑠にとりまとめをいただいた。編者たちのつたない英語の校閲には大変な苦労を強いたが、改めて御礼申し上げたい。

　本書を編集するさなかの2024年1月1日、石川県能登半島を中心とした大規模な地震・津波被害が発生した。現在もあらゆる分野における救済活動が進められており、同地における被災資料救済活動も行われることになるだろう。被害に遭われた方々にお見舞い申し上げるとともに、本書がささやかながらも今後の活動の一助になることを願っている。

Editors
AMANO Masashi
MATSUSHITA Masakazu

How to Preserve
Local Historical Culture

Methods and Ideas for Rescuing
Materials during Disasters

Foreword

▨ OKUMURA Hiroshi (Graduate School of Humanities, Kobe University)

This book represents a vital part of the research project "From Local Historical Material Studies to Regional Historical Culture: Creation of a New Research Field for Resilient Local Communities in a Country of Natural Disasters" (Principal Investigator: OKUMURA Hiroshi, Project Number: 19H05457), supported by the Grant-in-Aid for Specially Promoted Research.

Since the Great Hanshin-Awaji Earthquake, we have developed collaborative research in Local Historical Materials Studies (LHMS) nationwide. Seeing the recent challenges facing Japan, it became all the clearer that it gets increasingly and rapidly difficult to pass on local histories and cultures because of such factors as frequent large-scale natural disasters, population decrease due to the drastic changes in the social structure caused by globalization, greater mobility of population, and transformation in values since the economic miracle.

Empirical research using local historical materials (LHM) lays the academic foundation in humanities and social sciences, but it presupposes preserving the historical materials. Unless society recognizes that the preservation and inheritance of the materials have social value, they disappear. It is a vicious circle that diminishes the importance of related research, which weakens public awareness and causes further loss of the materials. Preserving historical materials unknown to academics requires the research community to collaborate with the locals to discover and evaluate them; those involved agree establishing new methodologies and research fields is also necessary for such a purpose (OKUMURA Hiroshi (ed). *Rekishibunka wo daisaigai kara mamoru: chiikirekishishiryogaku no kochiku*

[Protecting Historic and Cultural Resources from Natural Disaster: Construction of Studies about Local Historical Materials]. University of Tokyo Press, 2014).

The approach of LHMS, serving as the foundational study for civic society formation, inherits the challenges of post-war Japanese history, which aims to link specialized knowledge of university researchers with societal knowledge based on local communities to form civic values that support Japanese society after WWII; in practical research through responses to large-scale natural disasters, LHMS has become enriched over time (OKUMURA Hiroshi. *Daishinsai to reki-shishiryohozon: Hanshin-Awaji daishinsai kara Higashinihon daishinsai e* [Great Earthquakes and Historical Material Preservation: From the Great Hanshin-Awaji Earthquake to the Great East Japan Earthquake]. Yoshikawa Kobunkan, 2012).

Our research team have prioritized this aspect. AMANO Masashi and MAT-SUSHITA Masakazu have led practical research, consolidating and analyzing practical methods for historical material rescue activities during large-scale natural disasters and disaster prevention/reduction of LHM. This book, as one of the research achievements, presents a systematic approach to serve as a guide for practical activities in the actual large-scale disasters. We want it used across Japan and hope to receive feedback and suggestions from readers to improve and refine our work for the benefit of all.

It is worth noting that such trends in Japan align with global social changes and new developments in historical studies and historical material preservation worldwide. For further insights on this matter, see our publication, *Yoroppa bunk-aisankenkyuu no saizensen* [Front Line of Cultural Heritage Research in Europe] (Kobe University Press, 2023), authored/translated by Sonkoly Gábor, OKUMU-RA Hiroshi, NEMOTO Takeru, ICHIHARA Shimpei, and KATO Akie.

Introduction

▨ AMANO Masashi (National Museum of Japanese History)

■ How Can We Promote Material Rescue Activities Led by the Locals?

Disaster response is a critical issue in today's society, where natural disasters occur frequently. Natural disasters cause significant damage to human lives, their livelihoods, and various historical and cultural objects, requiring us to perform rescue activities for the damaged materials across Japan. Amidst the frequent occurrence of large-scale disasters, in which many areas are at risk of being damaged in the future, disaster response for the diverse historical and cultural materials handed down is being discussed. In particular, community-based activities to preserve and pass on historical culture, represented by the "Shiryo-Network" (Historical Materials Network) in each region, are actively involved in rescue activities for materials in a disaster. Within this context, handling materials damaged by water or due to other reasons which require unusual treatment has undergone trials and errors.

Many introductions and manuals on rescue techniques related to the response to disaster-damaged material rescue, from the Great Hanshin-Awaji Earthquake to the Great East Japan Earthquake up to the present day, have been presented. The outcomes of these disaster response experiences include detailed first aid methods, restoration techniques, and specific equipment. However, the damage varies greatly depending on the geographical situation and extent of the disaster, and the condition of the materials is not consistent. Therefore, to implement measures with past disaster response practices in mind, an approach based on specific practical examples is necessary. What should we consider when dealing with disaster-damaged materials, and under what objectives? Moreover, from what perspective should we observe them, and to what extent should we examine countermeasures? The methods to deal with damaged materials, examination of specific countermeasures, and selection of technology are important topics for promoting the material rescue activities led by the locals.

Bearing the above issues in mind, this book presents ideas for disaster prevention and risk reduction of local historical materials, including countermeasures from the finding of damaged materials to their temporary storage and emergency treatment, and tips for deciding what technique to choose for the rescue in anticipation of the disaster-stricken area. Along with the progress of disaster countermeasures, researchers have accumulated many case studies; while specific techniques gained across the country are available, we focused on the following two points in this book.

■ Organizing Purposes and Concepts of Disaster Response

First, we should organize the purposes and concepts of disaster response. As mentioned above, research has accumulated diverse case studies on historical material rescue; technology developments and manual formulations are in progress; the public has started recognizing disaster response as an important topic in efforts to preserve materials. However, while many detailed techniques are available, organizing information for practical use, such as which techniques are effective in which situations, to what extent we should apply them and for what purpose, is a major challenge. Experts in preservation and restoration techniques who handle the damaged materials are not always available. In Japan, it is not uncommon for municipality officials and the locals to take charge of the initial response, and various individuals often set the choice of technology and end goal. Thus, it is an urgent task to select the techniques from the vast amount of accumulated information and organize the points to be considered to take appropriate measures. In other words, the first objective of this publication is to organize material preservation as a disaster response from a practical perspective and to present ideas for setting specific work processes and goals to be achieved.

■ Organizing Purposes of Preparation and Discussion toward Disaster Response

Second, we need to organize the purposes of disaster preparation and discussion. Disaster response is one aspect of preserving and passing on materials. Although rescuing materials from a disaster site and saving them from extinction is a major objective in the preservation, for medium/long-term preservation and inheritance, in addition to the physical approach, we need to explore the materials' relationship with the people and society surrounding them. In recent years, the relationships of experts and expertise with civil society have attracted attention. In the venue of preservation and inheritance of materials, experts from various fields seek ways to engage in dialogue with the people at the site of material rescue and in the process of preservation and inheritance. This book focuses on the relationship between the people and communities surrounding the materials, and the challenge is to contemplate how we can utilize expertise in society through several initiatives practised during the process, from rescue to inheritance.

■ Hints for Practical Activities

This book has three parts. **Part 1, "Prerequisites for Materials Rescue,"** introduces methods to collaborate with organizations and groups surrounding the community regarding communication and cooperation in a disaster. **Part 2, "Approaches to Materials Rescue and Preservation,"** presents the goals and points to remember for preservation as an emergency response to rescue damaged materials, with the target being paper documents, photographs, folk implements, and artworks. **Part 3, "Preparation for Materials Rescue,"** introduces the purposes of disaster preparation simulations and communication with the community. Seeking to utilize expertise and techniques and collaborate with diverse actors to ensure their survival, local communities promote local practices that introduce diverse "specialized knowledge" and "social knowledge" to inherit historical culture. How can we preserve and succeed community histories in today's disaster-prone society? We hope this project provides hints for practical activities for preserving and inheriting historical culture in each community.

To convey the events introduced in each chapter more extensively, we translated this book into English (this part). We planned this in anticipation of future discussions on how to use the efforts undertaken in Japan globally. We hope that this will assist international collaboration in materials preservation and inheritance.

Part 1

Prerequisites for Materials Rescue

Chapter 1

Communities and Materials in the Event of a Disaster

▨ AMANO Masashi (National Museum of Japanese History)

Introduction

Part 1

In our life, the threat of natural disasters is ever-present. While people involved in local communities study and prepare for frequent earthquakes, windstorms, and floods in every way, those in history and culture also try to devise the means to protect and pass on the historical/cultural materials handed down from generation to generation in each community.

The historical and cultural materials handed down in a community are diverse: we generally think of written records (collectively called old documents), artworks like hanging scrolls, and folk tools revealing the lifestyle and culture in the community. In recent years, audiovisual records such as photographs and audio/video clips have gained attention as local historical and cultural information. Although these entities have many terms ("cultural assets," "cultural heritage," or "historical materials"), all of them are objects sharing or having shared historical and cultural values in a certain space. While the authors call them "historical materials" or "resources" in this book, in recent years, more and more researchers have begun to use the term "local historical materials (LHM)". When we use this word, we focus not only on the materials themselves but also on the agents and processes involved, and consider and practice initiatives to make people aware of the existence of "historical materials" in a local community. With this perspective in mind, it will be necessary for the local community to take initiatives in preserving and passing on the various materials handed down in the community, in addition to specific measures to implement the initiatives when historical materials are in a state of crisis, particularly due to natural disasters.

This chapter reviews the progress of disaster countermeasures for historical materials in each community and discuss the concept of community-based materials rescue.

1. Disaster Response Progress

After natural disasters, various activities relive the affected areas: first, those directly related to human survival and livelihood, for example, lifesaving and lifeline restoration; then, those for historical/cultural materials begin. Many of the materials rescued after a certain interval are likely at considerable risk of deterioration or disappearance due to destruction or water damage. Such damaged materials tend to be discarded during debris removal or cleanup activities; however, some researchers try to rescue not only symbolic properties like national treasures and important cultural properties but also diverse materials from critical situations. Collaboratively working with the locals, they pass them down to future generations.

Only after the Great Hanshin-Awaji Earthquake (1995) did we start to appreciate the importance of such efforts in Japan. While the Agency for Cultural Affairs led a rescue program, saving various materials held by private individuals became a challenge, which made a voluntary activity necessary to protect and pass on local materials. Later, during continuous disasters, similar projects started in each affected area: the organizations collectively known as "Shiryo-Network" spread throughout Japan.

This chapter reviews some examples of community-based disaster countermeasure practices, mainly conducted by Shiryo-Networks, and shows communal activity trends and characteristics. Around 2004, members of Shiryo-Networks began to discuss how to save affected materials. In Hyogo, after Typhoon Tokage (2004), Siryo-net (Kobe) surveyed the devastated areas and rescued water-damaged materials found in the survey. The main target was old documents and other paper-based materials stored in private homes. It was a volunteer activity by university students, local government officials, museum curators, and the residents in the Kansai region, headquartered in the Faculty of Letters of Kobe University (MATSUSHITA and KONO, 2009).

After Typhoon Nabi (2005), similar rescue activities in Nobeoka, Miyazaki, saved photographic materials in private homes. In addition to unfolding and drying the adhered parts, the participants digitized the images for preservation (YAMAUCHI, 2005; YAMAUCHI and MASUDA, 2007). These activities led to the establishment of the Miyazaki Shiryo-Network, which has organized activities for the preservation and succession of materials in Miyazaki.

Several subsequent efforts have saved materials from flood damage since then. Among them a major turning point was the Great East Japan Earthquake (2011). The tsunami that struck off the Pacific coast of East Japan devastated innumerable local materials, destroying museums and other storage facilities. Therefore, those involved in all fields related to history and culture, including history, folklore, archaeology, and fine arts, struggled to relieve them in the disaster areas. In addition, specialists from many fields examined and practiced concrete measures for saving endangered materials. Amid these efforts, local Shiryo-Networks also rescued materials, mainly from private homes, and sought to preserve and pass them on. Siryo-net (Kobe), in particular, emphasizes dialogue and practice to rescue, protect, and inherit the materials, with the local community playing a central role [See p. 15 Fig. 1: Activities in Hiroshima during the 2018 Torrential Rains in Western Japan (30 July, 2018)].

Since the 2011 earthquake, Japan has seen many large-scale torrential rains and typhoons nationwide, including the 2015 Kanto/Tohoku Torrential Rains, the 2016 Kumamoto Earthquake, the 2018 West Japan Torrential Rains, and the 2019 East Japan Typhoons. Confronted with these damages, Shiryo-Networks have implemented initiatives after earthquakes and windstorms across Japan and have continued the quest for materials inheritance.

2. Disaster Preparation Practices and Leaders

2.1. "Rescue" Developments

We often refer to rescue activities for materials in a disaster as "rescue" activities. After the 1995 earthquake, the term "cultural properties rescue" appeared, and since the 2011 catastrophe, "rescue" has been gaining currency. TATEISHI

Toru, for example, defines "cultural property rescue" as "the rescue and transportation of cultural properties, mainly movable cultural properties, from the disaster area to storage areas (including temporary storage), performing necessary emergency treatment" (TATEISHI, 2023, p. 43). This concept presupposes the fact that the "Tohoku Region Pacific Offshore Earthquake Disaster Relief Project (Cultural Property Rescue Project)" in 2011 aimed to "rescue cultural properties in need of urgent conservation measures, take emergency measures, and temporarily store them at museums and other facilities with conservation functions in the prefecture or neighboring prefectures." This was the background for "Cultural Property Rescue Projects"[1], and this understanding has been valid in subsequent disaster countermeasures.

Because of frequent tsunamis, typhoons, and torrential rains, it is impossible to complete the "rescue" only by moving them to a safe place; the objective is to get the materials out of hazards like water damage.

What kind of entities are responsible for activities mentioned above? In the case of a wide-area disaster, as in 2011, the government responds to it comprehensively and nationwide, but local governments, museums, and universities usually take the initiative for local disasters. In particular, as for Shiryo-Networks activities, the locals and those involved in the community lead the projects in addition to university faculty, museum curators, archivists, and other specialists from many fields. The distinctive feature of Shiryo-Networks is that the researchers from diverse fields aim to research, preserve, and pass on local history and culture, focusing on diverse values through dialogues with the residents. On the other hand, the networks do not necessarily have specialists in conservation or restoration, and participants still try and fail when handling damaged materials. When the damage is extensive, each practitioner has to deal with an enormous amount of materials. Usually, citizen volunteers help with the work. Thanks to the accumulated experiences, we have many reports on handling materials from the immediate aftermath of the disaster to their temporary storage. We need a summary of the achievements and issues related to disaster countermeasure practices based on a series of experiences and a proposal for future countermeasures.

2.2. Expansion of Disaster Preparation

Since the Great East Japan Earthquake, efforts to save archival materials have undergone several transformations. One is the involvement of conservation and restoration specialists in local activities. Of course, experts had saved local materials, particularly folk and art materials. However, it was after the great earthquake that we could see the practice of collaborative rescues by Shiryo-Networks and the residents more often across Japan.

For example, OKADA Yasushi, a specialist in the conservation and restoration of sculptures and cultural properties, led a rescue for Buddhist statues handed down in the communities and damaged or destroyed by the earthquake and tsunami during the 2011 earthquake. When restoring Buddhist statues, Okada does not move the materials to a workshop but restores them on-site and shares the restoration process with locals by opening it to the public. Okada explains that this aims to allow the public to feel the restoration process of Buddhist statues as symbols of the community while linking it to that of the disaster area (OKADA Yasushi. "Higashinihondaishinsai ni okeru chokokubunkazai no hisaigo no taio to hisaimae no taisaku ni tsuite [Dealing with Sculptural Cultural Assets before/after the Great East Japan Earthquake]", in: *Bulletin of Tokai National Higher Education and Research University Archives*, 2021). Such efforts to empathize with the local significance of rescued materials while confirming their contents with the residents in the recovery and reconstruction from the disaster were also carried out in the rescue activities of damaged folk tools (KATO Koji. *Hukko Kyureshon* [Restoration Curation]. Shakai Hyoron Sha, 2017), and are also notable as activities to reposition damaged materials as local materials.

Another characteristic of recent rescues is that they have become increasingly substantial and diverse. If we define the scope of "rescue" as the whole activity process, a series of community-based activities also need specific responses to damaged materials. Many practices nationwide try to save paper materials, such as old documents, based on the experience of the Great East Japan Earthquake, and participants tackle various issues like handling water-damaged or stuck materials and combatting mold and odor hazards. Indeed, conservation and restoration specialists sometimes take the initiative. However, the projects are usually volunteer projects led by a *Shiryo Net*: cultural property staff in local governments, museum curators, university faculty, and the locals play a vital part in it.

Part 1

3. Objectives and Goals of Materials Rescue

As we have seen, "non-experts" often lead recent community-based activities to save archival materials, prompting us to seek and practice measures that do not require advanced techniques or specialized equipment. However, we have different issues depending on the damage to the target materials. Various practical examples and reports are available, depending on the situation in the affected areas and the nature of the response personnel, and we have a wide range of manuals and other documents based on thumb rules. An overview of these manuals reveals that although they use the same terminology, they sometimes have different objectives and methodologies. Furthermore, participants do not always share the process and goals of the "rescue". To understand "rescue" as a generic term for on-site work in disaster response and to examine past efforts as practical examples for the future, it is necessary to organize the concept of the work required in "rescue" [Fig. 2: "Rescue" flow].

An essential task in the "rescue" process is first aid (treatment). HIDAKA Shingo clearly states the purpose of this process as follows:

First aid measures are to halt the deterioration of damaged cultural properties and to provide a bridge to the next stage of restoration, that is, the full-

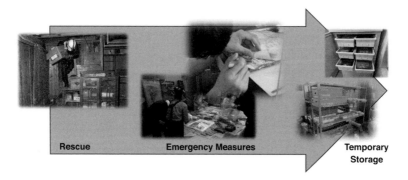

Rescue   Emergency Measures   Temporary Storage

Avoid disappearance and rapid deterioration of the material

Fig. 2

scale restoration. At the same time, keeping the temporary storage areas mentioned above clean is also essential (HIDAKA, 2015, p. 39).

According to him, emergency measures are temporary measures before we implement necessary "full-scale restoration", and in addition to controlling the progress of deterioration of the materials, they also include the maintenance of the storage space environment. In this case, emergency measures are positioned as a preliminary response before the restoration and differ from restoration activities. Symbolized by the word "rescue," the process of first disaster countermeasures is preliminary, and restoration actions involving dismantling and cleaning are not inevitable. However, with recent natural disasters becoming more frequent and severe, the "rescue" process tends to be time-consuming. In some cases, they carry out the work beyond the scope of emergency measures during long-term temporary storage.

Then, to what condition should emergency measures bring the damaged materials? Since many materials in various media are damaged, it is not realistic to immediately restore all the materials to their perfect condition. Therefore, it is crucial to avoid or control the rapid deterioration by applying emergency measures to as many materials as possible in the affected areas and formulating and implementing a work plan to proceed to conservation and restoration for the materials' expected subsequent utilization and succession. For details on specific methods for typical materials, see the discussions in Part 2.

First, let us discuss the purpose of emergency measures. With varying degrees of deterioration, the primary objective is to control the progression of deterioration of the target material. In other words, the primary objective is to eliminate the severe risks posed by disasters. For example, the primary objective for water-damaged ones is dehydration, which requires temporary treatment by freezing or drying. In the case of materials collapsed or damaged by the earthquake, it may be necessary to pick up the damaged parts or check the damaged areas.

Next, the criteria for the level of emergency measures differ in each region. The ideal situation would be to position the first aid phase as a temporary measure and focus on drying work, keeping the materials' shape intact, controlling deterioration factors such as mold, and simple cleaning for temporary storage. More specifically, emergency measures aim to bring the materials to a condition that will allow them to withstand temporary storage for two to three years. However, in the case of a great disaster like the Great East Japan Earthquake, "rescue" activities took more time than expected due to extended damage. As a result, they performed more than just temporary measures at the emergency measure stage. Some have started to call such practice "stabilization treatment" since the 2011 catastrophe, referring to actions that go beyond the scope of emergency measures and include some restoration actions. It is a measure that arose after a large-scale disaster where long-term temporary storage is necessary before restoration work. This concept applies to artworks, for which the practitioners need specialized techniques and knowledge even in the rescue stage. Based on this understanding, this book deals with the emergency measures stage rather than the "stabilization treatment" stage, and introduces its practice and concept.

As described above, the three stages of "rescue" activities generally include rescue, emergency measures as a subsequent response, and temporary storage. In principle, emergency measures should be temporary in anticipation of future restoration. However, depending on the damage and the nature of the materials, sometimes dismantling and cleaning may be necessary in the restoration process. In this regard, Prof. HIDAKA pointed out that "when considering the ideal emergency measures, it is necessary to seek for the ones that do not only seek to stabilize the condition of damaged cultural properties but incorporate the methodology of conservation and restoration of cultural properties for their subsequent utilization".[2] We, therefore, need to discuss ideas by paying attention to the social environment where the materials are, and not just by focusing on technological matters. To this end, it will be necessary to share the purpose and awareness of materials preservation and inheritance among the entities involved, and to discuss and confirm the goals.

Conclusion

This chapter reviewed the progress and situation of materials preservation as a disaster countermeasure and organized materials "rescue" activities in a disaster. Many private materials handed down in local communities are often stored in warehouses or storerooms. They are not always stable preservation environments, and it is difficult to receive public support for their restoration and conservation financially. When such materials are damaged, volunteers, especially those from a Shiryo-Network, often lead "rescue" activities. Local governments and museums do not always have specialists familiar with the target materials, so usually, non-specialists have to lead "rescue" activities. To prepare for such situations, it is first necessary to recognize the basic concept of the "rescue". It is also important to know about the fields and experts of materials preservation.

Notes

1 Decision of the Deputy Director-General of the Agency for Cultural Affairs (30 March, 2011), "Implementation Guidelines for the Tohoku Region Pacific Offshore Earthquake Disaster Relief Project for Cultural Properties (Cultural Property Rescue Project)". https://www.bunka.go.jp/earthquake/rescue/pdf/bunkazai_rescue_jigyo_ver04 .pdf (last viewed 25 December, 2023)

2 HIDAKA Shingo, "Daikibosaigaiji ni okeru bunkazaireskyu no kadai [Issues with Cultral Asset Rescue in Large-Scale Disasters]", in: *Bulletin of the National Museum of Japanese History*, 214, 2019, p. 50.

References

AMANO Masashi and GOTO Makoto (eds). *Chiikirekishibunkakeisho gaidobukku* [Guidebook for Community Hisorical Culture Inheritance]. Bungaku Report, 2022.

HIDAKA Shingo. *Saigai to bunkazai* [Disasters and Cultural Properties]. The Senri Foundation, 2015.

KOHDZUMA Yohsei, TATEISHI Toru, and KODANI Ryusuke (eds). *Nyumon daisaigaijidai no bunkazaibosai* [Introduction to Cultural Property Disaster Prevention in the Age of Great Disasters]. Douseisha, 2023.

MATSUSHITA Masakazu and KONO Mio (eds). *Suisonshiryo wo suku* [Rescuing Water-Damaged Materials]. Iwata-shoin, 2009.

OKUMURA Hiroshi (ed). *Rekishibunka wo daisaigai kara mamoru.* [Protecting Historic and Cultural Resources from Natural Disaster]. University of Tokyo Press, 2014.

Part 1

Chapter 2

People Involved in Materials Rescue

▨ MATSUSHITA Masakazu (Kobe University)

Introduction

As mentioned in Chapter 1, materials rescue involves more than specialists handling of cultural properties or restoring materials. In particular, as for privately owned materials rescue, the main target of Shiryo-Networks, a diverse group of people participate in it: in addition to cultural property researchers at universities or government officials, the locals and volunteers from outside the affected area are also a part of the project.

With Japan's population declining and aging at an accelerating pace and natural disasters occurring more frequently, fewer and fewer people can help with materials rescue; meanwhile, we have more and more materials to deal with. The challenge is efficiently rescuing materials with limited human, financial, and material resources. In addition to the technical and efficiency aspects of material rescue, it is necessary to explore materials rescue that allows the people who have inherited them to maintain their communities.

This chapter focuses on Siryo-net[1] (a volunteer organization based at the Faculty of Letters, Kobe University, established in the wake of the 1995 Great Hanshin-Awaji Earthquake) and their activities in Hyogo, analyzing what kind of institutions, groups, and people have participated in materials rescues. As a researcher at the university, I would primarily discuss the current situation and issues facing the preservation/utilization of "undesignated cultural properties": they are private properties, including various materials located in the private sector, which are unlikely to receive public support in a disaster.

1. Wide Area Collaboration System

1.1. Development of a Nationwide System for Rescuing Cultural Properties and Damaged Materials

Since the founding of Siryo-net (Kobe), more than 30 historical materials networks (Shiryo-Networks) have emerged throughout Japan—because of a large-scale disaster or as a pre-disaster preparedness measure (AMANO and GOTO, 2022). Since 2015, they have organized the "National Shiryo-Networks Research Meeting" to share information and prompt networking between them. In addition, based on the connections formed during the Cultural Heritage Rescue and Rescue Project after the Great East Japan Earthquake, 27 organizations (as of June 2023) related to various cultural heritage, including Siryo-net (Kobe), established the "Cultural Heritage Disaster Prevention Network Promotion Council". They share information during peace and launch a rapid, effective disaster relief activity when a disaster occurs. In 2020, the National Institutes for Cultural Heritage set up the Cultural Heritage Disaster Prevention Center as the headquarters facility to create a cultural heritage disaster prevention system, develop technologies, and support rescue activities in a disaster (KOHDZUMA et al., 2023). Furthermore, the National Institutes for the Humanities, led by the National Museum of Japanese History and Tohoku University and Kobe University, launched the "Inter-University Research Institute Network Project to Preserve and Succeed Historical and Cultural Resources". Working with other Shiryo-Networks, they create mutual support systems and wide-area networks for future disasters. Thus, compared to the 1990s, nationwide support systems at many levels have greatly advanced, as have the systems for dealing with various cultural properties and materials damaged in disasters and the networking for connecting organizations nationwide. To cope with increasingly diverse and complex natural and artificial disasters, disaster-related networking consisting of various fields is still necessary.

In addition, a system for cultural properties rescue aided by a wide-area framework is emerging; for example, in 2013, nine prefectural governments in the Chugoku and Shikoku regions, in addition to those of Hiroshima and Okayama City, already formulated the "Mutual Support Plan for the Protection of Damaged Cultural Properties in Chugoku and Shikoku". In 2018, the Kansai region made the "Guideline for Responding to Damage to Cultural Properties Based on the

Basic Agreement on Mutual Support in a Crisis in the Kinki Region" in anticipation of a Nankai Earthquake. The prefectures comprising the basic agreement are Fukui, Mie, Shiga, Kyoto, Osaka, Hyogo, Nara, Wakayama, Tokushima, and the Union of Kansai Governments (including Tottori); the Union of Kansai Governments includes Shiga, Kyoto, Osaka, Hyogo, Nara, Wakayama, Tokushima. As the 2011 catastrophe made clear, it is difficult for a disaster-affected prefecture alone to respond to a large-scale disaster, and a support system including multiple prefectures plays a significant role. For example, the Azuchi Castle Museum of Archaeology in Shiga vacuum-freeze-dried the water-damaged materials of Toyooka and Hidaka, Hyogo, when Typhoon Tokage (2004) hit Japan, using the mutual support framework by the Boards of Education of the then six Kinki prefectures (MATSUSHITA and KONO, 2009).

Thus, under such a comprehensive plan based on regional unions, actors prepare individual plans for cultural property preservation and sometimes support communities. We hope that a counterpart support system provided by Shiryo-Networks in a disaster will further develop for undesignated cultural properties.

1.2. Issues on Collaboration in Undesignated Cultural Properties Preservation

As mentioned above, Japan now has many Shiryo-Networks, which hold yearly meetings. When a large-scale disaster occurs, each Shiryo-Network gathers information. However, we need a platform for consolidating information on damage to undesignated cultural properties and effectively providing disaster areas with human, material, and financial support and know-how. Of course, this is not to say that each network cannot provide adequate support. In addition, the local network should take the initiative for small- to medium-scale disasters. However, in a large-scale disaster, if each local network were to request information from those in affected areas separately, the local governments would be overburdened with responding to repeated inquiries. It may be necessary to unify the contact points to reduce the burden on the areas, such having a specific Shiryo-Network as a centralized information center.

To facilitate damage assessment and restoration activities when staff in charge of cultural properties in the affected areas return to their original duties after completing lifesaving, evacuation shelter establishment, and lifeline restoration,

Part 1

Shiryo-Networks must prepare a logistical support system outside the affected areas. Specifically, this includes the following: obtaining information on the whereabouts of materials and damage in the affected areas; preparing personnel with rescue know-how and supplies for first aid; securing funds for activities through subsidies and donations; and accepting damaged materials (for first aid or cataloging). Many remote support activities have become feasible after online conferences using Zoom, Microsoft Teams, or Google Meet have become common due to the COVID-19 pandemic. Compared to public infrastructure, cultural restoration is a long-term process. When a large-scale disaster occurs, building a long-term support system incorporating logistical support may involve a diverse range of people, including those unable to visit the disaster area.

2. Prefectural Maintenance Systems

2.1. Preparation for Undesignated Cultural Properties in Prefectural/ Municipal Disaster Prevention Plans

In connection with the national basic plan for disaster reduction set by the Basic Act on Disaster Countermeasures, prefectures and municipalities have regional disaster reduction plans. We have pointed out the importance of including cultural property protection in regional disaster prevention plans and regarding damaged cultural property preservation as a part of reconstruction projects after a disaster (MATSUSHITA, 2014). In recent years, more and more prefectures have explicitly indicated that not only designated cultural properties but also undesignated cultural properties need identification, catalogue, preservation and handling promotion, damage assessment, information sharing, and manuals (see examples of Akita, Niigata, Ishikawa, Saga, Wakayama, Yamagata, and Oita). By specifying "designated cultural properties, etc."—this "etc." is the trick— in the plan, local governments can handle undesignated or unregistered cultural properties.

Recently, many prefectures have formulated "Cultural Property Disaster Response Manuals". Hyogo, for example, has developed a manual for its administrators in 2021 and one for cultural property owners in 2022. The latter manual covers cultural properties, whether designated, registered, or undesignated, although those for administrations cover only designated and registered ones[2]. The manual also states that they request Siryo-net (Kobe) for assistance in preserving historical and cultural materials when responding to windstorms and floods.

To support the possible participants, we should continue to encourage all municipalities in Japan to clearly state their response to undesignated cultural properties, including municipal and regional disaster prevention plans and cultural property disaster response manuals.

2.2. Shiryo-Networks in the General Guidelines for the Conservation and Utilization of Cultural Properties and the Regional Plan for the Conservation and Utilization of Cultural Properties

The 2018 amendment to the Law for the Protection of Cultural Properties newly institutionalized the formulation of a general plan for the preservation and utilization of cultural properties by prefectures and the preparation of regional plans for the preservation and utilization of cultural properties by municipalities, in addition to their approval by the Commissioner of the Agency for Cultural Affairs.

The former stipulates disaster prevention and response in a disaster as a basic measurement. This should be an opportunity to specify cooperation with universities and other private organizations like Shiryo-Networks and to create a cooperative system in a disaster. In the case of Hyogo, although it does not mention Siryo-net (Kobe), the general plan refers to daily cooperative relationships by specifying the names of universities related to cultural properties, for instance, Kobe University.

As of the end of 2023, 139 municipalities have prepared regional plans for preserving and utilizing of cultural properties[3], and some have attached a list of undesignated cultural properties to their plan. After the 1995 earthquake, research pointed out that a lack of information on the location of undesignated cultural properties in a disaster could delay the initial rescue (OKUMURA, 2012). Therefore, we hope these regional plans will lead to progress in the identifying undesignated cultural properties and their disclosure (but with attention to theft and other crime prevention measures).

Furthermore, in Hyogo, more and more cities and towns—as of the end of December 2023, Kamikawa, Kami, Akashi, Kobe, and Fukusaki—name indicates a Siryo-net (Kobe) as a partner for surveying the damage to historical and

Part 1

cultural heritage and their preservation/utilization. Thus, it will be necessary to recommend that the general guidelines and regional plans include each local Shiryo-Network.

2.3. Cooperation between Cultural Property-Related Organizations

Securing regular communication and cooperation routes in each field will also be essential. Along with the cooperation between those involved in cultural properties, those in social education need to organize a system. For example, in 2017, the Hyogo Prefectural Museum Association created a protocol ("Protocol of Mutual Cooperation and Liaison and Collaboration with Related Institutions and Organizations in a Disaster") that includes provisions for requesting the dispatch of staff from member museums to rescue disaster-stricken museums, and members have mutually signed this code. This system allows staff members to work not as volunteers but as part of their duties by submitting requests for dispatch to curators willing to provide disaster relief. The Gifu Museum Association has a system to contact the person in charge of cultural properties after a disaster to confirm the damage. When they contact the person in charge, sometimes they are unavailable; addressing the cause of the problem serves as actual disaster prevention training (SHOMURA, 2020). Making and confirming a contacts network will be essential for support and assistance in a disaster, even in regular times.

Some prefectures have established rules and agreements with Shiryo-Networks, governments, and various cultural property-related organizations to build partnerships and cooperative relationships in times of disaster and everyday life. For example, in 2015, Wakayama started the "Wakayama Prefecture Liaison Council on Disaster Countermeasures for Museum Facilities" for a cooperative relationship to rescue and conserve damaged cultural properties in the prefecture, including undesignated and private collections. *Wakayama* Shiryo-Network, Wakayama University, other research institutions, museums, libraries, prefectural government, and municipal boards of education participate in the council. Similar efforts are underway in Okayama, Tokushima, Ehime, and others.

Although Hyogo does not currently have such a protocol, it has some cooperative relationships: the Cultural Properties Division of the Hyogo Prefectural Board of Education has issued to the municipal boards of education in the prefecture a request for cooperation in the survey of Siryo-net (Kobe) when the network examined damaged historical materials in the prefecture. The Cultural Properties Division of the Hyogo Prefectural Board of Education, Community Outreach Center (Kobe University), and Siryo-net (Kobe) hold "Hyogo Prefecture Cultural Heritage Disaster Prevention Workshop" every year, where staff in charge of cultural properties in Hyogo practically practice the first aid for damaged cultural properties. While learning from the aforementioned advanced efforts in other prefectures to assess the damage in a disaster regardless of movable or immovable cultural properties, Siryo-net (Kobe) has held many discussions with members of the Hyogo Heritage Organization, to which many architects belong, the Hyogo Prefectural Museum Association, and the Hyogo Prefectural Board of Education. These collaborative relationships daily will make it possible to facilitate materials rescue activities in a disaster.

3. Connections with Diverse Sectors

3.1. Response to a Disaster

Once receiving a disaster prevention order, administrative staff in the affected areas cannot always deal with cultural properties. Even if they return to ordinary work, the first step is to examine designated cultural properties. Therefore, Siryo-net (Kobe), whose main goal is undesignated cultural property preservation, refrains from contacting the disaster areas immediately after a disaster strike when they are busy lifesaving and setting up evacuation centers to avoid burdening the areas as much as possible. When they have restored lifelines and established evacuation shelters, researchers visit the affected areas with staff in charge of cultural properties, members of community history research groups, and town chairpersons. Outsiders only visit the areas with the acceptance and approval of the residents. The first prerequisite for rescue activities targeting privately owned damaged materials is not to interfere with the reconstruction. In addition, securing a temporary storage place for the damaged materials is desirable. Cooperation with the governments, universities, and residents is essential (MATSUSHITA and KONO, 2009).

However, since the Great Hanshin-Awaji Earthquake, research has argued that a delay in visiting the disaster area leads to the disposal of materials (OKUMURA, 2012). The disposal of undesignated cultural properties and materials in private

Part 1

collections accelerates, especially when "free garbage disposal" and publicly funded demolition of houses begin after a disaster. Therefore, it is crucial to encourage the owners to prevent their disposal and to inform them of consultation services for temporary storage and emergency treatment. In recent years, on the Internet, more and more local governments and museums in disaster areas have called for preventing such disposal and publicizing their consultation services.

Unless immediately after a major disaster when infrastructure is unavailable, Siryo-net (Kobe) provides information on handling local materials to disaster victims through publicity from town halls (PR magazines, handouts for supporting victims, and community association liaison routes), information from social welfare councils and volunteer centers, and multimedia such as newspapers, TV, radio, CATV, and disaster prevention radio. Recently, SNSs like X and Facebook have been of use. However, sometimes, in disaster-stricken areas where infrastructure is unavailable, paper-based local media can be more effective in disseminating information. Before a disaster occurs, we have to prompt social welfare councils and volunteer centers to ask volunteers working on the front lines so that they can encourage the owners to handle the items related to "family memories" carefully. Siryo-net (Kobe) used to send faxes to local governments in the affected areas, asking them to prevent the disposal of materials. However, given the trouble it takes them, the network has reduced this to a notice on its website and, in recent years, has left it to local Shiryo-Networks in or near the areas to deal with the issue.

The Ministry of the Environment has formulated the "Guidelines for Disaster Waste Management" as a compilation of emergency measures for the proper, smooth, and prompt disposal of waste generated in a disaster[4]. The guidelines provide the handling of "mementos": albums, photographs, Buddhist mortuary tablets, certificates, planners, safes, and valuables (wallets, passbooks, seals, jewelry), and state that "municipalities need to pay attention to how to handle mementos and valuables when removing disaster waste, and should stipulate the rules in advance and make them public, after confirming the procedures and responses under the Lost and Found Law and other related laws and regulations. Possible rules for the handling may include their definition, ways of identifying the owners, collecting, storing, and returning". The authorities are to deliver the valuables to the police, so the guidelines ask them not to dispose of other mementos, to store them, and to turn them over to the owners as much as possible (*Disaster Waste Management Guidebook*). Since the guidelines do not cover historical and other materials, we propose that they include the issue of disposal of historical materials, collaborating with the Japan Society of Material Cycles and Waste Management and other organizations.

The "Earthquake Disaster Countermeasures Plan"[5] section of the Regional Disaster Prevention Plan of Kasai, Hyogo (revised in 2021), states that "if there are damaged cultural properties in the neighborhood, a temporary collection site for cultural properties will be set up at a temporary refuse collection site". It is a unique approach to securing a temporary storage site in the disaster area after a rescue operation.

3.2. Post-Disaster and Day-to-Day Activities

Fewer and fewer people are involved in the daily preservation of local historical materials: the nation's whole population is ever-shrinking; municipal mergers downsize the cultural property administrations; local historical societies are losing members; (junior) high school teachers, the important bearers of local history studies, are too busy to participate in community history societies.

In this context, what can universities do to preserve and pass on historic materials and records remaining in communities and homes, both in a disaster and everyday life, and keep the public interested in these materials? Naturally, we have to have those not involved with cultural properties understand the importance. Researchers need to develop a curriculum that explains the significance of record preservation in museology, archives-related studies, and first-year standard education courses for undergraduates in the social, natural, and life sciences in addition to for those in the humanities (OKUMURA, MURAI, and KIMURA, 2018). Since 2002, the Community Outreach Center (Kobe University) has been working with the locals and the governments to promote community development that makes use of their history and culture. The work tells the public the importance of local materials and records preservation regularly before a disaster strikes (Community Outreach Center, 2013).

Siryo-net (Kobe) makes a provisional catalogue of rescued materials and returns them after the locals and owners have restored their lives. At the time, we always explain the contents of the materials and the significance of the preservation. For example, for materials damaged by Typhoon Etau (2009), we worked with the Sayo Board of Education and the Sayo Community History Society members to rescue, provide first aid, and read the materials. The members have continued reading and transcribing the materials for publication (MATSUSHITA, 2013). In the case of the documents of the community association in Uruka, Shiso, ITAGAKI Takashi and YOSHIHARA Daishi, who belong to Siryo-net (Kobe), exhibited and explained the rescued documents at a community center, conducting joint research with the locals since then (Uruka Community History Editorial Committee, 2018).

In addition to undergraduates and postgraduates involved in cultural properties, many senior citizens participate in the volunteer activities of Siryo-net (Kobe) in providing first aid, organizing, and photographing damaged materials. Living in an urban area, many of the senior volunteers are "nomadic", who travel back and forth between the Hanshin area and the disaster-stricken areas, and have experienced different types of volunteer work such as removing the lining from sliding doors, reading old documents, and washing and joining earthenware. We hope to encourage the public to participate in Shiryo-Network activities by working with people with such diverse interests.

Conclusion

The foundation for responding to disasters is daily research, conservation practices, and the development of institutional and human networks. Our society has fewer children and more older adults. More than that: the population never ceases to decrease; more families have no heirs; more villages are disappearing; storms and floods become more frequent due to climate change; large-scale earthquakes continue to hit us. In short, it is no longer possible to force the individual locals (owners or property managers) to preserve the materials in the community.

The General Guidelines for the Conservation and Utilization of Cultural Properties call for conserving cultural properties by the "community as a whole". However, it is not enough to emphasize the negative aspects in this way, pointing out fewer people working on them due to the declining population. Some researchers study "public archaeology", arguing that archaeological sites are protected not just by researchers but by the public involvement and understanding of the significance (OKAMURA and MATSUDA, 2012). Similarly, the historical heritage remaining in a community gains more value through such involvement and understanding. How can we preserve private historical materials as "public property" through the involvement of diverse people? We will continue to learn from practices across Japan and deepen local historical materials studies with a focus on the rescue/utilization of damaged materials by the residents; at the same time, by making more people interested in and involved in the preservation and use of cultural properties, we will realize the participation by the "community as a whole" in the sense of giving meanings to and protecting cultural properties, and promote the creation of institutions and networks to maintain the communities.

Notes

1 For more information, see the website (http://siryo-net.jp/). (All the websites here last viewed on 23 January, 2024)

2 Hyogo Prefecture Board of Education. *Hyogo Prefecture Cultural Properties Disaster Prevention and Response Manual*. (https://www2.hyogo-c.ed.jp/hpe/bunka/cont_cate/兵庫県文化財防災・災害対応マニュアル/)

3 Agency for Cultural Affairs. *Regional Plans for the Conservation and Utilization of Cultural Properties, prepared by local governments*. (https://www.bunka.go.jp/seisaku/bunkazai/bunkazai_hozon/92040101.html)

4 Ministry of the Environment. *Disaster Waste Management Information*. (http://kouikishori.env.go.jp/guidance/guideline/)

5 Kasai City. *Kasai City Regional Disaster Prevention Plan (revised in 2021), Chapter 3: Disaster Emergency Response Plan* (https://www.city.kasai.hyogo.jp/uploaded/attachment/16252.pdf)

References

AMANO Masashi and GOTO Makoto (eds). *Chiikirekishibunkakeisho gaidobukku* [Guidebook for Community Hisorical Culture Inheritance]. Bungaku Report, 2022.

Community Outreach Center (Graduate School of Humanities, Kobe University) (ed). *"Chiikirekishiisan" no kanosei* [Potential of Community Historical Heritage]. Iwata-shoin, 2013.

Part 1

Japan Society of Material Cycles and Waste Management. *Saigaihaikibutsu kanri gaidobukku* [Guidebook for Disaster Waste Management]. Asakura Publishing, 2021.

Japanese Local History Research Association (ed). *Rekishishiryo no hozon to chihoshikenkyu* [Historical Material Preservation and Local History Studies]. Iwata-shoin, 2009.

KOHDZUMA Yohsei, TATEISHI Toru, and KODANI Ryusuke (eds). *Nyumon daisaigaijidai no bunkazaibosai* [Introduction to Cultural Property Disaster Prevention in the Age of Great Disasters]. Douseisha, 2023.

SHOMURA Misato. "Monobukai (Hokoku). Reiwa 2 nen 7 gatsu gou niokeru hisaianketo jissi to kekka nitsuite [Report at Monobukai. Questionnaire on July 2022 Heavy Rain Disaster]", in: *Museums in Gifu*, 187. Gifu Museum Association, 2020, p. 3.

MATSUSHITA Masakazu, KONO Mio (eds). *Suisonshiryo wo suku* [Rescuing Water-damaged Materials]. Iwata-shoin, 2009.

MATSUSHITA Masakazu. "2009 nen taifu 9 go hisaishiryo no hozen to katsuyo [Preservation and Utilization of Materials Damaged by Typhoon Etau (2009)]", in: *Saigai hukkou to shiryo* [Disasters, Restoration, and Materials], 2, 2013, pp. 27-38.

OKAMURA Katsuyuki and MATSUDA Akira. *Nyumon paburikku akeoroji* [Introduction to Public Archaeology]. Douseisha, 2012.

OKUMURA Hiroshi (ed). *Rekishibunka wo daisaigai kara mamoru.* [Protecting Historic Cultural Resources from Natural Disaster]. University of Tokyo Press, 2014.

OKUMURA Hiroshi, MURAI Ryosuke, and KIMURA Shuji (eds). *Chiikirekishiisan to gendaishakai* [Community Historical Heritage and Modern Society]. Kobe University Press, 2018.

OKUMURA Hiroshi. *Daishinsai to rekishishiryohozon* [Great Earthquakes and Historical Material Preservation]. Yoshikawa Kobunkan, 2012.

Sayo Community History Society. "Husuma no shitabarichosa kara shiru kyodo no rekishi [Community History Seen from Fusuma Undercoat Paper Research]", in: *Bulletin of Sayo Community History Society*, 6, 2018.

Siryo-net (ed). *Siryo-net katsudohokokusho* [Siryo-net Activity Report]. 2022.

Uruka History Compilation Committee. *Uruka no ayumi* [History of Uruka]. 2018.

Part **2**

Approaches to Materials Rescue and Preservation

Chapter 3

Rescuing Paper Materials

§ AMANO Masashi (National Museum of Japanese History)

Introduction

The paper materials covered in this chapter refer to records generated and accumulated by people during their lives. These materials, mainly written records, are made of various types of paper depending on the period and purpose, ranging from old documents with recognized historical and cultural value to everyday memos and journals. A vast, diverse group of materials remains across Japan.

While many public institutions such as museums, libraries, and archives hold paper materials, individuals have enormous materials at home, which they have inherited from ancestors to convey the history of the community and the family. They come in records maintained by organizations, personal diaries, writings, and books. However, in most cases, the owners treat them as a group, so in a disaster, those who rescue them must handle a massive amount at once; in such cases, they must accurately identify and treat water-damaged materials.

1. Rescuing Damaged Paper Materials

If a disaster damages the storage space, materials not contained in containers are at risk of being scattered. In addition, a tsunami or torrential rains can deteriorate paper materials—easily contain water—due to decay and mould, destroying some of the text and other material information, and even the materials themselves [See p. 38: Materials damaged by tsunamis (rescued on 23 March, 2012)].

Letters and documents are sometimes stored as a group of several items, tied together with string or in envelopes and bags. The custodian may have organized them by age and contents when storing them. In a regular organization of materials, the practitioner needs to record the condition and structure of the materials before transportation; it is fundamental to organize the materials while retaining their original shape and arrangement, as the storage space per se is essential information.

However, it is difficult to make such detailed records following these basic principles in a disaster because of the need to transport materials rapidly within a limited time. Therefore, it is desirable to record the on-site removal process with photographs or videos and keep them as reference information for later organization work. As for paper materials, it is not easy to determine whether they are historical at the on-site work stage. Usually, it is impossible to immediately grasp information on materials at the disaster site due to water damage or mud stains. Saving as many materials as possible requires removing them first and then sorting them out while grasping their contents during the first aid phase.

When handling, the practitioner should be careful to avoid damage or dissipation of the materials, as they are vulnerable when wet. Since most paper materials are groups of records accumulated by a house or organization, they are generally stored as a single group, often in boxes or containers. When transporting, it is necessary to keep them together as much as possible, and if stored in a container, move the container itself; if not, the practitioner needs to put them into plastic bags or cardboard boxes before transportation. The order should be maintained, but it is challenging to maintain detailed order under limited circumstances, so it is necessary to record the condition with photos or videos before transferring.

2. Condition Assessment and Temporary Storage

2.1. Grasping the Condition

Dealing with damaged paper materials requires the practitioner to confirm the presence or absence of breakage and water damage. Earthquakes can tear or break the paper materials, while water damage by rainfall, storm surges, and tsunamis sometimes destroy them, too. We should not leave them unattended, or water damage will lead to decay and mould, making it impossible to maintain and pass on the materials as historical ones. Therefore, the practitioner must check the following points.

(1) Approximate Number of Materials

Precisely counting the number of materials at the rescue stage is almost impossible: check the approximate number of items for planning the work process. Paper materials are usually lie in containers, so it is necessary to carry them as they are. Otherwise, put the materials into containers like cardboard boxes and count the number of the containers. In addition, check the forms of materials (books, documents, letters, postcards, coated paper) as best as possible.

(2) Water Damage

Determine the cause of water damage: rainfall, storm surge, tsunami, river, or moisture or leakage at the storage location. We can focus on dealing with the water in the case of rainfall or moisture. However, river or sea water may contain contaminants which need work other than drying.

Check the extent of the damage, whether entirely or partially, and see whether the water is so wet that it is dripping or has already started to dry.

(3) Damage level

Confirm mould, rot, odour, and paper adhesion. However, at this point, see only the extent of the damage seen by surface observation. Mould, decay, and odour can pose health hazards, so avoid putting your face too close to the material. Adherence can break the material if wet. Do not separate the sheets forcibly.

2.2. Temporary Storage After Transportation

Storing water-damaged materials at room temperature will cause them to rot; dry them as quickly as possible. If the total number is under 100, it may be possible to dry them immediately after transportation. However, many items need preparations for treatment, and immediate response becomes difficult. Frozen storage using a freezer is sometimes necessary during the preparation for treatment [See p. 40: Frozen-stored water-damaged materials].

The advantage of frozen storage is that it can control decay and deterioration, including biological damage. During frequent typhoons, high temperature and

Part 2

humidity aggravate the risk of rapid decay; temporary freezing and storage make it possible to adjust work timing, for example, to conduct full-scale work after the weather becomes cooler and drier.

If possible, pack each item in a plastic bag and frozen. However, if the items are in too poor a condition to separate one another, pack them in a plastic bag and frozen as a whole. Since it is not easy to immediately secure a large freezer, it is advisable to identify nearby facilities with large freezers before a disaster and ask them to cooperate in an emergency.

3. First Aid Measures for Damaged Paper Materials

Regarding the first aid measures of paper materials, many practical examples of disaster countermeasures and manuals are available in Japan and abroad, introducing detailed process techniques. This chapter focuses on the required response and the concept of first aid rather than presenting specific techniques.

One of the goals of such measures is to prepare for the data recording: count the number of materials and eradicate major concerns—decay, breakage, or mould—about storing and managing at average temperatures. Drying, cleaning, and adherence separation are necessary.

3.1. Drying

The drying process is the highest priority. However, we use different methods depending on the condition and scale of the materials and the number of practitioners. Methods practised or introduced are diverse and come into three patterns regarding methodology and purpose.

The first is air drying [See p. 43: Air-Drying (Hiroshima Prefectural Archives, 30 July, 2018)]. Practitioners spread the materials in a space out of direct sunlight and dry them with natural air or a circulator. This method is more cost-effective and technically feasible than others. However, considering the risk of spoilage, it is most effective when dealing with materials with only minor mould or stains and just beginning to dry out.

Next comes water absorption drying [See p. 43: Water Absorbent Drying (1): Wrapping materials in absorbent paper (Hiroshima Prefectural Archives. 11 December, 2018), Water Absorbent Drying (2): Degassing in a pouch (Hiroshima

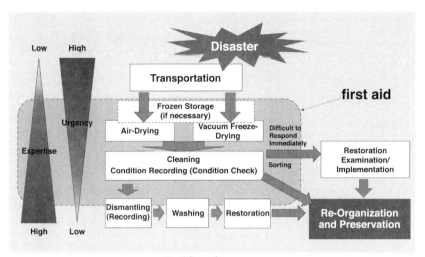

Workflow after rescue

Part 2

Prefectural Archives. December 12, 2018)]. Some researchers have recently proposed specific processes with various practical examples. However, the basic concept is the same: wrap materials in absorbent paper and squeeze out the moisture by applying pressure. This method is effective for materials containing a large amount of water. It can effectively extract water by wrapping each material or a single mass of materials in absorbent paper and applying pressure.

When handling large quantities, it is possible to squeeze out the moisture by placing the material in a pouch and deaerating it with a vacuum cleaner.

Water absorption drying alone takes a long. Therefore, this method is usually used for the preparation of air drying. When they can open the adhered paper roughly, the practitioners use air drying.

The third method is vacuum freeze drying. This method is large-scale, uses vacuum freeze-drying equipment, and effectively handles large volumes of materials (more than several thousand). In Japan, researchers used this method for the first time in 1992 in Soka, Saitama, to dry materials damaged by water due to a private house fire and firefighting activities. Since then, researchers have used this method for large-scale water damage, but it is not a silver bullet because coordination with facilities that own equipment is necessary and the cost is not low. Therefore, when we anticipate a large-scale disaster, we must coordinate in

Selecting an Appropriate Drying Method

	Air-Drying	Water Absorbent Drying	Vacuum Freeze-Drying
Cost	◎	○	△
Work Efficiency	△	△	◎
Versatility	◎	○	△
Anticipated Usage	Minimal mould and staining/minor water damage	Temporary treatment for air-drying; used when the material has a lot of moisture	In the case of extensive damage

advance with nearby museums and research institutions that own the equipment.

As described above, several methods are available for drying materials. However, selecting a technique that suits the situation and purpose is necessary rather than sticking to a specific one. Generally, when working manually, it is vital to avoid applying heat or other methods that may damage the materials and to avoid rapid temperature changes. In addition, coated paper sheets may adhere to one another too firmly if dried thoroughly.

In any case, it is often difficult to dry the materials completely using only one method. Combining several ways depending on the condition of the materials and the workforce is necessary.

For example, see the practice after the torrential rains in western Japan in 2018. The torrential rains caused water damage to several thousand paper materials (account books, postcards, letters, and paintings) stored in private homes in Hiroshima. The Hiroshima Prefectural Archive accepted these materials and carried out the drying process according to the following procedures.

(1) Classification

First, they classified the materials by genre (account books, pamphlets, postcards, letters, and paintings).

Then they sorted the classified materials into three categories: (a) those containing a large amount of water and are at a severe risk of decay, (b) those beginning to dry out, and (c) those already dry and with no evidence of water damage.

(2) Treatment

(a) They wrapped each item in a plastic bag, put them in a cardboard box to prevent odour and moisture, and stored them frozen.

(b) They prepared shelves and air-dried the materials in a well-ventilated place out of direct sunlight.

(c) They cleaned the materials after checking the mould and staining. At this stage, they focused on adherence separation described below rather than stain removal, confirming that they are dry to the depths.

(3) Thawing and Drying of Frozen Materials

For (a), since it was summer, they froze 17 cardboard boxes and stored them until when spoilage was less likely to progress. When winter came, they started the drying process.

Next, they removed the frozen materials from the plastic bags and wrapped each item with absorbent paper (newspaper).

Putting the materials into pouches, they observed the progress in deaeration. After about 1 to 2 days, the frozen materials returned to room temperature. Confirming that the paper absorbed the moisture, they took the materials out of the pouches, replaced the paper, and degassed them again.

Repeating the process several times to separate the adhered materials from one another, they finally dried them with air.

In this case, they could perform such a work process because they had ample space at the archive and could use freezers, and many workers helped them with the work. Depending on the location, it may be challenging to follow this process as the power supply and pouches may not be available. For example, we can prevent dehydration without pouches by wrapping the materials in absorbent paper, laying them on a flat surface, and placing something on top. The principle is the same, and selecting a method that does not damage the materials is crucial.

Condition As of 30 July

Partial air-drying at unpacking yard in Hiroshima Prefectural Archives
Groups of materials with different degrees of decay progression and dryness

[1] Cold Storage

[2] Continuing Air-Drying

[3] Dry Cleaning

10-13 December, 2018:
Thawing and Drying Operation

(1) Wrap each material with about 2 sheets of newspaper

(2) Put the material into a commercially available futon compression bag and vacuum it

Air-dryable material (pages open or surface dry)

(3) Leave it overnight, open, check the condition, and classify

Material with high water content (water soaks through to the touch)

Focus on adherence development
Make sure the material is dry to the inside

Store the materials temporarily after completion

Work process at Hiroshima Prefectural Archives during the 2018 torrential rains in Western Japan (Amano et al., 2019)

3.2. Purpose of Cleaning

Cleaning is necessary to make it possible to temporarily store the materials after drying. We have two options: dry cleaning (done in a dry condition) and wet cleaning (done with water). The purpose of cleaning is to remove any spoilage from the materials, but the extent of the treatment is an important issue. Since most paper materials are documents, the process includes separating the adhered materials to prevent them from sticking to one another.

If wetting causes the adhesion, we can separate them by carefully making a gap in the sticking area with a spatula or tweezers [See p. 48: Material adhered by water damage (sample)]. This process needs care and time: never run the risk of breakage, and try to open from a different part. The opening can be highly challenging if mud or mould causes the adhesion. It is a good idea to stop the work, document the current situation, pack the mouldy or dirty material to prevent it from scattering and focus on temporary storage to complete the emergency measures. In this case, it is desirable to remember that the first aid is only temporary and to proceed with arrangements for the repair plan.

Depending on the damage, the dried materials may still have mud, mould, or other contaminants [See p. 48: Material adhered by mould]. Therefore, it is necessary to remove mould spores on the surface by removing the mould with a cloth or paper dampened with ethanol. We can remove mud stains so that the process does not damage the materials, but dry cleaning has a limited effect. Moreover, brushing can run the risk of scattering. Therefore, during the dry cleaning stage, opening up adherence is better than struggling to remove all the stains. Health hazard measures are necessary for this work: wear industrial masks with high dust-proof performance and high particle collection efficiency to prevent inhalation of mould and other contaminants. In Japan, DS2 masks meet the National Inspection Standards set by the Ministry of Health, Labor and Welfare, as do N95 masks American standards and FFFP2 masks European standards, respectively.

Even if most of the work is adherence separation, mould and contaminants scatter to some extent, so sufficient ventilation is necessary. Install air purifiers to keep the work environment clean.

The first aid measures for paper materials aim to grasp the overall condition of the materials; completely separate the adherence caused by water damage; and prevent odour, mould, and stain spreading for temporary storage. As forcible attempts may result in large-scale damage, if even simple repair afterwards seems impossible, adherence separation should be temporarily suspended. Sometimes, wet cleaning may also be effective as an emergency measure to remove contaminants and odours. Usually, however, water-based cleaning requires the dismantling of the materials. In this case, too, it is a prerequisite to have the technology

Part 2

and equipment to handle the materials after cleaning. Depending on the damage, the dried materials may still have mud, mould, or other contaminants. In rescuing documents, we tend to focus on bringing the textual information to a readable state as quickly as possible. However, from a long-term perspective, it is effective for the preservation and inheritance of the materials to proceed in a step-by-step and systematic manner.

Conclusion

Paper materials remain in vast quantities throughout Japan, and when rescued, they are damaged, and the items come in large quantities. They are vulnerable to water and breakage and require an extremely rapid response from the rescue to the drying. Many practical reports are available, including those on familiar materials (refer to them for specific techniques and information). However, it is important to note that the work process should be simple and that the first aid should have specific goals. Thus, it will be essential to keep the following basic objectives in mind: (1) dry the materials to get out of the immediate crisis, (2) open the materials to get an overview, and (3) manage the materials to proceed toward a full-scale response. See the work mentioned in the reference for specific and simple ideas and methods in this process (YAMAGUCHI, 2022).

References

AMANO Masashi, YOSHIKAWA Keita, KATO Akie, NISHIMUKAI Kosuke, and SHIMOMUKAI Yuko. "Nishinihongou de suisonhigai wo uketa monjoshiryo kansoho no kento [Drying Methods for Water-Damaged Documents in Heavy Rains in Western Japan]". Poster presentation at Japan Society for the Conservation of Cultural Property 41st Conference, 2019.

MASUDA Katsuhiko. "Suigai wo uketa tosho monjono shinkutoketsukanso [Report on Vacuum-Freeze Drying of Books of Japanese Handmade-Paper]", in: *Hozonkagaku* [Conservation Science], 31, 1992.

National Institutes for Cultural Heritage founded the Cultural Heritage Disaster Risk Management Center (ed). *Fuyukabito karano jintai no bogo ni kansuru manyuaru* [Manual for Human Protection against Floating Mould]. https://chdrm.nich.go.jp/facility/2022/03/

post-49.html (last visited 25 Dec 2023)

NISHIMUKAI Kosuke and SHIMOMUKAI Yuko. "Hiroshima kenritsu monjokan niokeru 'Heisei 30 nen / gatsu gou' hisaibunsho no reukyu to hozenkatsudo [Rescue and Preservation of Materials Damaged by July 2018 Heavy Rains at Hiroshima Prefectural Archives]", in: *Bulletin of Hiroshima Prefectural Archives*, 15, 2020.

YAMAGUCHI Satoshi. "kamiseichiikishiryo wo nokosu gijutsu [Technologies for Preserving Paper-Based Local Materials]", in: AMANO Masashi and GOTO Makoto (eds). *Chiikirekishibunka keisho gaidobukku* [Guidebook for Inheritance of Local Historical Materials]. Bungaku Report, 2022.

Chapter 4

Rescuing Photographic Materials

▨ MATSUSHITA Masakazu (Kobe University)

Introduction

Historical materials, the preservation target of the Siryo-net (Kobe), are undesignated cultural properties in private ownership. The rescue of these documents, detailing the history of communities and families following the Great Hanshin Earthquake, focused on local records maintained by long-established families and neighborhood community associations. The aim was to understand the historical and geographical background essential for restoring areas affected by the disaster. Meanwhile, photographic materials are found in any typical household, and depict the history of each person, family, and community. Specifically, when the general public participated in rescuing and cleaning photographs damaged during the Great East Japan Earthquake and the Kii Peninsula flood disaster of 2011, volunteers in the affected areas were strongly impressed by the method as a means to rescue the records and "memories" of families and people.

Thus, in this Chapter, we specifically discuss rescuing photographic materials from among family records. Since the time when digital cameras and mobile phones became popular, photographic records have been stored as digital data in various recording media. Therefore, I should discuss the rescue, storage, and restoration of digital media as well. However, since the allocated space is limited, I will define photographic materials discussed in this Chapter as black-and-white and color prints of photographs (photographic paper), pocket photo albums, and adhesive mount photo albums. We will discuss the steps taken from the rescue,

Part 2

drying, and cleaning of such photographic materials that are stored in a typical household.

1. Rescue and Temporary Storage of Photographic Materials

Wind and water damage obviously affects documents, but following an earthquake, damaged buildings can experience water leakage. Subsequent rain, snow, and tsunamis can also cause water damage to materials. Since earthquakes often lead to fire, fire and associated water damage can occur. In any case, water damage of materials from disasters cannot be avoided; therefore, we discuss the rescue of water-damaged photographic materials.

As we saw in the areas affected by the 2011 great earthquake, all manner of materials affected by tsunamis and floods are washed away from their original locations. Some are recovered by the Japan Self-Defense Forces, but in the worst case, they are lost forever. Even if materials are not washed away, when silver halide prints (typical black-and-white and color photographs) and negatives are immersed in water for a long time, the image layer (gelatin, silver halide, and pigments) becomes deteriorated, leading to images disappearing, dissolving, discoloring, or fading [See p. 52 Photo. 1: Photographs with the image layer dissolved due to a long exposure to water]. Specifically, decomposition occurs rapidly in hot and humid disaster-affected sites during the summer, which makes decomposition of the gelatin layer on the surface of the photographs and biological damage by insects more likely. In the case of floods and tsunamis, domestic wastewater, salt from seawater, and so on become adhered to the surface of photographs, which further promotes deterioration.

While naturally drying water-damaged photographs, rescuers often discover that images are lost since some photographs have adhered to each other, albums are moldy, images have adhered to the protective film of albums, and so on [See p. 53 Photo. 2: Photographs that became adhered to the protective film of a pocket album due to tsunami damage].

Rescuing photographic materials happens more often by request than during patrols of affected areas. At rescue sites where the Siryo-net (Kobe) took the lead, such as during flood damage of Sayo, Hyogo Prefecture (Typhoon Etau, August 2009), a person found out about our rescue effort for damaged materials in a newspaper article and consulted us about photographs that had become adhered to water-damaged albums. We performed emergency treatment, such as cleaning the albums at the person's residence (removing mud), drying, and making copies by taking photographs with a digital camera. However, it was extremely difficult to perform tasks since there was no easy access to water and the missing floor provided no room to work [See p. 53 Photo. 3: Cleaning the damaged photographs in Sayo Town (Taken on October 12, 2009)]. Since 2011, we have been performing our tasks at locations with accessible water instead of the affected sites as much as possible.

As previously mentioned, if materials remain wet, deterioration of the surface will be promoted. To minimize the damage to the images, securing a freezer and temporary storage so that mold would not grow on photographic materials would be ideal. If a freezer cannot be secured, photographs should be dried in the shade using a fan, and so on. At temporary storage sites, humidity should be kept as low as possible.

When removing materials from the affected areas, a simple record of the current conditions, such as photographs of the damage, should be prepared. After confirming the number of damaged photographic materials (number of albums and so on), a written agreement of loan is created with the owners. Most important at such a point is a sufficient understanding by the owners regarding the treatment of damaged photographs. Since these tasks are mainly performed by volunteers with varying levels of skills, an agreement must be reached ahead of time that not all photographs will be fully restored, and photographic materials that are mostly of private information will be seen by many staff during the process. Specifically, cleaning makes a notable difference in how much of the image survives. In the case of heavily damaged photographs, cleaning will almost certainly remove the image layer. However, if left dirty, biological damage will further promote deterioration, thereby making the photographs impossible to view. Therefore, owners need to understand the advantages and disadvantages of each treatment.

2. Treatment of Disaster-Affected Photographic Materials

Below, we present the treatment policies for color photographs that have been water-damaged and soiled in floods and tsunamis by referring to the treatment of personal albums and photographs following the 2009 Typhoon Etau (flood damage of Sayo), tasks performed at Hiroshima Prefectural Archives following the torrential rain of August 2014, and tasks performed at Seki Cultural Properties Protection Center by the Gifu Museum Association following the Torrential Rains of July 2018.

The point to note while performing these tasks is not to inhale mold, mud, or dust when handling any other water-damaged materials. Therefore, we paid attention to the hygiene of volunteers by encouraging them to wear a dust mask and latex gloves, to practice hand washing and gargling, and to ventilate the rooms. Refer to the following in terms of materials used for the tasks [Photo. 4: An example of tools used to treat disaster-damaged photographic materials].

Depending on the damage to the photographs, these tasks were not always performed according to the procedure. For black-and-white and heavily damaged photographs, we recommend having professional photographers perform the repair.

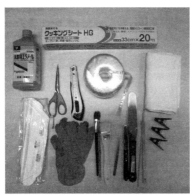

Photo. 4

Items required to remove a photograph from an album.

- Mask and rubber gloves (thin)
- Spatula (bamboo or rubber), brush, and tweezer
- Pallet knife, X-Acto knife, scissors, and cloth
- Ethanol (70%) for disinfection and spray bottle
- Newspaper and paper towel (for absorbing moisture)
- Parchment paper and rayon paper (for flattening)
- Digital camera for recording, air purifier, dehumidifier

Items required to clean photographs.

- Mask and rubber gloves (thin)
- Bucket for cleaning water (two: one for washing and one for rinsing)
- Small soft brush
- Sponge mat to drain water, towel, rack, or paper towel
- Clothespins to dry photographs, clips, laundry drying rope, and vinyl string
- Newspaper

From Hiroshima Prefectural Archives, *Doshasaigai de hisaishita arubamu shashin eno taishoho.*

2.1. Recording Current Conditions and Removing Photographs from Albums

(1) Numbering albums and taking photographs

As examples of damaged photographic materials, we consider cases of photographs stored in pocket albums and adhesive mount photo albums, and also cases where photographs are kept in a bundle that has become adhered together. In all cases, since these photographs must be dried, the first step is to remove one photograph at a time. However, when separating photographs, images may become damaged. In addition, to record the information such as the order of photographs in an album, before taking albums or bundles of photographs apart, the current conditions must be recorded using a digital camera.

Each album should be numbered, and where pages can be opened, the entire page should be photographed. Specifically, notes written or inserted in pocket albums and adhesive mount albums often preserve the information about the photograph and must be recorded along with the relevant photographs.

(2) Removing mud from albums

First, mud on the outside of albums is removed. Mud on the cover, back cover, and text block is removed using a bamboo spatula, brush, paper towel, or cloth. If possible, albums are wiped using a firmly wrung-out cloth or are disinfected with a paper towel soaked with ethanol. Subsequently, the album is opened one page at a time, and mud and soil are removed one page at a time.

Dirt on the protective film of pocket albums and the adhesive mount must be removed with a bamboo spatula or brush. However, if there is moisture between the protective film and the surface of the photograph, pressing firmly on the film could shift the image. Thus, cleaning must be done with utmost care.

(3) Photographing the conditions after the removal of mud

As each page of an album is opened, the entire page is photographed using a digital camera or scanned with a scanner. If possible, it would be ideal to record one photograph at a time. This is because, when the protective film is removed or cleaned, the image may be lost.

(4) Drying albums

If possible, albums should be dried with pages open and standing. Using an air purifier, dehumidifier, or a fan, albums should be dried in a clean temporary storage with low temperature and humidity and with as little direct sun as possible.

(5) Removing photographs

If the damage is severe, such as with dirty water inside of the protective film, photographs must be removed from pocket or adhesive mount photo albums to be dried. The protective film is removed by running a knife along the outline of a photograph [See p. 56 Photo. 5: Removing a photograph from an adhesive mount album (taken on September 8, 2014)]. If there is dirty water between the protective film and the photograph, and forcefully removing the film would damage the image, or if the image has transferred onto the protective film, the protective film should not be removed. When removing a photograph from adhesive mount albums, photographs are peeled using a pallet knife or bamboo spatula. If this is not possible, the mount should be separated into front and back sheets, removing the photograph with the mount still attached.

2.2. Cleaning and Drying Photographs

Soiled photographs removed from albums continue to deteriorate if left as they are; therefore, dirt must be removed. However, since the image may be lost through cleaning, a copy must be created by taking photographs with a digital camera before cleaning. When handling photographs, latex gloves and a dust mask are required.

(1) Cleaning

Soiled photographs are soaked in a tray filled with water. Soil from the image layer is gently removed using a small brush or the pad of a finger. At such time, a corner or an edge of the photograph should be dipped in the water to confirm that the water does not remove the image. Specifically, subjects such as people should not be washed too aggressively [See p. 57 Photo. 6: Cleaning a photograph with a small brush]. The back of photographs should be washed in the same manner. Attention should be paid to how photographs are held, such as pinching the edge of the photographs with fingers to avoid touching the image layer on the front. If the image layer of the photograph has already become dissolved and reds and yellows are marbled, the photograph should not be cleaned [See p. 57 Photo. 7: The surface of a marbled photograph].

(2) Rinsing

Lightly-washed photographs are placed in a tray with clean water and then lightly rinsed [See p. 57 Photo. 8: Rinsing a photograph].

(3) Draining water

Rinsed photographs are drained on paper such as newspaper or absorbent paper towel.

(4) Drying

Photographs are hung on a laundry rope or net using clothespins for drying. As much as possible, number tags for album and page numbers should be hung so that albums and orders are clear [See p. 58 Photo. 9: Drying a photograph]. If space for drying is limited, photographs could be placed flat on paper such as newspaper that absorbs water or placed on a slit board. If photographs have curled after drying, each photograph should be wrapped with rayon paper or parchment paper, then a weight placed on top to make them flat.

Dried photographs should be stored in a new pocket album if there is no stickiness. If stickiness remains after drying, a paper such as parchment paper is placed between the photographs before storing.

2.3. If Photographs Are Not Being Cleaned

As previously mentioned, if the image layer of a photograph has dissolved and appears marbled, the photograph should not be cleaned. In addition, if the damage to the album is limited (no mud on the surface, no odor), it should be dried without cleaning. If photographs can be removed from pocket albums or adhesive mounts, these photographs should be individually dried.

Generally, to maintain the subjects of photographs, the damage to the image layer should be kept to a minimum. Although photographs were not cleaned in the Hyogo and Gifu cases, there were requests to clean photographs in Hiroshima even if this damaged the images, since marbled images reminded people of the disaster. As such, the treatment policy for such private photographic materials will change based on the owners' wishes. Therefore, before starting the tasks, the treatment policy needs to be agreed on with the owner.

2.4. Challenges Associated with Cleaning Photographs

Deciding how to store severely damaged albums and photographs is difficult.

Wedding and birthday albums often have decorations on the surface, which should be maintained as much as possible. However, since damaged photographic materials deteriorate faster due to water damage, it is often difficult to keep the original. Therefore, along with the dried, damaged photographs, copies are prepared with a scanner or digital camera, and digital data are provided as DVD and so on. Furthermore, the Miyazaki Shiryo-Network used photographic data for digital restoration.

Photographs stored at typical households are not likely to receive government support, basically relying on volunteers. This is the same challenge as other undesignated cultural properties. However, in recent years, some companies have provided information on handling damaged photos or photography storage goods such as pocket albums. After the Torrential Rains of July 2018, the "Mono Committee" of the Gifu Museum Association led the treatment of damaged albums in Seki. Seki, Gifu Prefecture, mentioned the support they received on cleaning photographs and albums in their *Disaster Victim Support System Guidebook* that was distributed to disaster victims. Through this publication, disaster victims found out how to request cleaning of their damaged albums. These are cutting-edge attempts and model cases for the local government to handle disaster-affected photographic materials in the future[1]. Going forward, joint rescue activities by Shiryo-Networks, volunteer groups, governments, and companies with photography cleaning expertise will be effective.

Conclusions

Especially since printed photographs have gradually decreased since the start of 2000s, providing opportunities to inform people of how to give emergency treatment to photographs in albums from the pre-digital days is necessary. At the time of disasters, film companies and photography associations published guidelines on rescuing photos, and offered support, but it is also important to have the practical actions of volunteers who cleaned the photographs in the affected areas along with the rescue activities by Shiryo-Networks of each area[2].

By rescuing materials that are packed with people's "memories" and "attachments," perhaps we can help ease the sense of loss and help regain normal life for people in the affected areas. Furthermore, when people have lost loved ones and their homes in a disaster, having items that are associated with the family will give them strength for mental recovery. This has been documented in many disaster-affected areas. As photographic rescue following disasters becomes more known, we hope that it conveys the importance of preserving individual records not only during disasters but even during normal times, and the significance of our disaster-affected material preservation activities that save the history of families and communities.

Notes

1 Seki City prepared the *Disaster Victim Support System Guidebook* (First Edition) following Typhoon Lan of 2023, informing disaster victims of emergency treatment support for disaster-affected ancient documents and photographs.

2 A list of photograph cleaning volunteers is available on the Disaster-affected Photograph Cleaning Activities @ Nagareyama blog page (updated on September 20, 2023: https:// ameblo.jp/sunnyblog/entry-12744745156.html) (the website was last viewed on January 23, 2024).

References

Editorial Committee for the Rescue of Movable Cultural Properties (ed). *Dosanbunkazai kyusyutsu manyuaru* [Manual for Rescuing Movable Cultural Properties]. Kubapuro, 2012.

Hiroshima Prefectural Archives Leaflet, *Doshasaigai de hisaishita arubamu shashin eno taishoho* [How to Handle Albums and Photographs Damaged by Landslides] (December 2014), in: Hiroshima Prefectural Archives. *Hozonkanri koza* [Preservation and Management Lecture] (https://www.pref.hiroshima.lg.jp/site/monjokan/sub19.html)

ITAGAKI Takashi and KAWAUCHI Atsushi (eds). *Hanshin-Awaji daishinsaizo no keisei to juyo* [Formation and Acceptance of the Image of The Great Hanshin Earthquake]. Iwata-shoin, 2011.

SHOMURA Misato. "Heisei 30-nendo Monobukai Zigyo Sekishi no Suigai niokeru Osonarubamushashinto no senjoboranteia nitusuite no Hokoku [Report on the 2018 Mono Committee Project]", in: Gifu Museum Association "Koto Committee" (ed). *Museums in Gifu*, 183, Gifu Museum Association, September 2018, p. 3.

MATSUSHITA Masakazu. "Siryo-net (Kobe) ni yoru suison shashinshiryo no hozen okyusochi [Examples of Preservation and First Aid Measures for Photographs of Flood Damage by the Siryo-net (Kobe)]", in: *The Journal of the Society of Scientific Photography of Japan*, 84-2, 2021, pp. 72-79.

The Japan Society of Archives Institutes (ed). *Rekka suru sengoshashin* [Post-war Photographs that Deteriorate]. Iwata-shoin, 2010.

OHBAYASHI Kentaro. *Shashinhozon no jitsumu* [Photography Preservation Practices]. Iwata-shoin, 2010.

RD3 Project. *Hisaishashin kyusai no tebiki* [A Manual for the Salvage and Digitalization of extremely Damaged Photographic Materials. Kokusho Kankokai, 2016.

The 2018 Western Japan Torrential Rains "Preserve" Editing Team (ed). *Nokosu. Nishinihon Gousaigai* [Preserve. The 2018 Western Japan Torrential Rains]. ibid., 2021.

YAMAUCHI Toshiaki, "Taifuhigai ni atta shashinshiryo no hozon to shufuku ni tsuite [Preservation and Restoration of Photo Materials Damaged by Typhoons]", in: Kibi International University Research Advancement Center for Cultural Property (ed). *Kibi International University Research Advancement Center for Cultural Property Bulletin, Cultural Property Information Studies*, 4, March 2007, pp. 123-128; YAMAUCHI Toshiaki, "Shinkutoketsukansoho ni yoru shashinshiryo no hozonshori ni tsuite [Preservation and Treatment of Photographic Materials by Vacuum Freeze-Drying Method]" (ibid, pp. 129-134).

YOSHIKAWA Keita and YOSHIHARA Daishi. "Hiroshimadoshasaigai ni yoru hisaishashin arubamu no hozenkatsudo, "Preservation of Photo Albums Damaged by Hiroshima Landslides". The Siryo-net (Kobe) *Newsletter*, 77, December 2014, pp. 9-10.

Chapter 5

Folk Implements Rescue

▨ HIDAKA Shingo (National Museum of Ethnology)

Introduction

Cultural property rescue is an initiative undertaken by the Agency for Cultural Affairs to urgently preserve cultural properties, mainly arts and crafts, that natural disasters have damaged and to prevent them from being disposed of, dissipated, or stolen[1]. In the rescue of cultural properties, folk implements are the subject of many requests for help. These items originally existed in large numbers, so as a cultural property group, they provide an overview of the living culture of that community. Therefore, cultural property rescue activities will rescue enormous numbers of implements. Despite the number of requests for help, however, we need to understand folk implements more generally, regarding them as cultural properties of great importance at a local level, and herein lies a discrepancy. When a disaster threatens to wipe out a local community altogether, for the disaster victims, these folk implements their ancestors have handed down become an indispensable anchor for the identity of the disaster-affected community and the victims themselves. They endure as a representation of everyday life or the memory of the lives of ancestors, and in doing so, these folk implements also provide the whole community and the residents with a new opportunity to think about communal regeneration. This chapter focuses on folk implements rescue conducted as a part of cultural property rescue (rescue, temporary storage, and emergency treatment) after the Great East Japan Earthquake. Note that in culture property rescue, the activity's main pillars are "rescue, temporary storage, and

Part 2

emergency measures". Still, this chapter gives specific examples of treatment, so it uses the term "emergency treatment".

1. Disaster-Affected Folk Implements Rescue

Following the Great East Japan Earthquake, the rescue of folk implements first started with searching for buried items while removing the broken glass scattered across the floor and clearing away the sludge that the tsunami had brought with it. It was physically exhausting work, which soon had the goggles I wore clouded from perspiration and my body drenched with sweat [See p. 65 Photo. 1: Folk implements rescue at a disaster-hit museum (June 2011, taken by WADAKA Tomomi)]. I often couldn't tell whether I was handling folk implements or just rubble and detritus. The value of folk implements as cultural properties lies in their ability to preserve the memories of everyday life. In a sense, this scene of destruction, where everyday objects had become nothing but rubble and detritus, was perhaps their fate. As I struggled to judge whether I was handling rubble, detritus, or folk implements, I decided to rescue everything. If you discarded it, it would be gone forever; if it later turns out to be rubble or detritus while sorting, you could discard it. A worker's capacity for judgment inevitably diminishes when working in the harsh environment experienced during post-disaster rescue activities. Thus, it is necessary to err on the side of caution and rescue anything that could be a folk implement. Rescued folk implements are covered in dirt to varying degrees from the dust generated by the rubble [See p. 65 Photo. 2: Example of folk implements covered with dust following the disaster (February 2010, taken by HASHIMOTO Sachi)]. In some cases, disaster-affected cultural properties are no longer in their original shape due to damage from the impact of falling over or falling from a height or the shelf on overturning [See p. 65 Photo. 3: Folk implements damaged and no longer in the original form (June 2011, taken by the author)]. To find folk implements in this condition among the rubble and detritus, it seems essential for the rescue team to include curators from museums and art galleries, who are used to dealing with cultural properties daily.

Next, let us see the system for rescuing disaster-affected folk implements. Rescue is an activity which, above all, requires many people. Since the Great Hanshin-Awaji Earthquake, several big disasters have repeatedly hit Japan and damaged cultural properties. In response, a system has been established for staff from cultural property preservation institutions in addition to curators from public and private museums and art galleries, to assemble at disaster sites. Experience in rescuing disaster-affected cultural properties and museum materials has accumulated, leading to excellent results. However, the teams carrying out this work consist of curators and researchers from all over Japan with various areas of expertise. Therefore, if the team members work according to their value judgments and areas of expertise, their efforts would become disjointed, and achieving the overall objectives would not be possible. It is, thus, necessary to appoint a team leader in charge of the whole rescue site who can devise a work plan and give instructions to the rest of the team.

The team leader's job starts with a preliminary survey of the rescue site [See p. 65 Photo. 4: Preliminary survey before rescue work (June 2011, taken by WADAKA Tomomi)]. The team leader works out an effective plan to avoid accidents. Cultural property rescue takes place during the restoration phase of a disaster-hit area, so much of its road network is still in disrepair. The rescue activities following the 2011 earthquake were carried out in just such conditions, and it would generally take about three hours to get to the site—a journey time that would be inconceivable in normal times. It directly impacts the ability to secure enough working time at the site. In the preliminary survey, it was essential to devise a thorough plan that considers how to achieve results from the rescue activities most effectively within a limited timeframe.

Before the actual work begins, the team leader must first hold a pre-meeting to explain the objectives and plan to all [See p. 65 Photo. 5: Pre-work meeting in June 2011 (taken by KAWAMURA Yukako)]. If all the team members did not share the goals, work plan, and the work objectives for that specific day, it would be impossible to obtain effective results. Supervising the site is necessary to ensure regular breaks during working hours and to secure the site's safety to avoid accidents and prevent injury or illness. In particular, it is essential to adhere strictly to instructions about breaks. As described above, the rescue site is a harsh environment. Not taking proper breaks increases the risk of dehydration and heat stroke. When this happens, you ultimately rely on disaster victims' help: you need to take breaks to rest and regain your composure. One of the team leader's most important roles is to be aware of this and to share that awareness with the rest of

Part 2

the team. When I was team leader during the rescue activities following the Great East Japan Earthquake, we took 10-minute breaks every 40 minutes. As a result, no one got injured or sick, and we were able to carry out effective rescue activities.

Finally, the team leader writes a daily report of the rescue each day for the benefit of the next team leader. The area hit by the 2011 catastrophe was vast, and circumstances occasionally required a change of team leader. It is necessary to establish a system for doing a proper handover of the work by maintaining a daily report.

2. Temporary Storage and Sorting/Recording

Temporary storage means moving cultural properties from the rescue site [See p. 68, Photo. 6: Transporting items to temporary storage (June 2011, taken by WADAKA Tomomi)] and storing them safely [See p. 68 Photo. 7: Putting items in temporary storage (June 2011, taken by the author)]. The term "safe" in this context includes protection from wind and rain and security in terms of crime prevention measures, such as locking and managing the storage facility.

With temporary storage, the person in charge of the disaster-affected museum or other cultural property storage facility will only be present for a limited amount of time, so moving all cultural properties to the storage site in one go is necessary. You have no time for "art packaging" when transporting large quantities of folk implements in a limited timeframe. Apart from fragile items, therefore, all other items with a reasonable degree of robustness should be loaded onto the truck bed as far as possible [See p. 68, Photo. 8: Loading up a truck with as many disaster-affected folk implements as possible (July 2011, taken by the author)]. In addition, when transporting the disaster-affected folk implements, the truck drivers are not specialist drivers but people like the author, who are not used to this kind of work. The roads are often unstable, and the destination is some 50-100km away, so great care is required to avoid accidents. In these difficult conditions, expecting one person to manage all the driving safely on their own is unreasonable. Securing several drivers, taking turns driving, and being ever-mindful of safety while on the move is of great importance.

The work from rescue to temporary storage requires swift action within a limited timeframe. However, we should remember that we are dealing with many folk implements temporarily moved from their designated locations. It is also essential to keep a record of moved items. Suppose you have no record of the number of items of cultural property X at facility A. In that case, it will become impossible to confirm the number of rescued folk implements during subsequent rescue activities. Therefore, while doing the work of temporary storage, it is necessary to sort and record the items to confirm their overall number—even if it is only a rough count. However, it is not possible to draw up a perfect list when transporting disaster-affected cultural properties within a limited timeframe. In the case of the Great East Japan Earthquake, we counted the number of stacking boxes containing the rescued folk implements. To keep a record of which folk implements had been packed into the boxes, we took a photo of the contents of each box and saved the image data with the number assigned to the corresponding box [See p. 68 Photo. 9: Sorting materials using stacking boxes (May 2011, taken by the author)]. When we later came to perform the emergency treatment, we were finally able to sort and record each item.

Next, let us discuss the temporary storage environment. In addition to damage from the disaster, the wind, rain, and dust deteriorate folk implements. They are exposed to elements while rescued and moved to the temporary storage site, which is why we have to rescue, temporarily store, and perform emergency treatment as quickly as possible. However, the temporary storage site is not an environment where we can regulate the temperature, humidity, and light, like the storage area of a museum. In a large-scale disaster, various facilities sustain damage; we need to use most of the locations and environments that are still in relatively good condition as evacuation shelters for disaster victims and storage areas for relief supplies. Therefore, the locations provided as temporary storage sites for disaster-affected folk implements are not ideal for evacuation shelters or storage sites for relief supplies, and they are very often empty classrooms in schools or the entrance halls of unused facilities [See p. 68 Photo. 10: Temporary storage site at facility not currently in use (July 2011, taken by the author)]. Thus, trying to stabilize the environment at the temporary storage site is of importance. The places provided as temporary storage sites during disasters tend to have large windows and doorways, and the air conditioning system rarely functions. The large windows and doorways make the environment susceptible to the influence

Part 2

of the outside air. It can give rise to large fluctuations in temperature and humidity, which increase the risk of embrittled folk implements becoming damaged or deformed. Even small gaps in the rails, which the sashes for opening and closing large windows and doorways are attached to, can allow dust into the room, which then gets on the folk implements. These gaps can also allow insects to enter and feed on the folk implements, creating an environment susceptible to biological damage. Furthermore, the folk implements are exposed to other deterioration factors, such as the ultraviolet rays from sunlight coming through the large windows.

It is desirable to work with a conservation scientist familiar with museum environments to tackle these challenges. Conservation science is a field of research that takes an academic approach to conserving cultural properties, including museum environments. "Conservation of Museum Collections" was designated as a mandatory module (mandatory in FY2012) in the Course for Prospective Museum Workers in the Ministerial Ordinance Partially Amending the Ordinance for Enforcement of the Museum Act published on 30 April 2009; around this time, conservation science research results on the museum environment were published in various forms[2]. These publications itemize factors significant for temporary storage sites, such as temperature and humidity control and measures against biological damage, so we should refer to them to ensure the preparation of the best possible environment.

3. Emergency Treatment for Disaster-Affected Folk Implements

Emergency treatment is work to halt the deterioration of damaged cultural properties. When earthquakes or floods damage cultural properties, what we can observe first is surface contamination from dust, sludge, and sand. The impact of the disaster itself and damage sustained from falling or from shelves overturning can also be seen. The dust, sludge, or sand contaminating the surface attracts moisture, which in turn can encourage the growth of mold. Furthermore, this dirt makes it difficult to handle the folk implements themselves and significantly hampers the work of trying to sort them. Therefore, the first emergency treatment is cleaning to remove the substances that have soiled the disaster-affected folk implements [See p. 71 Photo. 11: Emergency treatment for disaster-affected folk implements (August 2011, taken by the author)]. However, this cleaning work is the absolute minimum. An important factor in rescuing as many disaster-affected cultural properties as possible is reducing the time spent on each folk implement. Since overly meticulous work will limit the number of items that can receive emergency treatment, the team leader must supervise the overall work while closely monitoring how the members implement the treatment. Cleaning the materials as part of emergency treatment, I distributed six cleaning kits to the members: a small, medium, and large paintbrush, a small and large scrubbing brush, and one type of calligraphy brush [See p. 71 Photo. 12: Cleaning set]. Of course, we may use fewer varieties of brush depending on the disaster situation. We then set a rule that the team should only do cleaning work using this cleaning kit and no additional cleaning. The curators and conservation specialists who work daily with museum materials and cultural properties probably felt that this cleaning work needed to be improved. However, we persuaded them that work requiring specialized skills, such as full-scale cleaning or fixing damaged parts using adhesives, would be carried out in the next phase of conservation and resto-ration activities.

Next, let us introduce the specific emergency treatment activities carried out after the Great East Japan Earthquake. In this case, sea sand contaminated the surfaces of the disaster-affected folk implements. Brushing with a scrubbing brush easily removes the sand once it is dried. Therefore, we brushed the sand off many disaster-affected folk implements using as little water as possible while sticking to the abovementioned rule: just removing what we could by using the cleaning kit.

The 2011 catastrophe was a tsunami disaster, a type of disaster I had not experienced before. A particular concern was that the salt content in the seawater would be a major cause of deterioration for the disaster-affected folk implements. Researchers tackled this problem for cultural properties, including excavated ar-tifacts, natural history objects, and ancient documents, by performing emergency desalting treatment at the cultural property rescue site. They hold training ses-sions on this kind of treatment, and the methodology is publicly available online. I also wanted to know whether desalting treatment is necessary for the folk im-plements affected by the earthquake. However, given the limited time they would have been exposed to seawater during the tsunami, it was necessary to carefully prioritize when removing the salt content that would have permeated during that time.

Compared to other cultural properties, folk implements are generally stable during regular times, mainly because people have used them until relatively recently in everyday life or for work. As they have been manufactured for practical use rather than for being admired as works of art, they have a certain degree of inherent durability. Therefore, the folk implements that seem to need desalting treatment for conservation and restoration are items exposed to salt water daily, such as fishing gears or salt-producing or soy sauce-manufacturing equipment regularly exposed to high salt concentrations.

In 2011, when I observed the condition of the folk implements affected by the Great East Japan Earthquake, none at that stage showed signs of deterioration due to salinity. Indeed, I felt that the desalting treatment would pose a more significant problem: that of the environment where researchers perform the treatment. Folk implements come in various shapes and sizes. While most are wooden, some are of various materials, including metal, paper, and lacquer. In addition, a large number of items need to be processed together at the same time. When desalting folk implements, therefore, it is necessary to observe the condition of multiple constituent materials. It is also necessary to prepare a large water tank [See p. 72 Photo. 13: Desalting tank for large artifacts (August 2012, taken by the author)] or lots of smaller water tanks [See p. 72 Photo. 14: Multiple desalting tanks for different types of artifacts (August 2012, taken by the author)] to perform mass treatment. In other words, when judging whether to carry out desalting treatment, we must consider whether we can prepare for this work environment. In addition, when immersing wooden objects in desalting solution, they need to be dried out after the treatment. When wood that has absorbed large amounts of water is dried out too quickly, it can shrink, become deformed, or crack. Therefore, preparing a place to dry the wood slowly over a certain period after the desalting treatment is necessary. Furthermore, metal parts will rust if immersed in water, so a space for performing anti-rust treatment is also required. Having managed to rescue items from the disaster site and transport them to the temporary storage site, it did not seem feasible to solve the problems mentioned above within the limited space available.

For the folk implements affected by the 2011 earthquake, we ultimately decided not to carry out desalting treatment; instead, we prioritized cleaning work focusing on removing sand and sludge adhered to the materials by the tsunami. However, that is not to say we shelved the salt issue altogether. After concentrating on the cleaning work in 2011, from February 2012, we carried out preliminary experiments in desalting, and then from March onwards, we provided technical instruction mainly within Miyagi Prefecture for full-scale desalting treatment [See p. 73 Photo. 15: Technical instruction for desalting treatment (2014, taken by WADAKA Tomomi)] [3].

Finally, I would like to summarize the procedures and ideas for emergency treatment of disaster-affected folk implements. When cleaning such implements in emergency treatment, the basic idea is to remove as much dirt as possible with cleaning tools but without water. However, in the case of items where mud has adhered to the surface and cannot be easily removed, or folk implements with complicated shapes where mud or sand has filled the nooks and cracks, you can immerse them in a tank filled with water [See p. 74 Photo. 16: Cleaning by soaking in a water tank (May 2011, taken by KAWAMURA Yukako)] or remove the dirt using running water [See p. 74 Photo. 17: Cleaning with running water (May 2011, taken by KAWAMURA Yukako)]. When using water for cleaning, it is necessary to prepare a space at the work site for drying the folk implements after washing them. If you clean using water in a work environment with high humidity or where there is no space for drying the folk implements, it can lead to outbreaks of mold, which then take time to deal with. For this reason, we should carefully decide whether to use water for cleaning.

In addition, note that emergency treatment is not an opportunity to show off one's technical skills. The priority should always be to stabilize as many folk implements as possible. When performing cleaning and other emergency treatment, we should always be mindful of the necessary work at any given moment and how that work will connect to the next phase of the work.

Conclusion

Based on the experience of dealing with folk implements in the immediate aftermath of the Great East Japan Earthquake, we have considered the main pillars of activity of cultural property rescue, namely rescue, temporary storage, and emergency treatment. However, this work alone is insufficient for the folk implements to be reborn as items handed down to future generations as local cultural properties. The work carried out after this point is also important.

That work involves conserving disaster-affected cultural properties deemed needing full-scale restoration by specialists [See p. 75 Photo. 18: Restoration of disaster-affected folk implement by specialist (June 2010, taken by HASHIMOTO Sachi)] and preserving folk implements at restored museums and other facilities [See p. 75 Photo. 19: Permanent storage of disaster-affected cultural properties (November 2010, taken by the author)]. The next step is to compile the findings from the cultural property rescue activities so far and specialist research activities at the museums and other facilities where the cultural properties are permanently stored, and link this to activities where those results are published and utilized [See p. 75 Photo. 20: "Rescuing History and Culture" Special Exhibition of disaster-affected folk implements (July 2010, taken by the author)]. Through these research and utilization activities, museums should fully use their function to firmly embed an understanding among the locals that folk implements are an inherent part of their community's identity. Based on this, by developing activities to think about how to mitigate against the next disaster together with the whole community [See p. 75 Photo. 21: Discussion forum with the locals on cultural property disaster prevention (November 2010)], I think it is possible for folk implements to be reborn as cultural properties the community will pass down to future generations.

References

1 Cultural Heritage Disaster Risk Management Center. *On Cultural Heritage Rescue.* https://ch-drm.nich.go.jp/disaster_response/rescue.html (last visited 21 July 2023)

2 MURAKAMI Takashi, *Hakubutsukan no tenjikankyo* [Museum Exhibition Environments], in: OKADA Fumio, Kyoto University of Art and Design (eds), *Bunkazai no tame no hozonkagaku nyumon* [Introduction to Conservation Science for Cultural Properties], pp. 314-325, Kadokawa, Tokyo, 2022.

MIURA Sadatoshi, *Shuzokonai no hokan kankyo* [Environment within the storage space], in: op. cit., pp. 323-33, Kadokawa, Tokyo, 2002.

MIURA Sadatoshi, SANO Chie, KIGAWA Rika, *Bunkazai hozon kankyo gaku* [Cultural

Property Storage Environment Studies], Asakura Publishing, Tokyo, 2004.

Tokyo National Research Institute for Cultural Properties (ed), *Bunkazai no hozonkankyo* [Storage Environment for Cultural Properties], Chuokouronbijutsu Shuppan, Tokyo, 2011.

ISHIZAKI Takeshi (ed), *Hakubutsukan shiryo hozonron* [Theory of Preservation of Museum Materials], Kodansha, Tokyo, 2012.

HONDA Mitsuko, MORITA Minoru (eds), *Hakubutsukan shiryo hozonron* [Theory of Preservation of Museum Materials], Foundation for the Promotion of the Open University of Japan, Tokyo, 2012.

INAMURA Tetsuya, HONDA Mitsuko (eds), *Hakubutsukan shiryo hozonron shintei* [Theory of Preservation of Museum Materials (revised edition)], Foundation for the Promotion of the Open University of Japan, Tokyo, 2019.

3 HIDAKA Shingo, *Saigai to bunkazai: aru bunkazai kagakusha no shiten kara* [Disasters and Cultural Properties: a Cultural Property Scientist's Perspective], Osaka: The Senri Foundation, 2015.

Part 2

Chapter 6

Rescuing "Works of Art"

▨ OHBAYASHI Kentaro (Kyoto University of the Arts)

Introduction

We use the term "Works of art" to refer to items such as paintings, calligraphic works, carvings, and handicrafts that have obtained artistic appraisal. The term is also employed to indicate items that have a certain commercial value, however this definition is regarded as imprecise. Certainly, items that have been officially recognized as cultural assets are easy to identify; however, this does not imply that such artworks are the only ones that should be saved. In some cases, cultural heritage items that have not been officially designated as such are still given appraisal for their historical or artistic value, as these are handed down for generations and have an emotional value for the owner's. Certain reproducible items, such as woodblock prints and photographs, that are also highly praised as works of art. When a disaster strikes and artworks get damaged or lost, it is difficult in pragmatic sense to use these as criteria for classification (triage). As such, we will vaguely bundle them all together under the definition of "Works of Art" (include works that have not currently received artistic acclaim and works that can be reproduced).

Furthermore, this chapter will focus on Oriental paintings and calligraphy with mounting. Regarding sculptures, crafts, and Western paintings such as oil paintings, the materials and structures are very different, so I hope that a report will be written by an expert on each in the future.

Part 2

1. The Materials and Structure of Japanese Paintings and Calligraphic Works

1.1. Paintings and Calligraphic Works with Mounting

Mounted works of art is a term that is not limited to any specific designation and, in principle, it refers to paintings and calligraphic works that have mounting. In other words, the work itself is the painting or calligraphy written or drawn on silk or paper (which is regarded as the main body of the work). The silk or paper is reinforced by pasting a backing paper on the back, and is mounted (=assembled) into forms such as sliding doors, folding screens, scrolls, bookletsthe (we usually use the term "binding" when assembling a booklet, but in this chapter, we use "mounting" instead), hanging scrolls, and picture albums, depending on the purpose for partitioning or reading or appreciation. The most distinctive feature of these forms is that the main paper is pasted and integrated with the mounting (lining and other parts). In other words, serious repairs for this type of works involve remove the paper lining from the main body, repairing the main body, giving it backing support, and shaping each part of the mounting. In the case of paintings and calligraphic works that have been handed down over a long period of time, multiple repairs should be done up to the present day. However, in an overwhelmingly large number of cases, the mounting is remodeled during repair, meaning the original mounting is not handed down. Mounting can be thought of as a garment that enhances the main body and, as it gets old and dirty, it needs to be replaced. Therefore, making new mounting is considered common sense, as repairing and reusing the old mounting represents a process that is too complex. This is precisely what happens in the tradition of paintings and calligraphic works in Japan. Unmounted items are also sometimes included in the category of works of Art.

1.2. Repairing the Main Body

The base for the main body is made of silk or paper; the majority of these works are on paper, but the status of the works is higher for those on silk. On this base material, the calligraphy or painting is expressed with ink or paint colors, respectively. The base and coloring materials (ink or paint) are usually fixed with some kind of adhesive, as it is essential for it to keep its adhesive strength. The goal of main body repair is to improve the flatness of the base material, the adhesive strength of the coloring material and the base material, and remove foreign substances on the surface so that the color and quality of the ink or paint can be clearly seen. To improve the flatness of the base material it is necessary to compensate for any missing parts and return it to a single-sheet structure; if the shape cannot be improved with the base material alone, it will need reinforcement from its backing. To ensure the strength of adhesion of the paint, peeling needs to be prevented. Further, to make the colors clearer, it is essential to clean the surface to remove or reduce impurities or stains.

1.3. Preparing the Mounting

After repairing the main body, the process for assembling the backing and the mounting begins; specifically, for works on silk, the most important process in repairing is replacing the backing (removing the old backing paper and affixing the new one). Some schools of thought include the removal of the first backing paper that is directly adhered to the main body as part of main body repair. Afterward, each form is assembled; however, since these differ greatly depending on the form, the structure and process of hanging scrolls and folding screens is shown as a representative example [Fig.1: Hanging scroll structure and 2: Folding screen repair process].

These show the general process lined up in order. Depending on the work's materials or state of deterioration, the process may involve more steps or have the order changed. For example, the "Limited Moisture Method for the first lining removal" may be used, in which a front support is added to the surface of the work and the first backing paper is removed. Furthermore, depending on the state of the paint, peeling prevention may be carried out not only in the first half of repairs, but also after treatment using water. Here, the tasks of recording and taking photographs during and after repairs are omitted.

For any of these forms, it is clear that, unless one is an expert, it is extremely difficult to assemble the mounting, even when following a manual. This is to say nothing of the fact that, in main body repairs, it would be unthinkable to grasp the materials and structure, scrutinize the level of deterioration and damage, and carry out proper treatment without an abundant degree of experience. Furthermore, the only professionals who are able to achieve long-term preservation

Part 2

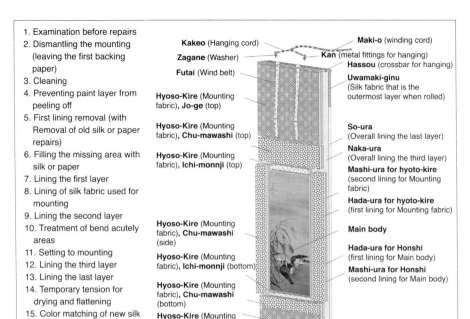

1. Examination before repairs
2. Dismantling the mounting (leaving the first backing paper)
3. Cleaning
4. Preventing paint layer from peeling off
5. First lining removal (with Removal of old silk or paper repairs)
6. Filling the missing area with silk or paper
7. Lining the first layer
8. Lining of silk fabric used for mounting
9. Lining the second layer
10. Treatment of bend acutely areas
11. Setting to mounting
12. Lining the third layer
13. Lining the last layer
14. Temporary tension for drying and flattening
15. Color matching of new silk or paper repairs
16. Final assembly of mounting
17. Conservation report

Kakeo (Hanging cord)
Zagane (Washer)
Futai (Wind belt)
Hyoso-Kire (Mounting fabric), **Jo-ge** (top)
Hyoso-Kire (Mounting fabric), **Chu-mawashi** (top)
Hyoso-Kire (Mounting fabric), **Ichi-monnji** (top)
Hyoso-Kire (Mounting fabric), **Chu-mawashi** (side)
Hyoso-Kire (Mounting fabric), **Ichi-monnji** (bottom)
Hyoso-Kire (Mounting fabric), **Chu-mawashi** (bottom)
Hyoso-Kire (Mounting fabric), **Jo-ge** (bottom)

Maki-o (winding cord)
Kan (metal fittings for hanging)
Hassou (crossbar for hanging)
Uwamaki-ginu (Silk fabric that is the outermost layer when rolled)
So-ura (Overall lining the last layer)
Naka-ura (Overall lining the third layer)
Mashi-ura for hyoto-kire (second lining for Mounting fabric)
Hada-ura for hyoto-kire (first lining for Mounting fabric)
Main body
Hada-ura for Honshi (first lining for Main body)
Mashi-ura for Honshi (second lining for Main body)
Jiku-gi (wooden shaft bar)
+Jiku-syu (shaft head)

Fig.1

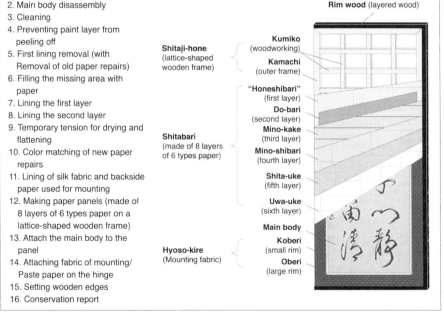

1. Examination before repairs
2. Main body disassembly
3. Cleaning
4. Preventing paint layer from peeling off
5. First lining removal (with Removal of old paper repairs)
6. Filling the missing area with paper
7. Lining the first layer
8. Lining the second layer
9. Temporary tension for drying and flattening
10. Color matching of new paper repairs
11. Lining of silk fabric and backside paper used for mounting
12. Making paper panels (made of 8 layers of 6 types paper on a lattice-shaped wooden frame)
13. Attach the main body to the panel
14. Attaching fabric of mounting/ Paste paper on the hinge
15. Setting wooden edges
16. Conservation report

Shitaji-hone (lattice-shaped wooden frame)
Shitabari (made of 8 layers of 6 types paper)
Hyoso-kire (Mounting fabric)

Rim wood (layered wood)
Kumiko (woodworking)
Kamachi (outer frame)
"Honeshibari" (first layer)
Do-bari (second layer)
Mino-kake (third layer)
Mino-shibari (fourth layer)
Shita-uke (fifth layer)
Uwa-uke (sixth layer)
Main body
Koberi (small rim)
Oberi (large rim)

Fig.2

of works at the cultural asset level are mounting technicians who specialize in assembling mounting and who are capable of designing and executing repair specifications in line with the principles and general rules of cultural asset repair. However, only a limited number of such specialists exist. It would be ideal for such specialists to be involved in everything from rescue during disasters, to emergency procedures and serious repairs. However, in Japan, professionals with this kind of knowledge, experience, and skills mainly belong to private organizations such as companies; therefore, it is quite difficult to have them on site from the time a disaster strikes. Nevertheless, the longer these tasks are postponed, the more likely it is for the work to have zero chances of being handed down with an official valuation as a work of art. This chapter will examine what can and should be done on site during disasters to avoid this consequence.

2. Works of Art as Victims of Disaster

From the standpoint of a repair technician, what is important is the state of the main body and the type and degree of deterioration, regardless of the type of disaster the artwork has suffered. This chapter will start by listing the nature of deterioration and damage that characterizes each type of disaster.

2.1. Earthquakes

When an area containing artworks is hit by an earthquake, physical deterioration caused by items falling from high places is assumed, as well as the artwork being crushed under collapsing structures. The main types of damage to main bodies are Damage caused by thrusting, snapping, missing parts, scratches, as well as damage to the mounting (hanging scroll, folding screens, sliding screens) [See p. 81 Photo. 1: Perforation, scratches (sliding screen owned by C Family in Ofunato City)]. However, earthquake damage is not limited to what happens during the initial disaster. It often happens that infrastructures are lost in the disaster, or that humidity and temperature can no longer be controlled, leading to biological damage from mold. Further, if buildings are destroyed, water damage to artworks can occur due to rain and water tank leaks.

2.2. Flooding, Tsunami (High Water), and Landslides

The deterioration caused by flooding, tsunamis, and landslides is classified under water damage. They differ from water leaks because works of Art themselves may go missing or be lost due to entire buildings being swept away, or the materials being dragged outdoors. Furthermore, Japanese painting and calligraphic works use paper and silk as base materials. This means that most of them use water-soluble adhesives as color fixing agents and many of the components of the mounting (including the lining) are assembled by being adhered with water-soluble wheat starch. Given this, being immersed in water is greatly damaging to these artworks. This damage is further compounded if it happens over a long period of time. The paint layer may suffer advanced peeling and, if the base material is paper, the hydrogen bonds could break, weakening it. If a hanging scroll is exposed to water damage while rolled up, the surface of the painting and the backing paper may cling to each other, with part of the paint layer possibly adhering to the lining [See p. 82 Photo. 2: Pasting part of paint layer to full lining (Nagano City, Chomei Temple). Paint is stuck to the back side (full backing paper). Of course, the paint remaining on the surface side had lost adhesive power and was at risk of peeling off.]. Not only the paint layer, but the paper of the main body itself may adhere to the lining, meaning the surface of the painting will be lost [See p. 82 Photo. 3 Front/Back: Pasting part of the main body paper to the full backing (Nagano City, Chomei Temple). main body paper is pasted to the back side (full backing paper) of the hanging scroll]. If folding screens are exposed to water damage while in a closed position, the surfaces of the paintings may stick together.

Despite being called water damage, it is rarely just water. In fact, even rain leakage on its path from the roof to the damaged materials becomes dirty water, containing various foreign substances. Moreover, it goes without saying that the water in floods, tsunamis, and landslides is dirty water, containing various dissolved and undissolved materials from the surrounding environment. Even if the water that reached the damaged materials was initially pure water, it would become dirty because of the dust and other foreign substances on the surface and interior of the work itself, resulting in deterioration. In fact, such dirty water can cause impurities to adhere to the surface of the painting [See p. 83 Photo. 4-1 Before repairs/After cleaning: Stains (mud) adhering to scroll (unmounted hanging scroll owned by S Family in Ofunato City) and Photo. 4-2 After cleaning: Breaks, missing pieces (unmounted hanging scroll owned by S Family, Ofunato City). The scroll was in a rolled up position when the tsunami hit and spent a long time with mud adhered to it. The paper of that section had decayed and broken, some parts were missing and even after cleaning not all of the stains could be removed.], cause stains, and leave boundary lines from drying, if it dries unevenly [See p. 84 Photo. 5 Before repairs/After repairs: Stains (with edges) (sliding screen owned by C Family in Ofunato City). The scroll absorbed seawater, leaving it with dark-colored ring stain (with edges) due to dirt sticking at the borders of where the water dried.].

Stains to works of Art are not only caused by dirty water from outside. If the works of Art themselves were made with coloring that is vulnerable to water, the color can move to places outside the original expression as it gets wet and elements that were originally part of the main body can cause visual damage. This can happen if dye-based paints were used [See p. 84 Photo. 6: Running of dye-based paint (ukiyo-e woodblock print owned by S Family in Ofunato City). Many of the carmine and composite dyes used in Meiji period woodblock prints are vulnerable to water and, since they were stacked in storage, the staining caused by water transferred and spread.], if water-based ink was used to write characters, or if the dyes used to color the mounting fabrics for hanging scrolls were not fixed [See p. 85 Photo. 7 Front/Back: Transfer of dye from mounting fabric (Nagano City, Chomei Temple). The scroll was stored rolled up, but the mounting fabric (middle layer) purple dye was exposed to water in a flood and transferred from the middle of the second inner layer to the main body, staining it.]; these can all cause visual damage in other parts of the main body.

Further, in most cases, after the disaster, water damage produces biological damage, with the most ubiquitous being damage from mold. This is not a merely cosmetic problem: fungal mycelium growth can destroy the color layer or the base materials themselves and, in the growth process, other darker colored substances are produced [See p. 85 Photo. 8: Coloring due to chromogenic mold production (Hand scroll Owned by S Family in Ofunato City)], causing visual damage. Furthermore, if the material is immersed for a long time, sclerotia will form when the fungal myceliums cluster together, potentially destroying the base material itself and germinating [Photo. 9].

Part 2

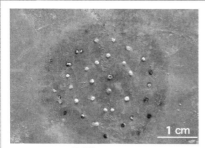

Folding screen

Hanging scroll

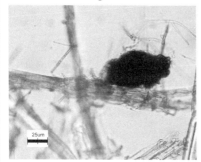

Micrograph

Photo 9. Sclerotia (Owned by S Family in Ofunato City)

If an item stays wet at low temperatures for a long time, fungal myceliums will form clusters called "sclerotia". When they germinate they penetrate the main body paper and produce white and black spot-like bumps on the surface. These are generally seen in crops such as cabbage, but, if the conditions are right, they also form in works of Art.

Book edge

Book surface

Photo 10. Paper breakage due to salt content crystallization (Owned by S Family in Ofunato City)

If the salt content in the paper repeatedly deliquesces and dries under specific conditions, crystals form clusters. This can be seen in the breakage that happens in some of the unions between the paper's fibers, so this may result in a decline in the base material's strength (this is not an art material, but the photo is placed here because the same thing could undeniably happen).

Micrograph

Immersion in seawater causes other forms of deterioration: when the surrounding environment drops below a certain humidity level, the moisture in salt water evaporates and dries, leaving the salt content inside the base material, Since salt content deliquesces (the phenomenon of a substance absorbing water vapor and spontaneously becoming an aqueous solution) when the environmental humidity level goes above a certain point, even if it is dry, it will approach a state of wetness when rainfall or other weather causes the humidity to rise, even if the material is not directly touched by water. If this is repeated, the material will remain wet for a longer period of time, which may aggravate deterioration. In some cases, as the salt content repeatedly deliquesces and dries, it can form concentrated crystalline clumps [Photo. 10]. In that sense, it is essential to remove the salt content.

2.3. Fire

In fire disasters, most materials get lost, but, luckily, some materials survive. This is because, although artworks featuring paper as base material carbonize in intense heat [See p. 87 Photo. 11: Burned sutra (Senpuku Temple sutra). When paper is charred and carbonizes it becomes brittle and could break or peel simply by being bent, so it will need a surface coating to cure the surface of the piece or some reinforcement from backing.], other artworks made of silver that has blackened over time may be deoxidized and return to the work's original white color. However, in disasters caused by fires, the water employed in firefighting may affect an item; this means that even when such artwork is not affected by high temperatures, it will still suffer water damage. Furthermore, in recent years, various firefighting substances are being used. However, research is still lacking on the effects of chemical firefighting substances on works of Art.

3. Stabilization Measures during Disasters

As mentioned above, when paintings and calligraphic works with mountings suffer a disaster, a suitable restoration period is needed to finish assembling the mounting, restoring their original shape and allowing for them to be handed down. This is not the kind of thing that can be done in a short period immediately following a disaster. Furthermore, disassembling works of Art must be done with an understanding of the main body's material structure and condition, as well as the structure of its mounting. This would be rather difficult without the help of a specialist. In that sense, the biggest issue is whether a specialist can be involved from the beginning of the restoration work. If it is possible to involve one, it would be preferable for that person to think of the entire journey up to the completion of repairs and decide on the spot which measures will be taken. If it is not possible to involve a specialist from the beginning, those involved should think of their objective while keeping the works of Art in a stable condition until a specialist can carry out the repairs. This is no easy task, considering the infinite variety of art material types, material structures, types and degrees of disasters, and conditions. Therefore, although it is not always possible, seeking the advice of a specialist at the very beginning is directly linked to the post-repairs outcome and will even influence the retaining of the artwork's value when being passed down.

Stabilization measures start from the rescue at the disaster site.

3.1. Grasping the Situation (Decisions at the Disaster Site)

The first decision to be made at a disaster site is selecting which items to rescue. This means deciding whether or not something should be kept as a work of art and therefore rescued and moved (if possible, after confirming with the owner). Further, at this time, the question of whether stabilization measures are needed is determined and, if necessary, the items in question are rescued with the assumption of moving them to a place where repairment measures can be taken. Sometimes the decision about essential timing for stabilization measures (namely defined as "urgent", or "can be handled later") will influence the decision about the destination the artworks will be moved to. Another important decision is whether the materials are in a condition that allows them to be moved as they are. Those involved will need to consider these aspects while conducting the rescue operation, give instructions on storage methods at the temporary storage space, give directions to workers on items that need immediate handling, or consult with a specialist, and so on.

3.2. Confirming a Policy for Storage Measures (Examination and Treatment for Temporary Storage Spaces and Work Spaces for [Stabilization] Measures)

After rescued items have been transported to a temporary storage space, it will be necessary to further assess and confirm how they will be stored and what kinds of measures need to be taken and when. To this end, the presence of a specialist who views the items directly would be useful; however, if that is not possible, those involved must gather information for consulting with a specialist at a later time. The following is an organized list of examples of minimum required information about the artwork.

-Condition of materials that have suffered the disaster

First, the overall state of the artwork must be grasped, meaning not only the main body, but also the mounting. Is there any physical damage, and has the material been damaged by submersion in water? If so, is it still wet, or has it already dried? Will its current condition allow it to be picked up and moved? Additionally, check whether the works of Art are in a storage box or wrapped in packaging, whether that packaging is protecting it, or if, instead, the packaging is causing damage to the main body. Then, proceed with checking the following key points.

-Damage from mold [See p. 85 Photo. 8]

The growth of colonies or production of pigmentation can be observed with the naked eye. With works of Art, the base material itself and the adhesives contain nutrients necessary for the growth of mold. As such, mold will invariably grow if the humidity level rises at a certain temperature. The likelihood of mold growth is especially high if an item has been submerged and then dried, whether in fresh or seawater. Mold damage is not only visual: it causes the base materials and adhesives to physically deteriorate, so disinfection measures are needed to keep mold from propagating any further. However, bacteria exist everywhere and there is a high likelihood of outbreak even after treatment is done. Therefore, once the treatment is complete, it is essential to consider the post-intervention storage environment at the same time.

-Adhesion and impregnation of substances that (may) accelerate deterioration

During disasters, foreign substances may adhere to the surface of the main body (base materials and paint layer) or impregnate and settle inside it. As previously mentioned, impregnation caused by submersion is especially likely to leave various organic and inorganic matter inside the main body, which eventually accelerates deterioration. It is not an exaggeration to say that cleansing work is the most important stabilization measure. Removing salt content is essential for metal materials and paper, which has also been seen to be worsened by salt, depending on conditions. Therefore, rinsing with water is essential for substances removal [See p. 87 Photo. 11].

-Paint layer deterioration damage

Due to the structure of pigment, fixing agent as animal glue or other materials is used to affix it to the base material (paper, silk, wood, etc.). If the material is stuck to the other side of a scroll mounting (hanging scroll or reel) or folding screen, it can be confirmed relatively easily by observing it with the naked eye. However, in some cases it may be difficult to detect a simple decrease in adhesive strength. Particularly in cases of water damages, if the material is submerged for a long time, the cement will lose adhesive strength and, even if it appears the same after drying, it has a greater likelihood of peeling off, especially with the artwork being subjected to even the slightest amount of physical force. In these cases, the artwork needs to be examined by touch, a task that is incredibly difficult to carry out without experience. Moreover, the choice of which stabilization measure to take is deeply related to the repairs that will take place later, so it is preferable to follow specialists' instructions. Dye-based colors (including ink) are highly likely to blur if submerged, moving not only laterally, but also transferring to the paper back side or to other materials, which can be confirmed with the naked eye [See p. 84 Photo. 6].

-Base material deterioration damage

If the material has been physically damaged due to the disaster, visual detection becomes simple; on the other hand, strength decrease due to deterioration is hard to detect with the naked eye. In certain cases, examination by touch can be helpful, although, it depends on experience.

-Mounting deterioration damage

If the mounting is broken, the immediate assumption is that it will be replaced. However, at this stage, what needs to be kept in mind are cases in which the mounting may damage the main body. It may not be much of a problem if the item is being placed in a storage case without any work being carried out on it, but the mounting may become a nuisance if other stabilization measures, such as rinsing, are being taken. For example, if the dyes used in the mounting fabric dissolve in water, the fabric will need to be removed first [See p. 85 Photo. 7]. Further, when removing foreign substances or dealing with mold, it may be complex and time consuming to completely remove the backing paper, if there is any. In those cases, it is best to consider the overall strength of the main body and remove the backing paper if necessary.

Other types of deterioration may occur depending on the type of works of Art and the type of disaster, meaning it will be necessary to ascertain and deal with each one separately.

3.3. Approaches to Stabilization Measures

Works of Art will eventually need to be brought into a specialized laboratory to have repairs done, or they will no longer be able to be handed down as works of Art. The stabilization measures mentioned here are carried out with the aim of preserving the materials' current condition, namely stopping or delaying the further deterioration until the item can be treated. They could also serve as measures for cases in which taking immediate steps would be more efficient than waiting for treatment if the date for serious repairs has not been set. Of course, there will be differences depending on the material structure of each main body, the state of the mounting, the degree of deterioration or damage, and the amount of time that has passed since the disaster. However, when it comes to works of Art such as paintings and calligraphic works, it is essential to think not only about what should be done to keep the deterioration from worsening, but also find a way to preserve the expression of the work.

In case of physical damage only, it is sometimes possible to package the item as is and setting it aside, if the storage environment meets the necessary conditions.

Moreover, in the case of submersion, drying is a necessary measure for curbing deterioration and preventing the growth of mold. However, works of Art often have paint adhered to the base material with resin and mountings whose structures are pasted together with starch glue. In these cases, drying them is not sufficient. The items will need to be dried in a way that does not alter their shape or structure: an extremely difficult task.

Furthermore, in the event of water damage from flooding, tsunamis, or other types of natural disasters, the water often contains both water-soluble and non-water-soluble foreign substances; if they remain in and on the main body, deterioration is likely to accelerate. Unless cold storage is used, mold damage will be inevitable. Therefore, removing these substances as much as possible is prerequisite while waiting for repairs. One thing that makes this task particularly difficult is when the mounting, which is the structure that supports the main body, is in contact with the main body while it has foreign substances on it that could aggravate deterioration. Therefore, because the backing paper is united with the main body, the task of rinsing and drying involves the backing paper too, meaning that it will require more water and more time, placing the main body under even more stress. In that sense, removing the mounting and only working on the main body is an effective part of stabilization measures.

Once the materials are rinsed, one method for drying submerged materials, such as books, is vacuum freeze-drying. Rinsing and then freezing the materials when they are still wet, and drying them in a vacuum, can prevent the pages from sticking together through hydrogen bonds. On the other hand, since this will release starch glue and other types of bonding, this method can only be applied to works of Art with specific conditions. In particular, it is limited to items that do not include paint. However, when disasters occur, there can be cases in which something must be necessarily done to keep mold damage in check.

Subsequently, to preserve the expression of the item as an art material, the structure of the base material and the paint layer must be preserved. However, even experts can have a difficult time determining whether materials can withstand methods such as rinsing, or whether they will weaken after undergoing such treatment. Nonetheless, neglecting to make such decisions may mean that the item will no longer be regarded to as an artwork. Taking measures to increase the paint's adhesive power and keep it from peeling is also a task that is safer in the hands of a specialist; when securing a specialist proves be too difficult, in some cases the item can be treated by pasting a covering paper to it. In any case, it is preferable to carry out these repairs under the guidance of a specialist.

Beyond stabilization measures, it is preferable to have definitive repairs done as early as possible. Since massive quantities of works of Art emerge during disasters, it is not realistically possible to repair all artworks at once. In such cases, once some time has passed since the disaster and those involved can think calmly, it is advisable to weigh the changes in artistic value caused by the disaster, as well as the meaning of the item when it was passed down. Once that has been done and the budget has been considered, those involved need to decide on the order and priority of repairs.

4. Examples of Stabilization Measures (Sliding Screen owned by C Family in Ofunato City)

4.1. Initial Examination

The site survey was conducted on May 6th, two months after the disaster. We were surprised to find that the main body was wet when we checked the sliding screen's damage conditions on that day; we later established that this was due to the deliquescence phenomenon from the salt content remaining in the main body [See p. 92 Photo. 12: Site survey]. We knew that as long as the salt content was not removed, it would get wet every time it rained or humidity levels rose and would dry again every time the weather cleared up. Repeating this cycle would clearly mean further deterioration, so we determined that stabilization measures to remove the salt content would be necessary. We considered whether to do these stabilization measures on site and realized that it would have been difficult to arrange the materials needed (a worktable on which to treat the sliding screen, equipment such as a sprayer, and materials such as absorption paper); therefore, we decided to transport the sliding screen to a lab to work on it.

4.2. Rescue

We tried to remove the sliding screen itself and transfer it, but the effects of the earthquake were such that the weight of the lintel above the screen made it impossible to remove it screen. Therefore, we hurried to remove the main body only and transfer it to a workable place. Plain paper was attached around the main paper to make all the works the same size, and then decorative paper with golden foil pieces scattered around it was placed around it. We decided to cut out the main body exactly where the decorative paper was and remove it with a bamboo spatula, together with the underlying floating layer [See Fig.2, Underlay structure diagram] [See p. 93 Photo. 13: Removing the main body].

4.3. Stabilization Measures

4.3.1. Survey

When the main body arrived in Kyoto, we examined it further to determine a policy for stabilization measures.

-Condition of the main body

During the tsunami damage, something that was flowing collided with it, and part of the main body was destroyed. Additionally, the lower third had been submerged in dirty water, thus, a dark brown mark was left around the edges that considerably hindered the appreciation of the piece. Upon closer inspection, a green discoloration was seen around the main body, where the decorative paper sprinkled with gold leaf pieces was joined. This indicates that the source of the inlaid gold leaf is not real gold leaf, but is actually brass leaf, which changes color when wet and takes on a greenish color.

The reason we transferred it to Kyoto was to remove the was salt content from the dirty water of the tsunami in the main body. The piece was in danger of suffering more physical deterioration and mold damage. The cause of this lied in the repeated phases of getting wet and dry, due to changes in environmental humidity levels. If this process was not stopped, it would not have been possible to keep it in a stable condition until official repairs. Thus, the most important measure to be carried out was that of rinsing with water and, essentially, the main body needed to be examined to determine whether it would withstand that treatment.

There were no significant traces of the ink used for coloring having bled or transferred, even if it did sustain damage. The paper was determined to be either bamboo paper or Xuan paper (Later identification revealed that it was bamboo fiber.), common in the calligraphy of Edo-period literary people (Confucian scholars). Constant exposure to outside air and light, which is the destiny of all sliding doors mountings, contributed to the surface of the paper already being deteriorated.

-Mountings

When the piece was transferred, the main body had been cut out and removed, but some decorative paper with brass pieces was still attached around the main body. It would not be possible to know how many layers of backing there were behind the main body without disassembling it, but it was clearly visible that missing parts had been mended in past repairs, and breaks (cracks) had been pieced together, showing that prior repairs had been done on the lining at least once. Furthermore, since it was removed with a bamboo spatula when it was dismantled on site, one floating layer from the underlayer was still attached to the main body side. In other words, it was clear that there were at least two layers of paper other than the main body.

-Previous repairs

Repair paper was attached to the missing part. However, there were some places where the direction of screen trace did not match the main body, and I felt that it looked strange.

4.3.2. Deciding a Policy for Measures

Based on the results of the examination, we set up a policy for stabilization measures.

The priority was to remove salt content and rinse with water. This was the same water rinsing method used for general repairs of mounted cultural asset works, which is to place the main body on top of ten layers of blotting paper, spray it with purified water (filtered water with metal ions and foreign substances removed) from the painting surface side, and use gravity and the capillary action of the paper to make the blotting paper absorb the water. This dissolved the foreign substances on and in the main body (for water-soluble substances) or moved them (for non-water-soluble substances small enough to pass through the gaps in the fibers of the paper), allowing to remove them from the main body. We considered what was needed to minimize the burden on the main body and maximize the effect of doing this treatment.

-Examining whether to remove things other than the main body

As mentioned in the previous section, since there was a possibility during rinsing that the brass leaf mounting paper would transfer substances that would give greenish discoloration caused by rust to the main body, this needed to be removed in advance. Moreover, the other two layers of non-main-body paper (floating paper) and backing paper that were attached needed to have their salt content removed. Doing so would have required greater volumes of rinsing water, making the treatment process longer and risking putting too much stress on the main body. Therefore, we decided it would be best to remove these as well. Initially, I had planned to replace the additional paper to make the different sizes of

Part 2

the main body uniform and use new paper, but since there was no major damage to the original paper, I decided to use it without removing it.

-Examining whether the main body can withstand rinsing

The expression of the main body was written in India ink and the included a red signature and seal. These are known to have a certain resistance to water, however, we still carried out a patch test (a test to determine whether there was any transfer after placing a small piece of wet blotting paper) and verified that there was no transfer.

4.4. Stabilization measures
4.4.1. Mounting paper removal method

We added a small amount of water to the seams of the mounting paper that remained around the main body to loosen and remove the adhesive glue.

4.4.2. Removal Methods for Old Underlayer Paper (Floating Paper) and Old Backing Paper

For old upper floating layer we placed the piece backside-up on the worktable, sprayed it with purified water and removed it [See p. 96 Photo. 14: Removing backing paper]. We removed the old backing paper in the same manner. When we started to remove it, we found that two layers of backing paper were present. The main body is made of short fiber paper and has deteriorated considerably (its strength has decreased), but the cracks have been connected with the old backing paper, and the missing parts have been filled in with another repair paper. In order to remove this first backing paper, it is necessary to remove the old supplementary paper in the missing area on the spot, fill it with new supplementary paper, and apply (paste) the new first backing paper, in other words, perform a full-scale repair. Therefore, we decided to leave this first layer of backing paper and wash it with water. Thus, we decided to leave this one layer of surface backing paper and proceed with the water rinsing treatment.

4.4.3. Water Rinsing Treatment

We conducted the water rinsing treatment, placing the main body with only the first backing paper remaining on top of the layered blotting papers and spraying it with purified water [See p. 96 Photo. 15: Water rinsing. To place less stress on the main body, we spray it and impregnated it with water; the excess was removed by being absorbed by blotting paper placed underneath.]. The water took a significant amount of time to penetrate the areas that contained salt from the tsunami. We repeated the spraying several times, measured the concentration of salt in the water in the blotting paper directly beneath the main body, and finished the rinsing when the paper's salt content was approximately zero [See p. 96 Photo. 16: Measuring salt concentration. We determined whether the salt content had been removed by measuring the salt concentration in the top layer of blotting paper.].

This rinsing also alleviated the brown edge line that had resulted from the borderline of where the sliding screen had been submerged, becoming nearly imperceptible.

4.4.4. Drying

After the rinsing was complete, we placed the main body on a blanket and let it dry naturally. It still had old backing paper and was secure, so there was almost no roughness after drying [See p. 97 Photo. 17: Drying. Abrupt drying causes ring stains, so we let it dry slowly and completely on a blanket.].

4.4.5. Storage

After drying, since there were no concerns about color peeling, we layered the main body and rolled it up for storage.

Above was the course of events and details of measures taken in 2011 to stabilize works of Art following the disaster. I think these measures could have been possible on site if the conditions had been met; on the other hand, it did feel remarkably more secure to treat this piece in a well-equipped, familiar environment, while checking the conditions of the artwork. This case example involved writings in India ink; however, if it had been an art material whose expression had been done with paint (color), I wonder what would have happened if we had had to treat it on site.

(Regarding this art material, we were able to ultimately complete the repairs in 2014, with special research funding from the Kyoto University of the Arts and aid from the Tohoku University International Research Institute of Disaster Science and the Japan Conservation Project. See Column below.)

Full Repairs

Three years after the stabilizing measures, our budget grew, and we were able to conduct a full repair. During the stabilizing measures we realized that it would be difficult to remove the old first backing paper without this overly stressing the main body; we have now reconfirmed that decision. It was confirmed again that it is difficult to remove the old first backing paper without putting a burden on the main body(paper). The old first backing paper was left as part of the main body, and the old repair paper was oriented diagonally, causing an odd feeling, so I removed it all and replaced it with a new repair paper that looked similar to the main body. A second backing paper was applied. The base frame was solid and didn't warp, so I added 6 types of 8 layers of underlay to create a panel, and pasted the main body on top of it. Brass foil had been used the decorative paper, which had stained the main body with a greenish copper rust color due to the water damage. Thus, we made a new mounting paper with real gold foil. We used the original handle and assembled it with a newly made black-lacquered wood. We fit it to the slope of the threshold, lintel, and pillars on site; then, we adjusted it and put it in place.

Lining (first backing paper)   Underlayer (second layer)   Attaching fabric of mounting

Antechamber (before repairs)

Repair paper (before repairs)

Repair paper (after repairs)

Antechamber (after repairs)

Conclusion

First, I would like to focus on the challenges of the status quo. In the present day, a very small number of people are capable of repairing and treating works of Art, aside from the specialists in workshops and other places. I feel that we need to create a system that allows these private sector specialists to be involved in the event of a disaster and that trains talent who have the knowledge and experience to consult with specialists, also handling emergency measures if needed. Even if they cannot do full repairs, in any event of a disaster, human resources are needed in handling emergency stabilization measures. Nonetheless, as this does not seem an immediately reachable goal, for now, people will have to rely on points of contact that can introduce them to specialists. Such consultations can now be made at the Cultural Heritage Disaster Risk Management Center of Japan National-al Institutes for Cultural Heritage, which deals with cultural assets. In the private sector, this is handled by the *Siryo-net*; however, for works of Art, specialists respond more directly through the NPO Japan Conservation Project, which also provides recommendations on affiliated specialists. Moreover, the Japan Society for the Conservation of Cultural Property can introduce their member specialist.

Finally, as the author, I would like to close with remarks about what I experienced during my involvement in the repair and treatment of several works of Art affected by disasters. When repairing works of Art which suffered a disaster, I feel that often measures for dealing with deterioration and damage from neglect and aging over many years have greater relative importance than the measures for damage from the disaster itself. In other words, I am encountering an ironic reality in which items that had reached the stage of needing repair were neglected only to then be repaired when disaster struck. Of course, it is reasonable to think about and prepare for measures and repairs when disaster strikes, but in the case of works of Art such as these (non-designated works of art), it is important to preserve their artistic value independently from the occurrence of a disaster. This highlights the question of what to do to protect these materials in the day-to-day, while conducting maintenance.

References

Tsunami ni yori hisai shita bunkazai no hozon shufuku gijutsu no kochiku to senmon kikan no renkei ni kan suru purojekuto jikko iinkai [Executive Committee of the Project to Establish and Conserve Restoration Techniques for Cultural Assets Damaged by Tsunami and Collaborate with Specialized Institutions] ed. Hideo Akanuma and Mahoro Suzuki *Antei-ka shori ~ dai tsunami hisai bunkazai hozon shufuku gijutsu renkei purojekuto* [Stabilization Treatments: Collaborative Project for the Storage and Restoration of Cultural Assets Affected by the Tsunami Disaster] (Executive Committee of the Project to Establish and Conserve Restoration Techniques for Cultural Assets Damaged by Tsunami and Collaborate with Specialized Institutions, Japan Museum Association, ICOM Japan Committee, 2018 (expanded edition)).

Dosan bunkazai kyushutsu manyuaru henshu iinkai [Editorial Committee for the Manual of Rescue of Personal Property and Cultural Assets] *Dosan bunkazai kyushutsu manyuaru omoideno-hin kara bijutsu kogei-hin made* [Manual of Rescue of Personal Property and Cultural Assets: From Keepsakes to Works of Art] (Kuba Pro, 2012).

Otsunami hisai shiryo renkei purojekuto anteika shochi [Stabilization Measures of the Collaborative Project on Tsunami Disaster Materials] (video) https://www.j-muse.or.jp/06others/stabilization.php (last accessed January 23, 2024).

Part 3

Preparation for Materials Rescue

Chapter 7

Rescue Simulation: Action Plan

▧ YAMAUCHI Toshiaki (Kyushu University of Health and Welfare)

Introduction

Disasters occur annually across Japan, and the number of damaged cultural properties is endless. Sometimes, disasters directly damage cultural properties, such as destruction or defacement; at other times, facilities storing or containing cultural properties get damaged, even if not directly. In any case, we must rescue the materials as soon as possible. The risk of loss or damage if left unattended during a disaster is high; thus, it is necessary to move them to a relatively safe location at some point after a disaster occurs. It is essential here for the people who are to take on the rescue in a certain area to know when they should perform the work and what kind of personnel and equipment preparations are necessary.

Modern administrative policies include regional disaster prevention plans as well as other plans and manuals addressing various natural disaster risks, and administrators modify them according to the situation—for example, "hazard maps" created from the perspective of damage forecast and disaster risk reduction; "evacuation planning" establishing evacuation actions such as identifying evacuation routes and sites; an "evacuation shelter management guidebook/manual" defining the process from preparation to closure of the shelters; "disaster waste disposal plans" for the disposal of waste generated during a disaster; and a "memorabilia handling manual" aiming to return the victims' cherished possessions to them instead of disposing as waste. These have been developed to examine many issues that have arisen in past disasters and to make it possible to respond to similar situations in the future.

Part 3

243

In the field of museum and cultural property protection, in some cases, actions in a disaster are still limited to confirming the condition of designated cultural properties; in other cases, a BCP (Business Continuity Plan) is unavailable, partly due to the limited number of staff responsible for disaster management. Although municipalities that have experienced major disasters usually have manuals, handbooks, guidelines, and the like in place in preparation for high risks in various areas of their administrative measures, they must also anticipate cases where the staff will not pass on know-how due to a change in personnel over time and other similar situations.

Hence, it is vital to continuously build and examine operational plans for disaster preparation in museums and cultural property protection. In this chapter, we examine activities that aim to establish disaster prevention and risk reduction management in municipalities, particularly at the city, town, or village levels, and to build consensus among related institutions, such as municipalities and private organizations, through simulations related to materials rescue in anticipation of a disaster.

1. Disaster Preparation Simulation

The plans and manuals prepared for a disaster often may not be followed exactly as described when a disaster occurs. However, the only way to react is, even if not perfect, through the process of exploring and developing the best possible actions by assuming possible conditions. This is why local governments responsible for disaster management activities, schools and companies that have long continued disaster prevention education, and community disaster prevention organizations develop such manuals.

It is necessary for us to "prepare", even in positions involved in the preservation of museums and cultural properties (both government and private).

The Aichi Prefectural Museum of Art holds "simulation meetings" for practical responses to expected situations in a disaster, and they repeatedly revise the response policy[1].

The Kanagawa Prefecture Museum Association holds "Comprehensive Disaster Prevention Planning Activities" every year; these include remote information transmission drills to consolidate information in multiple block units within

Kanagawa, and they set other conditions, such as the establishment of a system to enable backups if the pre-determined representative museum suffer from an accident[2]. In addition, they established a system to ensure that the staff can pass on know-how through continuous disaster prevention training, changing the personnel in charge.

In addition to museums, the administration of cultural property protection has widely started similar practices with the release of the "Cultural Property Preservation and Utilization Guidelines" in each prefecture. In fact, Gunma Prefecture has a section in its [Cultural Properties Disaster Prevention Guidelines] entitled "Disaster Preparedness Efforts: Creating a Disaster Prevention Plan" that states to "create a timeline in a disaster." The timeline is formulated by the Ministry of Land, Infrastructure, Transport, and Tourism and other ministries as a disaster prevention action plan related to disaster prevention and risk reduction actions[3], but Gunma Prefecture encourages cultural property owners and management organizations to formulate own timelines based on the flowchart, like *My Timeline*, an action plan for each resident.

In Kagoshima Prefecture, "Disaster Prevention, Crime Prevention, and Disaster Response" in its [Cultural Property Preservation and Utilization Guidelines] includes a section entitled "Providing Information in Online Workshops on Learning Skills and Knowledge for Materials Rescue in the Event of Flood Damage." They have held many workshops on disaster prevention of cultural properties and handling materials damaged by disasters. Now that the world is online, holding these workshops between remote locations has become more common.

Cities, towns, and villages that are directly involved in disasters need to ponder certain issues in recent years when dealing with disaster response for cultural properties, such as the possible inability to pass on knowledge and skills due to workforce shortages and transfers, including generational changes, caused by staff reduction and declining staff ratio. Sometimes, small municipalities cannot fill professional staff positions and instead assign their relevant tasks to the general administrative staff. Concerns arise about the decline of professional work not only in disaster response but also in museums and cultural property protection. Coordination in a wide regional area among municipalities and with private organizations such as Shiryo-Networks and Heritage Manager is also essential. Although, in many cases, municipalities take charge of both museums and cultural property protection, the conditions for rescue activities are different for museums, which are specified public facilities, and for cultural properties, which are widely distributed throughout the local community; thus, individual response for each case is necessary. Moreover, local history research groups are shrinking due to the ageing population, and schoolteachers have become increasingly busy and are more frequently transferred, which makes it difficult for them to deal with local materials; therefore, we need to develop and nurture new citizen volunteers who can help in the local scene.

In this sense, we must explore various activities for rescuing cultural properties and materials during disasters— "protection of cultural properties" in general— to build consensus among government officials and the groups involved in such activities.

Thus, the Miyazaki/Kagoshima Shiryo Networks hold DIG (Disaster Imagination Game), a simulation training that anticipates disaster, as a workshop for understanding the know-how of information, personnel, and equipment that changes on a timeline, the maintenance of facilities for evacuation of materials, coordination with external organizations, and safety management, in anticipation of the materials rescue in museum and cultural property protection [Fig. DIG of materials rescue in a disaster]. We originally designed this as an operational training exercise for coordination among local Shiryo-Networks, where labor-force

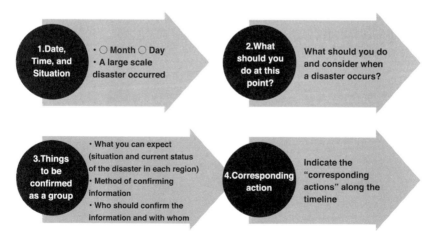

Fig.

shortages are common. However, in checking with persons in charge in munici-palities from preparation to implementation and assessment, we found it easy for all parties concerned to grasp, understand, and share the necessary systems and issues in a disaster in the municipalities in question. Participants have confirmed their understanding of the "lack of preparation for disasters" and the "importance of cooperation from diverse standpoints," and they have identified issues connect-ed to manageing cultural properties in a disaster.

1.1. Attempting DIG

DIG was initially developed by the (then) Defense Agency's National Institute for Defense Studies and Mie Prefecture in 1997 as a simulation of a municipality in a disaster, based on a command post exercise conducted by the Self-Defense Forces[4].

The objective is to prepare for disasters by examining methods of responding to one at a certain point in time and according to ever-changing situations. It has a wide range of applications, and currently, they often implement disaster prevention training for municipalities, volunteer groups, and other civic organi-zations all over Japan. The authors have applied this program to cultural property rescue with the advice of meteorologists and disaster prevention experts and have improved the program. Although we started it to confirm and strengthen the co-operative relationship between the two neighbouring prefectures of Miyazaki and Kagoshima in southern Kyushu in a disaster, we have extended it to municipali-ties protecting cultural properties, museum curators, lifelong learning institution staff.

Our DIG consists of three major phases: <preparation>, <implementation>, and <assessment>. Below are the specific steps for each phase.

1.2. Preparation

In the preparation phase, we decide the workshop's purpose, implementation timing, target, and the type of disaster targeted and prepare accordingly. Our workshop's mission is simple: "to transport materials from the disaster-stricken area to a safe place," we can change this to any other mission. It would be more effective to plan the timing of the workshop based on the season when weather disasters are most likely to occur and when earthquakes and tsunamis have occurred in the past.

The setting assumes the largest disaster that has ever occurred in the target municipality or region. Participants should, of course, use hazard maps and other topographic maps as references, but to establish a timeline, they must understand the progress on the disaster's time axis [Table]. In the case of weather disasters and earthquakes, the Japan Meteorological Agency discloses the chronology of the disaster since its occurrence. Information related to the maintenance of class A rivers is available at each region's river and national highway office affiliated with the Regional Development Bureau of the MLIT, where we can check the location of past disasters, records of rising water levels, and direct causes of disasters. Moreover, it is beneficial to read municipality magazines and disaster record magazines (if published) as resources for municipality information. With the cooperation of the crisis management division, these magazines can provide information on timelines documenting the municipality's response to disasters. Municipalities have fewer records of disasters from older periods, such as the Showa period (1926–1989), but we can utilize information from public information in the past and newspapers of that time. However, regarding a Nankai Trough earthquake, records that meet modern standards are limited; we need to pay attention to writing scenarios. Although records can help us understand not only the occurrence of disasters but also how municipalities and communities responded to them, when setting up a timeline as a scenario, since old disaster responses are different from the modern administrative countermeasures, we should modify the contents in the light of the current situation, even if only partially.

We examine a material rescue system along with the timeline. This includes checking the location of materials at high risk of being damaged, securing human resources, establishing a communication system, and setting up temporary storage after transportation. At this stage, we reaffirm the extent to which the relevant local material rescue system is organized. In particular, after the Great Heisei Mergers, even in the same municipality today, differences remain in the sense of land and understanding of the local communities, such as between the main office and branches of the former municipality, and we are often reminded of the need to confirm the conditions related to the materials rescue.

Table   Rescue timeline of materials based on past typhoon disasters
(from a case study in Takanabe Town, Miyazaki Prefecture)

[Premise]

On 19 September 1983, a weak tropical cyclone formed over Chuuk Lagoon and developed while moving west-north-westward, becoming Typhoon Forrest over the ocean south-southwest of Guam on 21 September. It rapidly developed into a ferocious typhoon with a central pressure of 885 hpa and maximum wind speed of 55 m/s over the ocean 1,000 km southeast of Okinawa on 23 September. Its direction changed from north to east in the northern East China Sea from the 26–27, gradually weakening as it moved eastward and making landfall near Nagasaki City at around 10:20 am on the 28. After making landfall on Kyushu, it accelerated its speed and moved eastward, crossing central Kyushu, and becoming an extratropical cyclone near Sukumo City, Kochi Prefecture on the 28. This low-pressure area then increased its speed and moved eastward over the southern sea of Honshu, and at 9 am on the 29, it advanced to a location about 450 km east of the Kanto region.

A fall rain front that had stalled over the southern Sea of Japan as the typhoon moved northward became active on the 25, and strong rains began to fall mainly over the Pacific Ocean side of the Kyushu-Kanto region. Heavy rains fell mainly in Kyushu and Shikoku from the 26-27, and the passage of the typhoon caused widespread heavy rains from Shikoku to Kanto. "Linear rainbands," as they are called in current meteorological terms, may have occurred in many areas.

This typhoon caused damage in 38 prefectures, and in addition to flooding and landslides from mountains and cliffs, notable drowning accidents occurred involving schoolchildren due to rising water levels. Many large and small rivers rose or were flooded, and considerable damage was made to transportation facilities.

[Damage]

The Miyazaki area was initially hit by the typhoon.

Torrential rains hit Nichinan City and Kushima City on the 26, and on the 27, small and medium-sized rivers overflowed one after another, mainly in Miyazaki City and Koyu district, causing a series of flood damage. In Takanabe Town, 85 mm of heavy rain fell between 3 and 4 am on the same day, causing the river to overflow in areas along the Miyata River. Floodwaters spread toward the Shiota River, which branches off from the Shiota sluice gate on the left bank of the Miyata River. The closing of the flood gates caused the water in the Shiota River to come to a standstill, making it flow back into irrigation canals and drains, flooding the center of town. In areas such as Matsubara-cho, Asahi-dori, Tokamachi, and Ikada district, 136 households were flooded above floor level and 445 households below floor level, and three households were partially damaged. The rainfall from the time it began on the 25 until 6 am on the 28 amounted to 494 mm.

Water from the Miyata River often flows back toward the Shiota River, causing the city area to flood, which also occurred with Typhoon Trami in September 2018.

Dates	Time	Timeline based on 1983 weather conditions	Situation	What should you do at this point?	What should be confirmed as a group	Reference materials to be prepared
25-28 Sep		Rain continues from midnight throughout Miyazaki Prefecture due to the approach of the huge typhoon from the 25	In areas such as Matsubara-cho, Asahi-dori, Tokamachi, and Ikada district, 136 households were flooded above floor level and 445 households below floor level, and three households were partially damaged.			
		Heavy rains in Kushima and Nichinan City on the 26				
		Torrential rains mainly on Miyazaki City and Koyu District on the 27				
		The typhoon passes through after making landfall near Nagasaki City				
		The total rainfall in Takanabe from the 25–28 reaches 472mm				

		A disaster response headquarters was established for precautionary measures.				
		The Nippo Line was closed early in the morning, and many trains were suspended. Both inbound and outbound lanes of the Kyushu and Miyazaki Expressways were closed to traffic.				
29 Sep		Many public institutions were suspended. According to JR Kyushu, all lines in Kagoshima Prefecture were suspended—particularly the Nippo Line, which had been cut off by landslides and other issues. This was expected to affect a total of 80,000 people in all prefectures on both the 6 and 7.	The typhoon passed through, and the full extent of the damage came to light. Inland flooding occurred due to the closing of the flood gates from Miyata River to Shiota River. Since there was information that several historic buildings and public facilities in the city are being flooded, the City Cultural Properties Division staff went to confirm. ⇒ Two warehouses, including the former Meirin-do library on library grounds, and a historical building managed by the Council of Social Welfare (the old SUZUKI Masaya villa, a registered tangible cultural property) were found to be submerged in water/it was speculated that the historical materials in these places may have been damaged.	• What should you implement when confirming the situation and communicating information? • What should you prepare and expect during this period?	• What should be the methods and objects when confirming the situation, and how should you handle correspondence with the agencies concerned? • To which groups of people should you send the information on the whereabouts of the materials? • How should you consolidate information at this stage? • How should you secure and allocate the personnel and materials? (Which groups of people? What is necessary?)	• Flood Hazard Map and Landslide Disaster Prevention Map
30 Sep		Start of acceptance of bulky garbage due to disasters	With the start of the acceptance of bulky garbage due to disasters and the establishment of volunteer centers, cleanup work begins simultaneously in the affected areas.			
		Establishment of volunteer centers				

1 Oct			Municipal employees were given priority in managing evacuation centers; thus, work on cultural assets was postponed to a later date. However, since the Council of Social Welfare had jurisdiction over the old Masaya Suzuki villa, they offered to coordinate its cleanup with the Board of Education as it was a registered tangible cultural property. The Council of Social Welfare requested that the building be cleaned as soon as possible, especially with the removal of tatami mats and the removal and drying of sludge that had accumulated under the eaves.		
3 Oct			A plan was made to remove the materials from the affected areas. The materials were to be moved to the general gymnasium archery field.		
5 Oct		JR Kyushu suspended all train service until the morning of 5 October. Power and phone outages remained in some areas of the prefecture. Some sections of the Kyushu Expressway and national roads also remained closed. Many major roads, including prefectural roads, were closed or have only one side of traffic open.	Ascertain damage information while determining the timing of on-site materials rescue	• How should you confirm the safety of the site? • How should you confirm the travel route? • What precautions should you take for the staff? • Shouldn't you reconsider the travel route?	• A travel route map to Kagoshima, Miyazaki, Nobeoka, and around Koyu District would be useful.
			The library staff kept the doors of the warehouse open during the hours when they were able manage the collection and dry out the room. Water damage to the materials was confirmed during this time.		

6 Oct			The Council of Social Welfare contacted the Social Education Division about the condition of the interiors of the old SUZUKI Masaya villa, confirming that the fusuma was partially damaged by water and that a piece of paper with words written in them was affixed to it.		
			Preparations were made for the treatment of waterlogged materials.		
			Coordination with the Miyazaki Prefectural Board of Education and the Miyazaki Shiryo-Network for technical and material support was ensured.		
8 Oct	8:00		Town staff and Miyazaki Prefecture/Shiryo Network Members who could participate in rescue activities gathered in front of the Takanabe Town History Museum. Everyone moved to the site after role assignments were confirmed (car and pull cart).	• What should you do when travelling to the site and after arriving?	
	9:00		Rescue activities begin. Water damage to materials is greater than expected.	• What do you need during record keeping? • What should you do when the work ends, during transportation and storage?	
	10:30		• Records were created if possible, then the materials are moved out. If creating records is difficult, photographs of the situation are taken, and the materials are moved out. • The condition of the materials varies, with some identified as partially muddied and others as relatively lightly muddied.		

		⇒ Checked for items that have begun to dry with mud stuck on them, or records (photos, etc.) that have begun to deteriorate due to foul odors, mold, or bacteria. • Difficulties were observed in moving and temporarily packing materials from the site, and by 3pm, workers were fatigued. The removed materials were taken to the parking lot. Workers temporarily packed and loaded materials into vehicles in the parking lot.		
16:00		Work ends at the site.		
17:00		Materials are transported and placed in temporary storage.		

1.3. Implementation

The reasonable number of participants in the workshop would be 4–7 per group. Groups unfamiliar with the workshop may not know the procedure, in which case, a table facilitator[5] can facilitate the process.

The organizers prepare a map of the target area (enlarged to A1 size), a hazard map (about A3 size), records of past disasters, pens (water-based and oil-based fine-point ones that can write clear letters), sticky notes (square, preferably with solid adhesive, at least two colours), thick mounting paper (A3 size) to attach sticky notes printed (see below), transparent sheets for writing (writing sheets or a whiteboard), a projector, and a PC. The projector projects the timeline created with PowerPoint on one side of the screen and a hazard map (MLIT's "overlapping hazard map" is helpful but needs a network connection) with targeted points on the other. Desks are arranged, and the enlarged map, hazard map, and sticky notes are placed on top. Having a transparent sheet to write on overlaid on the map is functional. Moreover, the timeline should be tabulated and distributed to each table for easy reconfirmation of the participants.

Along with the primary facilitator who oversees the entire process, having an expert in conservation science or conservation and restoration as an advisor can provide a broader knowledge of material preservation and more persuasive ex-

Part 3

planations. At this time, the organizers should be ready to present helmets, masks (DS2/N95 or their equivalent), dust-proof glasses, and nitrile gloves, which will be required during the rescue.

The primary facilitator explains the workshop's content and develops scenarios according to the timeline. In addition to confirming the situation during the disaster, the damage and response, and the restoration status of the affected areas and roads, the facilitator states that materials were damaged and need to be rescued; moreover, they talk about the process from preparation for implementation and the actual rescue of materials to moving them out and setting them in a temporary storage area.

The organizers ask questions now, and the authors have chosen the following three questions.

Question 1: What should you implement when confirming the situation and communicating information?
What should you prepare and expect during this period?
Question 2: What should you do when travelling to the site and after arriving?
Question 3: What do you need during record keeping?
What should you do when the work ends, during transportation and storage?

In this way, we ask participants to examine the "actions they should take, their response behaviours," to describe them on the sticky notes, and then paste them onto the A3-sized questionnaire [See p. 113: Photo.1: Ideas written on sticky notes are pasted onto the mount]. We can modify the questions if necessary. For each question, participants have 15 minutes to think and write down their ideas on a sticky note; during this time, they must write one text per sticky note as, if they list multiple items on one, it will be difficult to classify them later. Each participant is responsible for writing on a sticky note. Next, they classify these sticky notes as a group according to their contents and place them back on the mount. Through this activity, they exchange opinions and reconfirm their ideas. After the prescribed 15 minutes, the advisor explains each question. If an expert in conservation science is not available, the primary facilitator explains; however, it would be best to obtain advice from an expert beforehand in this case as well.

During the explanation, it should be noted that no "right answers" exist and that presenting diverse ideas is the goal.

After completing the timeline, each group makes a presentation; this allows participants to reflect on the workshop and consolidate what they have learned. The time required to reach this point is approximately 2.5–3 hours from the start, with breaks in between. We can hold such programs online; in these cases, it would be practical to use online whiteboards such as "miro." Holding them online allows a broader range of audiences across regional locations to participate.

1.4. Assessment

After the workshop, the organizers ask participants to fill out a questionnaire. They list what they understood through the workshop and what they think should be issued and receive feedback on the results.

Below are some examples of the questions.

- What did you understand the most from this workshop? Select only one.
  The process of materials preservation activities / What preparations are necessary for materials preservation activities, and what preparations you did or did not do/ Knowledge and skills necessary for materials preservation/ The current state of local communities, such as declining population, ageing population, and an increasing number of vacant houses/ The difficulties and importance of collaboration among private organizations (here activities related to materials preservation) and with the government
- What did you find most confusing about the content of the workshop?
  I did not understand the methods to anticipate damage and what information I should collect/ I did not understand the procedures for materials preservation/ I did not understand what equipment and tools are necessary for materials preservation / I did not picture the geographical image in my head because I am unfamiliar with the area/ I did not sense anything particularly difficult.
- What were you able to sense the most regarding the significance of this workshop? Select up to two from the following eight options.
  Protecting cultural properties and museum materials from disasters leads to the maintenance and sustainment of local communities/ Protecting cultural

properties and museum materials from disasters leads to preparation for future large-scale disasters/ In many cases, materials are held not only by museums and other institutions but also by individuals, and it is important for the owners and the local communities to protect them/ Cooperation among people in various positions is necessary to preserve a community's history and culture / Collaboration among neighbouring communities is extremely important in a disaster/ To prepare for future disasters, the younger generation should get involved/ Although I could somewhat understand the significance of the activity, in terms of the details of the work or the relevant roles, I did not understand well / I did not understand the significance of the activity or the importance of the various roles at all.

2. Future Development

Municipalities across Japan are formulating the "Regional Plan for the Conservation and Utilization of Cultural Properties," and in many cases, they include the preservation of cultural properties in disasters. Next, although an implementation plan to address this issue is necessary, it is crucial to establish disaster management and disaster prevention in advance, and simulation is a process for establishing such management [See p.115 Photo.2: Workshop in Takanabe Town, Miyazaki Prefecture]. Moreover, we can improve the simulation mentioned here by adding an activity that involves handling actual disaster-damaged materials after the simulation.

One of the lessons learned from the Great East Japan Earthquake disaster response was the phrase "the only thing that was useful was what had been prepared," and "only being prepared was insufficient."[6] We need activities that enable a certain level of reaction to disasters, even if imperfect.

Notes

1 SOEDA Kazuho. "Shumireishon miitingu to bousaikunren [Simulation Meetings and Disaster Drills]", in: *Report on "Museums for Everyone," a project to support the creative activities in art and history museums in collaboration with local communities FY2014*, "Museums for Everyone" Project Executive Committee, 2015, pp.169-173.

2 Kanagawa Prefectural Museum Association Comprehensive Disaster Management Plan Promotion Committee. "Kanagawa-ken hakubutsukankyokai sogobosaikeikaku katsudohokoku [Kanagawa Prefectural Museum Association Comprehensive Disaster Prevention Plan Activity Report", in: *Kanagawa Prefectural Museum Association Bulletin*, No, 88, 2017, pp.62-79.

3 The definition of timeline includes the following: "A plan that organizes disaster prevention actions and their implementation entities in chronological order, focusing on the 'when,' 'who,' and 'what' will be done based on the premise that a disaster will occur and on the assumption that disaster prevention-related organizations will work together to anticipate and share the situations that will occur in the event of a disaster." (MLIT Disaster Prevention and Disaster Risk Prevention Headquarters for Water-Related Disasters Working Group for Disaster Prevention Action Plan, *Timeline (Disaster Prevention Action Plan) Development and Utilization Guidelines*)

4 HIRANO Atsushi. "Saigaikyuuenji ni okeru atarashii borantia no arikata to saigaizuzyoukunren-DIG [New Methods of Volunteerism in Disaster Relief and the Disaster Simulation Training DIG]", in: *Modern Firefighting*, 36-3, 1998, pp.148-152.

Mie Prefecture Fire and Disaster Prevention Division, Promotion Department. "Shiminkeihatsugata no saigaizuzyoukunren-DIG no gaiyou to kadai [Overview and Issues of Citizen Awareness Disaster Simulation Training DIG]", in: *Fire Science and Information*, No.63, 2001, pp.44-48.

KOMURA Takashi. "DIG (Disaster Imagination Game)", in: *Fire and Disaster Prevention*, Fall 2004, 2004, pp.92-102.

5 The types of facilitators are two: floor facilitators who oversee the entire workshop venue, and table facilitators who work together to facilitate small groups ("squads"); in particular, to "create the venue" as well as the "atmosphere" for the workshop is considered the table facilitator's main job. (The Great Hanshin-Awaji Earthquake Memorial Disaster Reduction and Human Renovation Institution, *Saigaiboranthia jissen wakushoppu gaido* [Disaster Volunteer Practice Workshop Guide], 2006, p.19.

6 The Tohoku Regional Development Bureau, MLIT. *Higashinihondaishinsai no jittaiken ni motozuku saigaishodoki shikikokoroe* [Disaster Initial Response Command Guidelines Based on Actual Experiences during the Great East Japan Earthquake]. (2013)

Part 3

Chapter 8

Rescue Simulation:
Disaster Preparation Practices

▨ AMANO Masashi (National Museum of Japanese History)

Introduction

Promoting materials rescue prerequisites the training of personnel. As described in Part 2, we must rescue various materials and take emergency measures when a disaster strikes. However, it is the staff members of museums, libraries, and archives that lead the practice in a disaster area, some of whom do not have special knowledge and skills for materials preservation and restoration. After a disaster, when information gets tangled up, accurate judgment of the situation and prompt work planning are inevitable. Thus, to develop human resources for disaster response, we must train the staff to select specific techniques and think in a way that enables them to plan a series of tasks from rescue to emergency treatment and then adjust for permanent preservation.

In this context, we have hold workshops for disaster preparation. The contents vary, but in recent years we have the following three types.

The first is an enlightening one. *Shiryo-Networks* and museums promote this type, whose purpose is not to specify the target materials but to introduce practical practices to publicize the activities of material conservation and expand the bearers for future preservation and inheritance. They try to let the public understand the importance of materials preservation by introducing water-absorbing drying of water-damaged materials using familiar household utensils and other materials.

Next is a technical training one. Its main target is technicians involved in materials repair and preservation, aiming to train specialists with the necessary

Part 3

techniques for first aid treatment and for subsequent full-scale repair— developing such techniques is also its aim.

The third is an action-planning one. This type studies the communication system and the transportation of the materials to the site in a disaster through tabletop exercises with the stakeholders in a specific community [Fig. 1: Types of workshops designed for disaster preparation] (See Chapter 7 for details).

While these workshops are effective in grasping the required actions for materials rescue, what the practitioners need in a disaster is to analyse the situation and manage the whole project by planning the work process from rescue to temporary storage, including negotiations with outside experts and coordination with volunteers. During the work process, observing the target materials and planning the workflow based on the observation are important, and it is necessary to select the most appropriate method using various techniques and knowledge. Therefore, in addition to understanding the entire work process, understanding the focus on the materials and simulating specific measures are necessary: training and examination through workshops are quite effective. In setting up a workshop, we need to provide participants with an opportunity to experience the actual work process from the planning stage to see what was influential in the process they devised

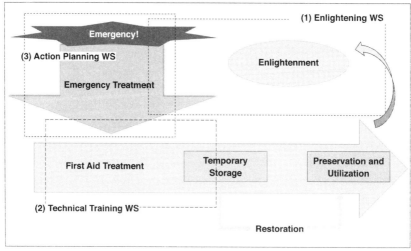

Fig. 1

and what the problems were, including failures, so that they can share the concept of disaster countermeasures and a concrete image of actions.

In this context, this chapter presents the objectives and methods of a work-shop designed for material rescue, aiming at improving skills in total rescue management.

1. Purpose

The author has held workshops mainly for those in charge of on-site work to rescue materials, such as local government officials, museum curators, university faculty, staff, and students. The central theme is to examine specific measures after rescuing damaged materials, especially water-damaged and challenging ones. Rather than a one-way introduction of ideas and techniques, the workshop aims to allow participants to discuss specific issues and engage in trial-and-error.

This workshop is a practical examination of what, to what extent, and how to tackle the series of work processes from first aid after the rescue to temporary storage. It emphasizes material observation upon seeing the damaged materials besides the practice and concept of handling them based on the observation. Frequent natural disasters led to the accumulation of disaster response experiences, thanks to which many reports and manuals are now available. Reading them, even those inexperienced can get some idea of the proper countermeasures; on the other hand, to put the acquired knowledge into practice, it is necessary to understand the full scope of the work, at what stage they should use the knowledge and skills, and specifically for what conditions they are effective. Participants need to observe the materials in our workshop and think about the proper measures. Furthermore, by discussing the results with other participants and attempting to put them into practice, these challenges enable them to acquire the necessary skills and improve disaster management.

2. Preparation

Part 3

2.1. Preparing Samples and Tools

The workshop simulates the first aid treatment of damaged materials. Organizers prepare sample "damaged materials", because it is difficult to offer actual ones. This section introduces samples of paper-based materials.

The target materials are old documents from the Edo period onward, many of which remain in museums, libraries, archives, and private homes across Japan. Using Japanese paper (Kozo paper), organizers make paper bundles imitating account books, letters, and attachments and then damage them intentionally by putting them in plastic bags, soaked with black or green tea leaves (or used coffee beans) and lukewarm water to simulate staining, and left overnight at room temperature to fasten staining and deterioration. Mixing mud to simulate defacement is possible, but materials should be as non-harmful as possible, considering the venue's environment and participants' health [See pp. 120-121 Fig. 2: Sample of simulated old documents, Fig. 3: Mixed with tea leaves and steeped in lukewarm water, and Fig. 4: Sample of pseudo-afflicted condition].

Other samples should be as general as possible. For example, for absorbent paper, use newspaper or kitchen paper; for tools, prepare items that anyone can obtain at a home improvement store, such as tweezers and brushes. Sometimes, it is possible to encourage participants to bring what they consider necessary for material salvage. The trick is to use only vague words such as "material rescue". Such a drill enables organizers to understand how the participants perceive material rescue and what tools they think they need.

The facilitator who supervises the entire workshop should preferably be someone with experience in disaster site management or an expert in conservation science or restoration, but others can serve if advice is available.

2.2. Setting Tasks

Organizers set tasks assuming the response immediately after the rescue. Participants can obtain the whole picture of material rescue by taking part in this type of workshop and action-planning workshop (introduced in Chapter 7 in detail) in succession.

When assuming a disaster, it should align with the geographical environment of the participants' residential areas. For example, if the area has a large river flowing nearby, assume river flooding; if on the coast, assume storm surge and tsunami; if along a mountain, assume landslides caused by heavy rains. In this way, assuming damage based on past disasters in the area makes it possible to share a more concrete image.

The participants play a role as on-site personnel responsible for materials rescued in a disaster, and each participant shall be given a group of prepared sample materials and examine how to treat them. They shall examine the following: (1) material observation, (2) goal setting, and (3) work process.

(1) Material Observation

Observe the images of the damaged materials projected on the screen and the sample materials distributed. Determine the initial task, considering the risks related to deterioration and damage.

When dealing with the risks, identify the points that need attention regarding the work environment and health.

(2) Goal Setting

To develop a work process within the scope of first aid, determine the specific conditions to which the materials should be brought. In addition, examine the points to remember when temporarily storing the materials after the first aid.

(3) Work Process

Determine the work process to put (1) and (2) into practice.

First, each participant considers the above on themselves. Then, in groups of three to five, participants discuss what they have examined and formulate a work process as a group [Fig. 5 and Fig. 6: Sample text for discussion].

3. Practice

Each working group has 3-5 participants. After the facilitator explains the tasks mentioned above, the participants consider the issues independently for 10 minutes, then discuss them as a group for 20 minutes and implement the work based on the process that each group has derived. The facilitator watches the discussion, and the participants are responsible for reviewing and implementing the

Part 3

Question 1: If you were asked to deal with a huge amount of water-damaged materials, what risks of the materials would you first focus on?

(1) Mould on the material
(2) Mud stains on the material
(3) Odour resulting from decay
(4) Moisture absorbed by the material
(5) Others:

Question 2: Based on the risk you focused on in Q1, what work goals would you set?

(1) Goals of "rescue": what and to what extent do you respond?

(2) Points to keep in mind for temporary storage

Question 3: What methods do you envision to achieve the goals of Q2? Work out specific work procedures.

Fig. 5

For summarizing group opinion

Question 1: If you were asked to deal with a huge amount of water-damaged materials, what risks of the materials would you first focus on?

Question 2: Based on the risk you focused on in Q1, what work goals would you set?

Question 3: What methods do you envision to achieve the goals of Q2? Work out specific work procedures.

Fig. 6

process [See p. 125 Fig. 7: Workshop (20 May, 2023, Fukushima University) and Fig. 8 Workshop (27 November, 2023, Saitama)].

After completing the work, each group presents their review, and then all the participants review. During the discussion, the facilitator comments on the evaluation, issues, and suggestions for improvement, particularly on the following points.

First, the validity of the observation. The critical point is whether the participants can concretely envision the damage situation based on the season and the time required for rescue, the scale of the materials as a group, and the nature of the materials. The facilitator needs to explain the damage that participants cannot perceive through images or samples, especially the risk of odour and mould, and to encourage them to pay attention not only to the approach but also to health hazard measures and environmental measures at the storage destination as part of the preliminary preparations.

As for the goal setting and work process, the facilitator evaluates whether the participants could make a feasible plan, presupposing that first aid is only temporary. Suppose some participants have experience in rescue activities. In that case, the facilitator sometimes comments on the importance of flexibly responding while respecting their experience and achievements and presents the need for a comprehensive review considering various opinions and methods depending on the situation.

After commenting on each opinion, the facilitator explains the basic concept of the process from rescue to first aid, summarizing the overall discussion. In workshops, the author presupposes the concepts introduced in Parts 1 and 2 of this book. Based on the concepts, the facilitator reviews the work to identify safer and more effective processes, showing them to the participants with samples. Finally, the participants confirm which stage in the overall disaster preparation process the work practised during the workshop belongs to.

Conclusion: Experiencing and Validating Failures

The workshop aims to allow participants to examine and discuss proactively and to acquire ideas on the work process planning for damaged material rescue and the selection of necessary skills. When we conduct a workshop, we focus on confirming what role the knowledge and skills possessed by the participants can play in the actual work site rather than on delivering a one-way lecture. Indeed, sometimes participants damage the sample materials during examination and practice, but failures enable them to verify the causes by themselves and to work out solutions through mutual discussion. Experiencing failures that cannot be experienced in the actual field and learning lessons from them are important opportunities in a workshop.

In the future, it would be ideal if a curriculum to develop the ability to manage a series of work related to material rescue is provided in university education and training programs for local government officials and museum curators. In addition, it is also necessary to cultivate the ability to deal comprehensively with diverse materials that are not limited to paper-based materials: we need to discuss and deepen the methodology of material rescue training.

References

AMANO Masashi. "Shiryohozon no ninaite to gijutsu wo tsunagu [Linking Conservation Practitioners and Technology]", in: *Chiikirekishibunkakeisho gaidobukku* [Guidebook for Community Hisorical Culture Inheritance]. Bungaku Report, 2022.

AMANO Masahi. "Kamibaitaishiryo no Kyusai wo soteishita shimyureshon wakushoppu no kento to zissen [Study and Practice of Simulated Workshops for Paper-Based Materials Rescue]", Poster presentation at the 45th Congress of the Japan Society for Conservation of Cultural Property, 25 Jun 2023.

KOHDZUMA Yohsei, TATEISHI Toru, and KODANI Ryusuke (eds). *Nyumon daisaigaijidai no bunkazaibosai* [Introduction to Cultural Property Disaster Prevention in the Age of Great Disasters]. Douseisha, 2023.

MATSUSHITA Masakazu and KONO Mio (eds). *Suisonshiryo wo suku* [Rescuing Water-Damaged Materials]. Iwata-shoin, 2009.

Part 3

Chapter 9

Communicating with Local Communities

▨ ABE Koichi (Fukushima University)

Introduction

This Chapter covers the challenges associated in communicating with local communities, which is necessary in disaster countermeasures and material rescue for preserving local historical culture. The target of our discussion is mainly the Siryo-net (Kobe) that rescues and preserves historical materials that are mostly in private ownership (for further information on the Siryo-net, see Part 1). When rescuing materials in disaster-affected areas, rescuers are rarely familiar with the area through surveys and research. In most cases, rescuers are visiting the area for the first time because of a disaster. Under such circumstances, for external experts to meet the local government officials in charge of cultural properties, local historians, owners, and residents, and perform material rescue activities smoothly, communicating with local communities is obviously an important key. It is clear that, if opportunities for locals and outsiders to become acquainted prior to a disaster exists, work would be more effective, thereby leading to better results.

However, "communicating with local communities" is not simple as it is extremely difficult to generalize how people will convey their ideas to each other, which is the core of diverse communication. It is also not suited to the creation of models or manuals. Japan has about 30 Shiryo-Networks (historical materials networks) across the nation, some of which have ample experience and have achieved notable results. However, given the page allowance limit, I focus on the Fukushima Shiryo-Network of which the author is the representative, and the Soma Shiryo-Network of which the author is an executive.

Part 3

269

1. Launching the Fukushima Shiryo-Network and Challenges Faced

The Fukushima Shiryo-Network was launched in November 2010 as a liaison for experts, government, and citizens by progressively disbanding the Fukushima Cultural Heritage Preservation Network established in 2005 by Fukushima Prefecture Cultural Promotion Corporation (Corporation, presently called Fukushima Prefecture Cultural Promotion Foundation) with the Corporation, Fukushima Prefectural Museum, Fukushima Prefectural Historical Society, and Fukushima University as promoters. The idea of HONMA Hiroshi from the Corporation, who liaised and coordinated each facet, was that the participation of citizen volunteers is essential in the comprehensive understanding and preservation of historical and cultural heritage including undesignated items. To gain the trust of owners, the participation of government personnel in charge of cultural properties is also recommended, which allows for a horizontal link beyond municipalities.

However, merely four months after its launch, the Great East Japan Earthquake and Fukushima Daiichi Nuclear Power Plant Accident occurred in March 2011. The Fukushima Shiryo-Network chose the representative and secretariat in April and took on the work of rescuing materials of municipalities and individuals who requested support. By June, the Fukushima Shiryo-Network had surveyed and conducted rescue in 25 cases, but the challenges faced were diverse. The main challenges were as follows:

(1) Inadequate data on the location necessary to perform the rescue: There was no location list, leaving volunteers to rely on the *Fukushima Prefecture Ancient Documents Location Confirmation Survey Report* compiled in 1980 by the Fukushima Prefecture Board of Education, or on individuals providing the materials.

(2) The local government not participating with the Fukushima Shiryo-Network: Presently, the relationship is still one-sided, limited to e-mails.

(3) Inadequate communication with local communities: The presence of the Fukushima Shiryo-Network is not well known, and even if there are materials needing rescue, the requests do not reach the Fukushima Shiryo-Network. This situation has not improved.

(4) A lack of citizen volunteers: From the viewpoint of crime prevention, the information on the disaster-affected areas was only shared among those involved. This limited the rescue activities to those who were available from the promoting agencies, limiting the recruitment of volunteers.

(5) Issues associated with being the liaison: The Fukushima Shiryo-Network was unable to take on responsibility for the management of rescued materials. It was also difficult to secure temporary storage and a place to work.

In terms of the topic of this Chapter, the activities that began while "communicating with local communities" remained inadequate.

In May 2012, the Fukushima Prefecture Damaged Cultural Properties Relief Headquarters was established. When rescue activities began at museums of the former restricted areas of Futaba, Okuma, and Tomioka Town in the summer, interested parties' interests shifted to the former restricted areas. The Fukushima Shiryo-Network, as merely the liaison, could not get involved in any way. As the author put effort into tasks at a temporary storage outside of the former restricted areas as a member of Fukushima University, promotors worked on the rescue of the cultural assets through each of their official positions. However, rescue cases in private ownership decreased in number, and the presence of the Fukushima Shiryo-Network was forgotten. This was a challenge unique to acting as the liaison.

2. Development of the Fukushima Shiryo-Network

The author became the representative in July 2012 and worked to overcome the challenges by shifting the axis of substantial activities to the university and continuing the routine activities with students while keeping the Fukushima Shiryo-Network as the base liaison for the promotors.

(1) Regarding the inadequate data, with the support of a research assistant, a list of owners in the prefecture was organized using Microsoft Excel wherever possible so that they could be searched and identified as needed. As a result, in Shinchi Town, which was affected by an intensity 6+ earthquake during the 2021 Fukushima Earthquake, we compared an owner list, *Shinchi Town History* (as the regulations on personal information were not strict at the time, owners' ad-

Part 3

dresses were recorded in full) with an older residential map to prepare a list. We cooperated with the Miyagi Shiryo-Network and attempted to conduct a location survey on-site. During this process, we were able to rescue materials from three commercial storage locations that were not on the list. This is a good example of how true information cannot be found unless one goes to the site.

(2) There is no change in the lack of participation by municipalities in the Fukushima Shiryo-Network. A network between municipalities was realized through the "Agreement on Mutual Support during Disasters Regarding Cultural Assets in Fukushima Prefecture" between Fukushima Prefecture and 59 municipalities, which was the result of the formulation of the Fukushima Prefecture Cultural Assets Preservation and Utilization Guidelines in March 2020. In November of the same year, the "Agreement on Support Activities during Disasters Regarding Cultural Assets in Fukushima Prefecture" was signed between the prefecture and four involved organizations including the Fukushima Shiryo-Network. Information is exchanged and training is provided once a year through a liaison meeting. The Fukushima Shiryo-Network was to indirectly cooperate with municipalities through liaison meetings, finally taking the steps it should have been able to take in the beginning. However, the rescue targets were limited to cultural assets managed by municipalities during disasters, and mutual support of routine removal activities was not assumed. The Network is not utilized to rescue undesignated cultural assets that are privately owned. As such, many challenges remain.

Tomioka Town and Fukushima University have signed an agreement, and the project team at the town hall continues to receive support with the storage and recording of materials rescued via donations and requests. The Fukushima Shiryo-Network offers support by recruiting citizen volunteers during busy times.

(3) Regarding the inadequate communication with communities, we attempted to solve this problem through student education. In Kunimi Town, located in the northern part of the prefecture, we conducted a damaged material survey with cooperation from those in charge of cultural assets, local history research associations, and neighborhood associations. As a result, we confirmed multiple unintroduced materials that were not known by *Kunimi Town History*. Based on this result, we rediscovered local cultural assets from the perspective of students while learning from the locals, and developed the "Local Marugoto Museum"

activity, which leads to material preservation [See p.130 Photo.1: Marugoto Museum (Kaida, Kunimi Town)]. This activity shifted the stage to the Yanagawa neighborhood of Date City, where the students' survey study was advanced with the cooperation and guidance of local historical research associations and NPOs. Even during the COVID-19 crisis, we cooperated with the locals of Kanayagawa Ward where the university was located, and conducted a survey study of Kannon worship, hymns, and history. These were all successful thanks to the understanding and cooperation of historians and the residents who know the local communities well. The students' survey results were summarized in a pamphlet and are being used for a better understanding of the area and tourism.

(4) Regarding the lack of citizen volunteers, by shifting the axis of routine activities to the university, the initial plan of citizen volunteers became impossible. Even then, we held night classes on the organization of documents called paleography training, which allowed people to participate after work. Nearby residents with interest responded to the advertisement by the Fukushima Shiryo-Network and attended voluntarily, taking photographs of ancient documents and making a list of contents with the students. They sometimes brought documents they had preserved themselves and took photographs. From 2014, we began holding a two-day summer camp in August, which has become an annual event where citizen volunteers both from, and outside of, the prefecture gather.

Regardless of participation in the activities at the university, citizen volunteers' interest in the local materials is quite high. Citizen volunteers gathered every time to participate in the preservation work of water-damaged materials at the Motomiya City History and Folklore Museum that was heavily damaged by the 2019 Typhon Hagibis [See p.131 Photo.2: Preservation activities of water-damaged materials in Motomiya City]. Many of these volunteers are seniors who participate in cultural assets lectures and citizen circles. There was definitely something to note about the skills and personalities of staff who are routinely involved with citizens. Every community has a coordinator with skills to make projects work smoothly by connecting people. To say that communicating well with such a key person is an important element in succeeding in communicating with local communities and building networks is not an overstatement.

The last item (5) is a challenge unique to the position of liaison. The problem of inadequate temporary storage locations and spaces to work was resolved by the

Part 3

establishment of the Fukushima University Fukushima Future Center for Regional Revaitalization (presently Fukushima University CommunityFuture Design Center), completion of center buildings (presently converted to the Faculty of Food and Agricultural Sciences building), appointment of a historical document manager, and securing of a material storage room. Presently, we have shifted the storage to the Faculty of Administration & Social Sciences and are continuing the preservation work in practice rooms and such.

The Fukushima Shiryo-Network still does not have a corporate status and remains a voluntary organization acting as a liaison. The reason we are still able to work is that, for the last 12 years, ironically, Fukushima has faced numerous disasters. Material conservation activities in a nuclear disaster area are described with the words, "in progress," but the meeting of the Fukushima Prefecture Damaged Cultural Property Rescue Team Headquarters that audits the countermeasures was a place for the Fukushima Museum, Fukushima Prefectural Museum of Art, Fukushima Cultural Property Centre Shirakawa Branch (Mahoron), Fukushima Prefectural Archives, Fukushima University, and Fukushima Shiryo-Network to meet in person and continuously exchange information and opinions. During the 2019 Typhoon Hagibis, the mutual support agreement imagined by the prefecture was implemented early, and related organizations arrived to provide support. Among these were the promotors of the Fukushima Shiryo-Network. We heard encouraging statements that when these members participate in an official manner, they act as representative of the affiliated organization, but when volunteering they act as a member of the Fukushima Shiryo-Network. This was an opportunity to confirm the manner in which the Fukushima Shiryo-Network functions as a liaison. Cooperation between experts functioned in rescues during the 2021 and 2022 Fukushima Earthquakes, thereby preserving materials from the perspectives of diverse experts.

When we look back, the result was quite different from what was initially imagined. However, we were able to establish a certain path to solving the problems initially faced. We are halfway through building a comprehensive cultural asset network that connects the government, academia, business, and citizens of Fukushima. To this end, we need to value connections with municipalities, local communities, and owners that came out of the material rescue and preservation on site and keep building upon them. That being said, since disasters keep occurring in such a wide area, rescue and preservation of materials often remains incomplete as those tasked to do so cannot keep up. In parallel to material rescue activities, our next challenge is to build a foundation so that not only the continuing support from external sources, but also long-term material preservation activities can continue within local communities. A method that is usable for non-experts also needs to be established.

3. Launch of the Soma Shiryo-Network as a citizen network

While Shiryo-Networks are centered around universities, museums, and municipalities, the Soma Shiryo-Network is the first Shiryo-Network in Japan that is organized and operated by citizens [See p.133 Photo.3: Preservation activities of fusuma underlay document rescued from the residence of SUZUKI Tatsuro].

The Soma Shiryo-Network was launched in September 2022, and consists of citizens and those born in Soma, with a Japanese painter, SUZUKI Tatsuro, as the representative. SUZUKI works on his creative activities in Tokyo, but after the Great East Japan Earthquake, he became involved in the support of his birthplace, Soma. His home in Soma is located on an estate that belonged to a samurai within the former Nakamura Domain. It is a building with both Japanese and Western aspects, built during the early Showa Era. The building withstood the Great East Japan Earthquake, but it suffered cracks in its pillars during the 2021 Fukushima Earthquake. While repairs and seismic updates were being considered, the 2022 Fukushima Earthquake occurred, which made the house lean. To see the main entrance built to welcome the head of the Soma household collapse due to the weight of ceramic roof tiles was especially shocking.

The Fukushima Shiryo-Network worked with the Miyagi Shiryo-Network, and following Shinchi Town in 2021, an interview of material owners began in 2022 in Kashima Ward, Minamisoma. At that time, the author was able to contact SUZUKI with the information received from NHK staff visiting Soma City.

While being a disaster victim, SUZUKI saw old buildings in the neighborhood destroyed, historical materials ruined, and traditional crafts facing extinction. He was alarmed by the loss of the history and traditional culture of Soma. SUZUKI's old classmate and the Chairman of the Fukushima Prefecture Folklore Society, IWASAKI Masaki, and KUSANO Kiyotaka, the Chairman of the Soma

Chamber of Commerce and Industry who operates a construction business, were also concerned that houses were demolished after each disaster while vacant lands increased, thereby leading to the loss of the historical landscape of the town around a castle. In this manner, local volunteers and staff from the Fukushima and Miyagi Shiryo-Networks all met in person, proposing the launch of a network from the common understanding that there needs to be an entity that receives all the information gathered to rescue materials. With the proposal from KUSANO, this network was named the Soma Shiryo-Network. Subsequently, along with the rescue of materials at the SUZUKI home, members of the organization were carefully selected, and the network was officially launched in September 2022, six months after the Earthquake.

The Soma Shiryo-Network with its characteristics as the liaison is filled with residents of Soma, and those who were originally from Soma, with which the Fukushima and Miyagi Shiryo-Network are involved. It is an industry-academia-public network consisting of coordinators, the head of the Soma Chamber of Commerce and Industry, Soma Local Study Group chairman and members, Bajokai (Soma High School Alumni Association) chairman, Fukushima Prefecture Folklore Society chairman, chairman of the Association of People from Sendai, journalists, tax accountants, Tohoku Gakuin University faculty members, and Fukushima University faculty members, with the faculty members of Soma High School serving as secretary general. At its core is the connection between alumni of Soma High School and interested parties. According to SUZUKI, staff was recruited from those associated with Soma High School in consultation with TAKEUCHI Yoshiaki, the secretary general and faculty of the school. Soma High School is a long-established school that began as Fukushima Prefecture Daiyon Junior High School in 1898 (Soma High School Auditorium built during the time of the old Junior High School is a registered tangible cultural asset). Many talented graduates have come from this school, succeeding both locally and in a wide range of fields. For a community-based network, to have the alumni association of a long-established school as the parent body is an advantage. When attempting to communicate with a community from the outside, an existing network is extremely helpful. The reason they were able to put activities on track in just one year and achieve successive results is exactly because of this advantage. We are thankful for the keen eyes of SUZUKI and others who focused on the alumni network.

The advantages of a community-based citizen network are ease of collecting information on the location of materials to be rescued, and the ability to flexibly respond to sudden requests. When a long-established restaurant in the city decided to close and tear down the building owing to the earthquake damage and the sudden passing of the owner, local study group members led the preservation of the paintings created by the owner along with historical materials. Their passion was obvious during the exhibition of rescued materials planned in conjunction with the first symposium.

Another characteristic of the Soma Shiryo-Network is that the coordinator is a journalist who is also an alumnus. TERASHIMA Hideya presents activity reports based on detailed interviews on an online news site, TOHOKU360. A Shiryo-Network with a dedicated journalist is surely rare. Another strength of the Soma Shiryo-Network is that their activities are shared across Japan.

Although the Soma Shiryo-Network has its advantages, disadvantages also exist. Generally, the alumni organization is dominated by seniors who miss the old days. This is also the case for the Soma Shiryo-Network. This makes the Soma Shiryo-Network unsuitable for physical work on-site, for example. They have no experience in material rescue activities such as clearing a storage shed, no human resources, or expert knowledge and know-how of material preservation. However, a system is in place where the representatives of the Fukushima and Miyagi Shiryo-Networks play the role of coordinators to provide experience and know-how to the Network, reaching out to experts, students, alumni, and citizen volunteers to secure enough staff to provide support.

In this manner, in September 2023, a year after its launch, a symposium was held at Soma High School to share the results and challenges of the Soma Shiryo-Network with citizens of Soma and interested parties across Japan. On the day, more people attended than expected, and there were many reactions to the report and the presentation of new materials. The current challenges confirmed at the symposium were securing long-term storage for rescued materials and a framework for expanding the scope of citizen participation. Cooperation of the government is the most urgent challenge at the present time. In the long run, the organization must be set up and human resources must be secured to maintain the ground-breaking attempt known as the citizens' network. In addition, a culture

Part 3

needs to be established for citizens to protect their history with their own hands. We hope that the ground-breaking attempts of the Soma Shiryo-Network operated by the citizens are a major inspiration, encouraging similar attempts across Japan.

Conclusions

I must apologize that we could not meet the task of communicating with local communities that is needed in disaster countermeasures and materials rescue of local historical culture. However, I believe there were some key findings. In local communities, there are always people who care about the local history and culture, know the locations of materials, and are ready to act out of concern over loss. Furthermore, these people are often equipped with the characteristics to become local coordinators. To achieve results with material rescue and disaster prevention measures in communities, cooperation with key people from local communities must be prioritized, and the circle of cooperation with residents must spread from there. Connection with existing networks, such as local history study groups, neighborhood associations, citizen circles, and alumni associations is also quite effective. Building networks with the government is just starting in many areas, but if there are opportunities for a Shiryo-Network to participate, sharing of disaster-affected material information and setting up of support systems might drastically advance. The role demanded of Shiryo-Networks is to create close cooperation between experts and act as a liaison connecting existing and diverse networks horizontally. This must lead to the true meaning of "passing on cultural assets including those undesignated by the entire community and society," indicated in the outline of the Amended Cultural Assets Protection Act.

References

ABE Koichi and The Fukushima University Fukushima Future Center for Regional Revitalization (eds). *Fukushima Saisei to Rekisi, Bunkaisan* [Fukushima Revitalization and Historical/Cultural heritage]. Yamakawa Shuppansha, 2013.

ABE Koichi, "Fukushima no Genba kara furikaeru 11 nen [Reflections from Eleven Years after the Fukushima Disasters]. *Shigaku*, 92-1/2, 2023.

TERASHIMA Hideya, "Fukushimaokizishin [The 2002 Fukushima Earthquake]", in:

TOHOKU360. https://tohoku360.com/316-soma/ (last viewed on September 12, 2023)

The Fukushima Prefecture Damaged Cultural Properties Relief Headquarters (ed). *Fukushim akenhisaibunkazaitokyuenhonbu katsudohokokusho* [The Fukushima Prefecture Damaged Cultural Properties Relief Headquarters Activity Report]. 2023.

Soma Shiryo-Network. *"Soma no Rekishi wo Mamoru Tsutaeru" 2023 Hokokusho* [2023 Annual Report]". 2024.

Chapter 10

Specialized Knowledge and the Preservation of Historical Documents

▨ ICHIZAWA Tetsu (Kobe University)

The following is an abridged version of the Japanese chapter by the same author in this volume.

Introduction

In this chapter, we will re-examine three topics that have been discussed throughout this volume: **knowledge**, **methods**, and **activities** for the conservation of historical documents in the event of a disaster. We will discuss these topics while keeping in mind the problems surrounding the role of specialized knowledge in modern society. Historical preservation activities bear fruit when specialists and non-specialists combine their skills together, so I would like to consider the potential that **knowledge**, **methods**, and **activities** might have for dealing with these larger problems.

1. The Present State of Expertise

TAKEKURA Fumito's *Dogu o yomu—130 nenkan tokarenakatta Jomon shinwa no nazo* was awarded the prestigious Suntory Prize for Social Sciences and Humanities in 2021, the same year it was published.[1] The debate that surrounded TAKEKURA's book is a noteworthy commentary on the standing of "specialized knowledge" in modern society. The problems of the book have already been discussed from several perspectives in *Dogu o yomu wo yomu*, but

Part 3

here I would like to review the issues raised by this book that relate to the topics of this chapter.[2]

As it is well known, TAKEKURA, who is not a specialist in archaeology, presents his own views in *Dogu o yomu*, and his work was not received well at all by archaeologists. As explained by SUGA Yutaka in *Dogu o yomu wo yomu*, *Dogu o yomu* mainly summarizes TAKEKURA Fumito's interpretation of *dogu*. Beyond its main arguments, however, the book was perceived as a critique of specialists.[3]

As SUGA points out, this point is well illustrated in an interview published in *The Asahi Shimbun GLOBE+* under the title *"Dogu o yomu no ura theme wa senmonchi e no gimon 'shiroto' to yayu suru fucho ni kikikan"*.[4] As implied by the title, TAKEKURA's *Dogu o yomu* is appraised as a book that raises doubts about specialized knowledge and criticizes those who disregard "amateurs."

In the interview, author TAKEKURA says the following:

Actually, the reason I decided to write *Dogu o yomu* like this was the distrust toward expertise that came out of the 3.11 nuclear disaster.

No matter how many times the local citizens pointed out the dangers of nuclear power, experts treated their concerns as "amateur opinions" and did not take them seriously. Nevertheless, the nuclear power plant that we had been told was absolutely safe had a meltdown before our eyes.

Without a doubt, specialists are necessary, but instead of being condensed into practical knowledge that can improve our lives, their expertise is locked away and monopolized as a vested interest. This way of handling specialized knowledge continues in various fields.

So how can we transform specialized knowledge into a more practical knowledge? The answer is to make it available to the public through liberal arts education and networking. I hope movement in that direction accelerates going forward.

TAKEKURA criticizes the closed and privileged nature of specialized knowledge, but this kind of criticism is certainly nothing new. One could say that it is a variation of the "absent-minded professor" trope that has often been made about specialists. Regarding the issue of the nuclear power plant in Fukushima, while

TAKEKURA claims that specialists ignored citizens' opinions and set up a power plant in a high-risk location, he himself completely ignores the fact that there were also specialists who argued that it was dangerous.[5] The fact that the media has made such a big deal about this unoriginal, clumsy argument shows just how strong our society's negative opinion of specialists has become.

Also in the GLOBE+ interview, Nakajima Takeshi says the following:

Archaeology cannot be the only way that we approach our thinking about antiquity. I believe many possibilities will open for us if we confront antiquity with the collective wisdom of philosophy, anthropology, and other disciplines. I think it is important to use this kind of approach to antiquity when we think about the Jomon period today.

Nakajima's opinion that we should study the Jomon period not only through archaeology, but also by marshalling the wisdom of other fields, is completely respectable. However, it is also an interesting phenomenon that this respectable opinion is tied in with a theory that so clumsily criticizes specialists.

2. Expertise and Daily Life

Moving on, let us consider the actual task of preserving historical records. Even in this field, there are problems related to specialized knowledge.

For example, there is the "Okuri-ie Project," in which volunteers clean out homes that are abandoned or will be abandoned, and hand them over to new residents. In an interview with YAMADA Noriko, the leader of the project, I heard the following story.[6] While cleaning out the former residents' belongings at one old house, they found a large number of old documents. The volunteers could not handle it, so they called a researcher to the site. The researcher said they would need to conduct an examination and asked the volunteers not to touch anything. However, the researcher's examination did not progress quickly, delaying the volunteers' work at the house. The researcher's schedule and the lives of the townspeople who were cleaning out the house did not align.

In a similar vein, psychologist TOHATA Kaito has cautioned that while mental disorders are determined to be illnesses and given proper medical treatment by specialists, these are problems that originally would have been addressed in people's daily lives but have been turned into a medical problem.[7] TOHATA's argument that there is a negative side to specialized knowledge and that specialists cannot operate effectively without worldly wisdom, is similar to the point made in the interview mentioned above.

The activities of ANDO Ryoko and others in the Suetsugi district of Iwaki City, Fukushima Prefecture, are also very helpful in considering the relationship between daily life and specialized knowledge.[8] Amidst anxiety over the amount of radiation from the Fukushima nuclear power plant meltdown, specialists presented various safety standards based on their own theories, and authorities repealed safety standards without satisfactory explanation. This all caused confusion in the region and conflict of opinion among residents intensified. Naturally, distrust toward specialists also increased. As their livelihoods were shaken, ANDO took action to restore residents' confidence in their local environment by helping them to measure radiation levels themselves. This project has been supported by specialists who have been involved consistently and provide expert advice based on the measured values. The project of ANDO and her colleagues was to restore trust in the local environment—including healthy relationships among the local people—and their work is a rare example of connecting specialized knowledge to our daily lives.

With these examples in mind, let us once again consider those three topics discussed throughout this book: knowledge, methods, and activities.

3. The Aim of Activities for the Preservation of Historical Materials

The three topics discussed throughout this book (knowledge, methods, and activities) are characterized by the fact that they have been developed through the actual rescue of historical materials and restoration of damaged materials during disasters in collaboration with various actors, including local citizens. In such a setting, specialists inevitably share their expertise and reconcile problems of daily life with specialized knowledge.

So, what kinds of methods, based on what kinds of assumptions, should be used to realize this "reconciliation"? Let us broaden our perspective a little. A

2022 book entitled *"Senmonka" to wa dare ka* grapples with this question head-on.[9]

The book works with the premise that there is a certain inflexibility of specialized knowledge. OKI Sayaka, for example, discusses how experts are called upon to give their opinions in a "hybrid forum" (Michel Caron), where a wide variety of topics intersect, including science, technology, society, politics, economy, and government regulations. The experts who are summoned to these forums are asked to answer questions outside their own fields of expertise. The specific issues are often interdisciplinary, and there are often strict time constraints on their answers.[10]

KAMISATO Tatsuhiro describes parliamentary briefings in which the government consults a council of experts as an oppressive "yoke." Some of the questions asked in these briefings cannot be answered by the research available at the time. However, the council members cannot fulfill their role by answering, "We don't know." As a result, they give the best assessment they can and the government then cherry-picks what it deems convenient from the council's report, which is limited to begin with. The constraints of these rules are like a heavy yoke on the shoulders of the council members. Kamisato further asserts that behind this "yoke" is a system in which "one part of the administrative structure, the secretariat, sets the agenda for the council, gathers the experts, and manages the council under secretariat leadership."[11]

So, what steps ought to be taken to apply specialized knowledge, which is inherently narrow, to real-world problems? On this question, the articles in *"Senmonka" to wa dare ka* make the following points.

The first is that actors other than specialists in a narrow field should also be involved in discussions to resolve a problem. In his proposed solution to the "yoke" problem mentioned above, Kamisato draws on the work of Erik Millstone and suggests that before a council is formed to assess risk, there should be a "social framing" stage in which there is discussion about what exactly specialists will be asked to assess, what range of specialists ought to be invited (for example, specialists not only in the natural sciences, but in the humanities and social sciences, as well as citizen representatives from local communities), and how much time will be allotted for the council to prepare answers.

SUGA Yutaka also argues for the importance of such a forum for specialists and non-specialists (which includes specialists in other fields) in his call for **knowledge governance**. According to SUGA, knowledge governance is the ideal "quality control" of knowledge, "a networking of specialists and non-specialists to perform quality control of knowledge from multiple perspectives, and to understand the multifaceted nature of one another's knowledge."[12]

In the case of the preservation of historical materials, there are various actors involved besides the owners and researchers. In *Link*, a periodical published by the Kobe University Community Outreach Center, we have conducted a series of interviews with individuals who are not historical researchers but are involved with historical documents or with the retelling of history through popular media, christening them "neighbors of historical research." We have heard from people such as a house clearance agent,[13] an antiquarian bookstore owner,[14] an editor of history books aimed at the general public,[15] a representative of the "Okuri-ie Project" discussed above,[16] and a newspaper reporter.[17] In these conversations, it became clear to us that researchers are only one of the many actors who handle historical materials.

The second point is a focus on the role of facilitators who connect specialists and society.[18] The SMS (Science Media Centre), which facilitates the distribution of information between the mass media and researchers in science and technology fields, was established as an organization to play such a mediating role.[19] In addition, there is a need for "cultural translators" who can communicate what is happening in other fields and link specialists with other specialists.[20]

The third point is the encouragement of research that involves participation in the subject. Rather than separating themselves as observers looking at a subject "objectively," researchers ought to become involved with the subject and transform themselves through their research.[21] This way of doing research has a lot in common with the participatory development theory advocated by NAKAMURA Hisashi, in which "outsiders" participate alongside locals in a regional development project, and through this process become personally vested in the project.[22]

The above problems concerning specialized knowledge (the gap between the range of knowledge possessed by experts and the answers sought from them) and the prescriptions for these problems ([1] participation of diverse actors, [2] mediation between specialists and society, and among specialists, and [3] research that involves the researcher with the subject) are also applicable to the rescue and preservation of historical materials. Rescue and preservation cannot be realized without the collaboration of various actors, and researchers in the field must be in a position to connect their expertise with society. At the same time, historical document specialists, conservation scientists, government officials, and experts involved in disaster recovery and reconstruction need to work toward mutual understanding. And finally, without a deep commitment to the people and places that have preserved and passed on the materials, it would be impossible to fully convey the meaning of these materials to future generations.

The knowledge, methods, and activities involved in the rescue and preservation of historical materials are deeply related to the problems surrounding specialized knowledge and have meaning as a practical way to overcome those problems. The knowledge, methods, and activities were born through experience in the field and refined through a reflective cycle with each new project. I think this process itself is a working example of the three prescriptions described above.

Conclusion

In this chapter, we have re-evaluated the meaning of the methods, knowledge, and activities in the preservation of historical materials by looking at problems relating to expertise. Returning to the topic of historical materials as a matter of historical research and study, we must of course also mention the issue of public history.

According to OKAMOTO Michihiro, public history is a somewhat ambiguous term, but "We can basically divide it into two categories: 'history *to the public*' and 'history *in the public*.'" The former refers to history as it is presented at museums and other institutions that educate the public, as well as archaeological sites and artifacts, novels, films, comic books, and other media produced by specialists. In contrast, the latter refers to history based on customs, oral traditions, and memories created by ordinary people, and was formerly outside the scope of professional research. Rather than thinking of these two categories as being in opposition to one another, healthy debates among scholars tend to emphasize their interdependence.[23]

One can argue that the preservation of historical materials is an activity that

Part 3

is both **to the public** and **in the public**. Moreover, if we consider the fact that it fosters collaboration between various kinds of actors in addition to specialists, we might say that the preservation of historical materials is an activity in which people with various skills and interests related to historical documents work together and create a new public space—to adapt OKAMOTO's theme, they **make the public**.[24]

In modern society, anyone can freely communicate about history to the world. We often see discourse in which a person's desires masquerade as history. Conspiracy theorists claim that experts know the truth but are covering it up. In such times, a public space where people, including experts, can work together toward the goal of preserving documents that communicate history, and exchange opinions about how to rescue and restore such documents, is extremely important.

The knowledge, methods, and activities for rescuing historical materials are designed to achieve a specific objective. However, they also have value in that they connect the research of specialists with citizens and society. I hope that this point will be investigated more deeply in the future.

Notes

1 TAKEKURA Fumito, *Dogu o yomu—130 nenkan tokarenakatta Jomon shinwa no nazo*, Shobunsha, 2021.

2 Jomon ZINE, (ed.), *Dogu o yomu wo yomu*, Bungaku Tsushin, 2023.

3 SUGA Yutaka, "Chi no 'kanteinin'—Senmonchi hihan wa senmonchi hitei de atte wa naranai", Ibid.

4 The Asahi Shimbun GLOBE+ interview is available online at https://globe.asahi.com/article/14400149 (Accessed September 9, 2023).

5 SOEDA Takashi, *Genpatsu to otsunami: Keikoku o homutta hitobito*, Iwanami Shoten, 2014.

6 YAMADA Noriko et al., "Interview Series *Rekishi kenkyu no rinjin-tachi* Dai-nikai dai-sanbu: Ikkyu kenchikushi Yamada Noriko-san", *Link*, no. 13, 2021, pp. 52-83.

7 TOHATA Kaito, "Shakai kihyo", The Asahi Shimbun Morning Edition, June 6, 2021.

8 ANDO Ryoko, *Umi o utsu—Fukushima, Hiroshima, Belarus ni te*, Mizuho Shobo, 2019; ANDO Ryoko, *Steve & Bonnie—Sabaku no Genshiryokumura in America*, Shobunsha, 2022.

9 MURAKAMI Yoichiro, (ed.), *"Senmonka" to wa dare ka*, Shobunsha, 2022.

10 OKI Sayaka, "Kagaku to 'senmonka' o meguru sho-gainen no rekishi", Ibid.

11 KAMISATO Tatsuhiro, "Risk jidai ni okeru gyosei to senmonka—United Kingdom BSE mondai kara", Ibid.

12 SUGA, op. cit.

13 YAGI Akihito, et al., "Interview Series *Rekishi kenkyu no rinjin-tachi* Dai-ikkai: Ie-jimai adviser® Yagi Akihiko-san", *Link*, no. 11, 2019, pp. 63-88.

14 HARA Tomoko, et al., "Interview Series *Rekishi kenkyu no rinjin-tachi* Dai-sankai: Shoshi Hara Tomoko-san", *Link*, no. 14, 2022, pp. 64-96.

15 YAMAZAKI Hiroshi, et al., "Interview Series *Rekishi kenkyu no rinjin-tachi* Dai-nikai dai-ichibu: Shinsho henshusha Yamazaki Hiroshi-san", *Link*, no. 13, 2021, pp. 8-42.

16 YAMADA, op. cit.

17 This will be published as the fourth interview in the series in *Link*, no. 15 (Forthcoming).

18 KOBAYASHI Tadashi, "Shakai to kagaku o tsunagu atarashii 'senmonka'", MURAKAMI, op. cit.; SUZUKI Tetsuya, "Undo toshite no senmonchi", MURAKAMI, op. cit.

19 SEGAWA Shiro, "Journalists to senmonka wa kyodo dekiru ka", Ibid.

20 See KOBAYASHI, op. cit. In addition, FUJIGAKI Yuko draws on the European discussion of "Responsible Research and Innovation" (RRI), which advocates for collaboration among actors in society. She asserts that "meddling in neighboring fields and flexibility through exchanges are essential" for this. FUJIGAKI Yuko, "Tonari no ryoiki ni kuchi-dashi suru to iu koto", Ibid.

21 SUZUKI, op. cit.

22 NAKAMURA Hisashi, "Tojishasei no tankyu to sankagata kaihatsu—Sri Lanka ni miru daigaku no shakai koken katsudo", SAITO Fumihiko, ed., *Sankagata kaihatsu—Mazushii hitobito ga shuyaku ni naru kaihatsu ni mukete*, Nihon Hyoronsha, 2002.

23 OKAMOTO Michihiro, "Public history kenkyu josetsu", *The bulletin of the Institute of Human Sciences, Toyo University*, no. 22, 2020.

24 For more on this way of thinking about "public," see SAITO Junichi, *Publicness*, Iwanami Shoten, 2000.

Conclusion

◪ MATSUSHITA Masakazu and AMANO Masashi

This book is part of the results of Group A, "Inheritance of LHM" of the Grant-in-Aid for Specially Promoted Research Project "From Local Historical Material Studies to Regional Historical Culture: Creation of a New Research Field for Resilient Local Communities in a Country of Natural Disasters" (Principal Investigator: OKUMURA Hiroshi, Project Number: 19H05457). The members of this joint research project are working to rescue, preserve, and pass down various historical materials in each community in response to the natural disasters that have frequently occurred across Japan since the Great Hanshin-Awaji Earthquake in 1995. Moreover, by examining the issues confronted in the process, the authors have made practical progress in finding a foundation for the inheritance of historical culture in local communities. Each author is still promoting own activities, and this publication is a condensed version of the philosophy of historical material rescue and inheritance discovered through these efforts.

To pass on historical materials within a community, it is only natural to protect the materials themselves. Therefore, we need to take prompt and appropriate measures to handle damaged materials, but handling the large number of materials scattered all over Japan takes much work. An overview of past efforts shows that municipality officials, the locals, and other individuals who are not experts in preservation and restoration often take the lead in responding to disaster-affected areas. These days, cases of disaster response activities in the past are available on many occasions, and encountering these activities enables us to get an idea of what they entail. Conversely, disaster situations differ depending on their timing, historical and geographical background, scale, and type of disaster. The target materials are also diverse depending on the activities' composition. Disaster response requires efforts beyond specific techniques and manuals; putting them into practice is always challenging. After much discussion among the authors, we decided that the chapters would not end with an introduction of methodologies and practices but would present ideas for rescuing of each material. Our purpose is to organize what the situation is like during the stage of material rescue and escape from immediate danger, what to keep in mind, and the critical points for achieving that goal so that readers can use them as references for future field responses.

Relationships with the people surrounding the materials are essential elements in preserving and passing them on. In particular, the locals in each community have passed down their materials while keeping close contact with them. Confronting local materials requires dialogue with the histories and people of that community. How do history and culture experts get involved in the process? We need to develop a method of passing on historical and cultural traditions through dialogue. In this book, ICHIZAWA Tetsu describes "make the public" as the dialogue between experts and the local community, symbolized by the Shiryo-Network activities in the recent materials rescue. Suppose we form such a public space through new relationships developed by activities. In that case, efforts to preserve materials will have to play a sustained role that goes beyond the rescue of objects. Many pursue the efforts to this end across Japan, and we can expect further development. During the planning, we discussed how our practices and investigations in Japan can be understood to benefit international efforts. Hence, we prepared the English and Japanese versions and had them publicized online so that more people can read them. NEMOTO Takeru supervised the English translation. Again, we would like to thank him for his hard work reviewing our English.

On 1 January 2024, just during the compilation of this book, a massive earthquake and tsunami hit the Noto Peninsula in Ishikawa Prefecture. Rescue activities are still underway in all fields, and those for disaster-damaged materials will follow. We would like to express our deepest sympathies to the victims of the disaster and hope that this book will assist them in the future.

Part 1

執筆者一覧 (五十音順)／List of Authors

［所属は 2024 年 3 月 31 日時点］

阿部浩一　ABE Koichi

所属（Affiliation）

福島大学行政政策学類教授　Fukushima University

研究分野（Field of Study）

日本中世史　Japanese Medieval History

主要著書・論文

『戦国期の徳政と地域社会』（吉川弘文館、2001 年）、『ふくしま再生と歴史・文化遺産』（編著、山川出版社、2013 年）、「ふくしまの現場から振り返る 11 年－できたこと、できなかったこと－」（『史学』92-1・2、2023 年）など。

天野真志　AMANO Masashi

所属（Affiliation）

人間文化研究機構国立歴史民俗博物館准教授　National Museum of Japanese History

研究分野（Field of Study）

日本近世・近代史、資料保存

Early Modern to Modern History of Japan, Preservation of Materials

主要著書・論文

『幕末の学問・思想と政治運動』（吉川弘文館、2021 年）、『地域歴史文化継承ガイドブック　付・全国資料ネット総覧』（共編著、文学通信、2022 年）、『古文書の科学』（共編著、文学通信、2023 年）など。

市沢　哲　ICHIZAWA Tetsu

所属（Affiliation）

神戸大学文学部教授　Kobe University

研究分野（Field of Study）

日本中世史　Japanese Medieval History

主要著書・論文

『太平記を読む』（共著、吉川弘文館、2008 年）、『日本中世公家政治史の研究』（校倉書房、2011 年）、「視点 6：中世の武士の「家」意識～『難太平記』を読む～」（佐藤昇編『歴史の見方・考え方 2 史料から広がる歴史学』山川出版社、2023 年）、「歴史－市民として／研究者としてどう向き合うのか」（松田毅・藤木篤・新川拓哉編『応用哲学』昭和堂、2023 年）など。

大林賢太郎　OHBAYASHI Kentaro

所属（Affiliation）

京都芸術大学歴史遺産学科教授　Kyoto University of the Arts

研究分野（Field of Study）

装潢文化財、歴史資料（写真、近現代紙資料）の保存修復
Restoration of Oriental Calligraphy, Paintings, and Paper Materials

主要著書・論文

『文化財の保存修復を学ぶ』（うち第二章「装潢」担当、京都芸術大学東北芸術工科大学出版局
藝術学舎、2022 年、共著）、『装潢文化財の保存修理－東洋絵画・書跡修理の現在－』（国
宝修理装潢師連盟、2015 年）、『写真保存の実務』（岩田書院、2010 年）など。

奥村　弘　OKUMURA Hiroshi

所属（Affiliation）

神戸大学大学院人文学研究科教授　Kobe University

研究分野（Field of Study）

日本近代史　Modern History of Japan

主要著書・論文

『大震災と歴史資料保存』（吉川弘文館、2012 年）、『歴史文化を大災害から守る』（編著、
東京大学出版会、2014 年）、「視点 12：地域歴史資料のもつ豊かな役割　〜阪神・淡路大
震災から考える〜」（佐藤昇編『歴史の見方・考え方 2　史料から広がる歴史学』山川出版社、
2023 年）など。

松下正和　MATSUSHITA Masakazu

所属（Affiliation）

神戸大学地域連携推進本部・特命准教授　Kobe University

研究分野（Field of Study）

日本古代史・被災資料応急処置論
Ancient History of Japan, First-Aid Treatment for Disaster-Damaged Materials

主要著書・論文

「史料ネットによる水損写真資料の保全・応急処置─「思い出」をレスキューするた
めに」（『日本写真学会誌』84-2、2021 年）、「民間所在史料保全のためのネットワーク形成」
（奥村弘編『歴史文化を大災害から守る─地域歴史資料学の構築』東京大学出版会、2014 年）、『水
損史料を救う　風水害からの歴史資料保全』（共編、岩田書院、2009 年）など。

日髙真吾　HIDAKA Shingo

所属（Affiliation）

国立民族学博物館教授　National Museum of Ethnology

研究分野（Field of Study）

保存科学　Conservation Science

主要著書・論文

『災害と文化財―ある文化財科学者の視点から』（千里文化財団、2015年）、『継承される
地域文化―災害復興から社会創発へ』（編著、臨川書店、2021年）、『復興を支える地域の
文化 -3.11から10年』（編著、国立民族学博物館、2021年）、『記憶をつなぐ―津波災害と
文化遺産』（編著、千里文化財団、2012年）など。

山内利秋　YAMAUCHI Toshiaki

所属（Affiliation）

九州保健福祉大学薬学部准教授　Kyushu University of Health and Welfare

研究分野（Field of Study）

博物館学、文化財の保存と活用
Museum Studies, Conservation and Utilization of Cultural Properties

主要著書・論文

「史跡整備と遺跡の意味の変化―国家の表徴としての空間が、市民協働の場にかわる
まで―」（安斎正人編『理論考古学の実践』同成社、2017年）、「学芸員養成における課題解
決型教育」（『博物館学雑誌』41-1、2015年）、「災害と社会を学芸員養成の中で考える―
地域課題をテーマとした博物館実習での展示活動と自己評価―」（"Journal of Health and
Welfare Investigation" No.6、2024年）など。

■英訳監修

根本峻瑠　NEMOTO Takeru

所属（Affiliation）

翻訳・教育業　Translator/Educator

研究分野（Field of Study）

オーストリア＝ハンガリー帝国史　History of Austro-Hungarian Empire

主要著書、翻訳書、論文

バルバラ・シュトルベルク＝リーリンガー『マリア＝テレジア―「国母」の素顔』（共
訳、人文書院、2024年刊行予定）、『ハプスブルク事典』（共著、丸善出版、2023年）、『ヨーロッ
パ文化遺産研究の最前線』（共著、神戸大学出版会、2023年）など。

編 著

天野真志　AMANO Masashi
松下正和　MATSUSHITA Masakazu

［執筆］
阿部浩一／市沢　哲／大林賢太郎／奥村　弘／日高真吾／山内利秋

［英語監修］
根本峻瑠

地域歴史文化のまもりかた
災害時の救済方法とその考え方【付・英語版】

2024（令和6）年3月31日　　第1版第1刷発行

ISBN978-4-86766-043-0　C0021　Ⓒ著作権は各執筆者にあります

発行所　株式会社 文学通信
　〒113-0022 東京都文京区千駄木 2-31-3 サンウッド文京千駄木フラッツ 1 階 101
　電話 03-5939-9027　Fax 03-5939-9094
　メール info@bungaku-report.com　ウェブ http://bungaku-report.com

発行人　岡田圭介
印刷・製本　モリモト印刷

※乱丁・落丁本はお取り替えいたしますので、ご一報ください。書影は自由にお使いください。

ご意見・ご感想はこちら
からも送れます。上記
のQRコードを読み取っ
てください。

人間文化研究機構「歴史文化資料保全の大学・共同利用機関ネットワーク事業」［監修］・天野真志・後藤　真［編］

地域歴史文化継承ガイドブック
付・全国資料ネット総覧

地域の歴史や文化の、何をどう守り伝えていけばいいのか。最新の研究と実践からその方法を紹介する入門書。自治体、博物館、文書館、図書館、また地域資料の災害対策、保存・継承に興味のある方必携！

ISBN978-4-909658-72-2 ｜ A5 判・並製・248 頁
定価：本体 1,600 円（税別）｜ 2022.03 月刊

渋谷綾子・天野真志［編］

古文書の科学　料紙を複眼的に分析する

古文書や古記録類に用いられた紙は、果たしてどんなモノなのか。人文学ではなく、古文書を自然科学的に調べていくと、そこから何がわかるのか。古文書研究に自然科学を結びつける入門として、基礎的な情報を紹介していく「古文書の科学」のガイドブック。

ISBN978-4-86766-004-1 ｜ A5 判・並製・240 頁
定価：本体 1,900 円（税別）｜ 2023.03 月刊

国立歴史民俗博物館・天野真志・吉村郊子［編］

REKIHAKU　特集・歴史をつなぐ

過去を振り返るために、人びとは様々な媒体を手がかりとし、資料を通して歴史をつないでいる。地域歴史資料概論から、多くの事例の紹介まで。さらには、近年の歴史資料保存活動を主導してきた久留島浩、奥村弘両氏のインタビューまで。過去を伝える資料を、未来につなぐことの意味をトータルに考え尽くす。

ISBN978-4-86766-023-2 ｜ A5 判・並製・112 頁
定価：本体 1,091 円（税別）｜ 2023.10 月刊
発行：国立歴史民俗博物館